BREATHTAKING

BREATHTAKING

A Field Guide to
Living Your Epic Life

SHELLI JOHNSON

EPIC LIFE ✦ PRESS

Published in the United States by Epic Life Inc.

First Edition, July 2025

ISBN: 979-8-9989619-0-8 (ebook)

ISBN: 979-8-9989619-1-5 (paperback)

ISBN: 979-8-9989619-2-2 (hardcover)

Advance Praise for Breathtaking

"*Breathtaking* really is one of the best manuals you'll ever discover for an adventurous life lived in holistic communion with nature. But it's also so much more than that. Shelli has mined her experiences to deliver sage advice on living bravely and selflessly."

—Jon Dorn, CEO of Teton Gravity Research, author,
and former Chief Entertainment Officer at *Outside*

"This book is captivating—I couldn't put it down. So many important lessons, all in one place. If you're seeking a life that feels more meaningful, inspired, and truly alive, this book is your guide."

—Susan Johnson, C-suite executive, athlete, volunteer

"*Breathtaking* is not just beautifully written—it is deeply lived. Shelli doesn't just write about wilderness or resilience; she embodies it. She has walked the walk—literally and spiritually—and returned with stories that matter."

—Jamie Leachman, Entrepreneur, Clinical Herbalist, MSW

"Reading *Breathtaking* feels like sitting by a campfire with a wise friend who reminds you, with love and clarity, that your life is meant to be lived fully awake."

—Joel Krieger, VP, Head of Creative & Experience, Magic Leap

"*Breathtaking* awakened parts of me I hadn't realized were waiting to emerge—parts I now understand are essential to living my most expansive, epic life. With authenticity, humor, and deep relatability, Shelli delivers a captivating and potentially transformative read."

—Stephanie Somersille, mathematical data scientist, PhD

"Shelli is a humble storyteller with infinite knowledge and inspiration she will selflessly gift to any fellow seeker and life explorer."

—Tina Postel, CEO of Nourish Up, Adjunct Professor at UNC

"This book is a gift. It's a call to be bold, to rest when needed, to seek adventure, and to face life with courage."

—Shay Runion, Chief HR Officer, Arrow Exterminators

"*Breathtaking* is a must-read for anyone ready to explore not just the great outdoors, but the depths of their own inner landscape."

—Ilana Tolpin Levitt, LPC, LMHC, NCC

"Shelli helped us strip away the labels and the roles, and reminded us who we are at our core. I can't wait for the world to experience her magic in *Breathtaking*."

—Doreen Rose, Chef, chef instructor, and health coach

"In this chaotic, overly busy time we live in, Shelli's wisdom is especially valuable. I plan to buy this book for the members of my leadership team."

—Wendy Mullen, Chief Administrative Officer, First Manhattan

"*Breathtaking* is a transformative guide to discovering your passion and purpose, paving the way to a more meaningful and epic life. A true breakthrough, it brings forth essential principles to elevate your leadership and inspire personal growth."

—Mona Harty, Chief Purpose Officer, board member/advisor

"Reading *Breathtaking* is like you're sitting in a good friend's kitchen drinking a cup of tea and talking with someone who really cares about your well being."

—Karen Monson, Backpacker and outdoor enthusiast

"*Breathtaking* is an inspiring guide that is ultimately a call to action—reminding us that an epic life is not about grand achievements alone, but about living each day with intention, courage, and a commitment to personal growth."

—Brian T. Brouillette, Vice President, CrowdStrike (retired)

To Jerry, the love of my life, and to my beloved sons, Wolf, Hayden, and Finis. *I love you more than words can say. I couldn't have written this book without your love, support, and presence in my life.*

To my mom and dad. *Thank you for giving me life, for your love and support, and for inspiring my love of Wyoming. I love you so much.*

To Jamie. *For seeing the writer in me and calling her forth!*

"It hurts just as much as it's worth."

—Zadie Smith, quoting from a condolence
letter in "Joy," *New York Review of Books*

"The gods envy us. They envy us because we're mortal, because any moment might be our last. Everything is more beautiful because we're doomed. You will never be lovelier than you are now."

—Achilles, *Troy* (2004), written by David Benioff

"I was much further out than you thought / And not waving but drowning."

—Stevie Smith

Table of Contents

Lesson 4 **101**
Appreciate Your Setbacks and Failures

Lesson 7   **171**
Tend to the Pebble in Your Shoe

Foreword
by Jon Dorn

Deep in the ancient, seemingly barren recesses of the Grand Canyon, there lives an exquisite—and very deadly—plant rarely noticed by the thousands of hikers who traverse the park's trails each year. It's a mystical species long used in carefully controlled doses by Native American shamans and medicine men from southwestern tribes like the Havasupai and Zuni to induce trance states, treat illnesses, and relieve pain. Consumed in powdered form or as a steeped tea, its roots and leaves are said to produce prophetic visions and to open communication pathways to the spirit world.

Datura wrightii, better known as sacred datura, belongs to the nightshade family and typically grows from spring through fall in sandy, sun-baked washes at elevations from one thousand to six thousand feet—a perfect match for much of the park's eighteen-hundred-square-mile ecosystem. A perennial herb, sacred datura likes to spread and climb, its vines sprawling up to eight feet wide and several feet high. If you were to pass a cluster during the day, you wouldn't stop to snap a picture. Though common along paths like the North Kaibab Trail, it looks like an everyday weed with toothy, dark-green leaves that are usually tinted gray and covered with fuzzy white hairs. Its nondescript appearance is why so few hikers notice it. Therein lies the secret of the sacred datura, whose appearance undergoes a radical transformation when the sun goes down.

At dusk, large, white, five-lobed flowers begin to emerge from the plant, their edges often tinged lavender. A fragrant odor wafts across the trail, attracting moths, deer, and rabbits. The beauty, however, is fleeting. By midnight, typically the petals have fallen off. But if, during the first few hours of the evening, you were to sweep your headlamp across a patch of sacred datura, your jaw would hit the two-billion-year-old sandstone beneath you. The pearly blossoms turn the monochromatic desert floor into a field of luminescent, platter-size flowers, revealing one of nature's truly magical phenomena.

To witness this brief efflorescence is to understand why Grand Canyon aficionados like to say that "half the park is after dark." In the cooler hours following sunset, the desert comes alive with bats, owls, ringtail cats, deer, coyotes, insects, and other creatures. To see the sacred datura bloom is also to understand why it's popularly known as the moonflower.

It was shortly after dark on May 20, 2010, an hour or two past Phantom Ranch at the bottom of the Grand Canyon, when Shelli and I chanced upon a patch of blooming moonflower as we ascended the North Kaibab Trail. To this day, I remember the moment with crystal clarity, both for its astonishing beauty and for the rapturous look on Shelli's face. This was the first time she'd ever seen the plant—or even heard of it—and for someone as passionate about outdoor adventure as she is, it was like stumbling across lost pirate treasure. ("Pay attention," she advises in the first chapter of this book, which is apt counsel should you visit this park.)

The mess of vines, leaves, and glowing white blossoms were so thick that we wondered if someone had planted a garden. I knew not to touch them—every part of the moonflower is loaded with toxic, psychoactive alkaloids—so we stood back, snapped a few photos, and counted ourselves lucky to have the fitness and resources to attempt a rim-to-rim-to-rim hike in the Grand Canyon. Little did I know how agonizing a crucible the rest of that night would be for Shelli.

We were six or seven hours into a twenty-four-hour hike that would take us from the park's South Rim to its North Rim and back again, a journey of forty-five miles and twenty-three thousand vertical feet—roughly the same elevation gains as summiting Mount Everest. Back at Phantom Ranch, I'd inspected and bandaged the blisters that were already turning her feet into a pulpy mess, and I'd recommended we turn back. But, as you'll discover later in this book, Shelli is made of tougher (and, yes, more obstinate) stuff—so, we soldiered on. But that decision came with an excruciating price.

As Shelli's feet exfoliated, the top layers of skin peeling away one by one, every step became an exercise in mind over matter. Blood soaked through her socks and eventually her shoes, and the hundreds of steep switchbacks stabbed like shards of glass slashing through her soles. Not wanting me to worry, generous soul that she is, Shelli hung back and wept out of earshot when the pain became intolerable.

The decision to continue also came—against all odds—with a few rewards. There was the magic moonflower moment. Bats winging close enough to our heads that we could hear and feel the *whoosh* of their tiny wings. A sky so full of stars that I couldn't possibly count all of them in ten lifetimes. And the adrenaline rush of sweeping our headlamps across the desert floor to see beady eyes peering back at us and dozens of scorpions skittering across the sand.

But the biggest dividend, especially for Shelli, was a psychic breakthrough that led to a life-affirming surge in resilience and self-awareness. Gaining courage and strength through adversity is a theme that runs throughout this book, and the experience of overcoming her physical agony as well as her doubts and fears has informed how she approaches every moment of her life.

I consider myself lucky to have witnessed Shelli's transformation and subsequent trajectory as an in-demand coach, speaker, and guide. Like the moonflower, something beautiful emerged for her during that dark night. Fresh shoots of joy and determination sprouted from the unforgiving terrain, and a new sense of confidence and purpose bloomed in her. Shelli's suffering on that hike yielded a renewal of sorts, a gift that she is now dedicated to sharing with others through her business. In so many ways, the moonflower strikes me as an appropriate image to keep in mind as you read this book.

Of course, *Breathtaking* is not just a "dark night of the soul," a concept from a sixteenth-century Spanish mystic that she references midway through the book. There is also joy in these pages, and humor, and tales of friendships and summits and parenting that will inspire every reader. There are "holy crap" moments when you suddenly realize how not normal this woman is. I mean, she's walked 35,000 miles in the last fifteen years! Do the math. Those numbers are bionic.

Indeed, this is a book that I wish I'd been given at the start of my days as a backpacker, climber, and skier. It contains so much hard-won outdoor wisdom, so many kernels of advice that could've helped me avoid the many errors I made in learning how to survive—and thrive—in the wilderness. *Breathtaking* really is one of the best manuals you'll ever discover for an adventurous life lived in holistic communion with nature. But it's also so much more than that.

Beyond the tips on backcountry travel and safety, Shelli has mined her experiences as a business owner, entrepreneur, coach, writer, guide, mom, daughter, friend, and wife—and as a very human seeker with unparalleled humility, integrity, and curiosity—to deliver sage advice on living bravely and selflessly. If only I'd gotten my hands on it as I was becoming a husband, father, and business leader! In all these pursuits, Shelli's insights would've helped me develop more fully into my best self as a spouse, dad, friend, and boss.

On the toughest wilderness trips, those spectacular epics that verge off the beaten path into unknown terrain, the most important member of your team is not the strongest, fastest, most confident, or most experienced hiker. It's the navigator, the person who can study the hieroglyphic squiggles on a topo map and divine the truest course through the challenges ahead. Such is the case in life, too; for my money, Shelli is the companion you need, and *Breathtaking* is the compass you've been seeking.

—Jon Dorn, CEO of Teton Gravity Research, author,
and former Chief Entertainment Officer at *Outside*

Introduction

It's May 20, 2010, and I'm standing on the South Rim of the Grand Canyon, waiting for my friend Jon to arrive. I'm looking across the great abyss to the distant North Rim, trying not to shit my pants. *What was I thinking?*

I had trained for the adventure. And yet, nothing could have prepared me for what unfolded over the next twenty-three hours. The physical agony and emotional unraveling I experienced in the depths of the Grand Canyon were brutal. That journey broke me open. When it ended, I wasn't the same person who had entered the canyon. Something inside me had awakened. I met parts of myself for the first time—and I was more than I was before. The experience transformed me—and changed the trajectory of my life. (You'll find the full story about that reckoning in the *Dare to Fail* section.)

Soon after I returned home to Wyoming, I embarked on what would become a fifteen-year trek. I would walk hundreds—and eventually thousands—of miles. From 2010 to 2020, I walked twenty-six thousand miles, the equivalent of circling the Earth once. All told, I've probably walked about thirty-five thousand miles in the last fifteen years. Not all of these have been hiking miles—many were walked during coaching calls, throughout my daily life, and during travels. All those miles of walking, wandering, and sauntering have been a sort of *thru-hike of midlife*.

My wanderings have taken me to some of the most breathtaking places on Earth. I've explored national parks and wilderness areas of the American

West—Yellowstone, Grand Teton, Zion, Arches, Canyonlands, and the Grand Canyon. With my family, I've wandered beaches, rainforests, and wild coastlines from Vancouver, B.C., through the Pacific Northwest to the Marin Headlands in California. I've explored Hawaii and Mexico, backpacked 160 miles of Spain's Camino de Santiago, climbed volcanoes and walked on glaciers in Iceland, and tackled epic hikes in Switzerland and Italy.

But my favorite place on Earth is my backyard—the Wind River Range of Wyoming. These mountains have become part of me. I've lost and found myself, again and again, in them.

The Wind Rivers are extraordinary—but don't move here. Seriously. The winters are long and brutal. The closest major airport is hours away. There are no shopping malls. The roads to the trailheads are rocky and ruinous for cars. It's the frontier—and conditions can be severe.

While I've been lucky to adventure in some spectacular landscapes, my journey has been mostly an internal one. Walking in the wilderness has helped me understand myself and my place in the world.

In 2010, I dedicated Fridays to long, solo walks. These were meant to be "work-free" days. But ironically, it was during my solo wanderings in the woods that the insights and inspirations for my work came flooding in.

Writing is how I make sense of the world. It's how I find my way. As a writer, I see everything as potentially interesting. I've always loved reading, collecting, and writing stories—mining them for wisdom and meaning— and sharing what I find.

In elementary school, I wrote notes to my best friend in the form of stories. (She reminds me, all these years later, that I told her I was going to be a writer when I grew up.) I studied journalism at the University of Montana, and my first jobs were in newspapers before launching my own in 1994.

As the founder of *Yellowstone Journal* and YellowstonePark.com, I went "into the field" with the park's wolf, bear, geology, botany, bird, and other experts, and immersed myself in the region's activities and cultural attractions, reporting on and writing over one hundred thousand words of original content each year for our magazines, website, and travel guides. I've published hundreds of adventure and travel-related blog posts.

While operating our Yellowstone business, my mission was to inspire people to experience a vacation of a lifetime. Since founding Epic Life Inc. in 2011, my mission has been to inspire people to experience the life of their lifetime.

Living the life of your lifetime—what I call your *epic life*—means saying yes to the whole experience. It will break your heart *and* take your breath away. It takes tremendous courage to live the life you want to live. Most of us won't do it. In fact, the top regret of the dying is that they didn't have the courage to live the life they wanted to live.

I take this work seriously. Our time is our life, and none of us knows how much we have. It is deeply personal work.

For the past fourteen years, I've worked as a coach, leadership consultant, keynote presenter, and adventure guide. I've gone "into the field" with individuals, leaders, teams, and organizations. I've guided many on Epic Adventures in the wilderness—and all through the one inside themselves.

I've learned so much from the wonderful people who've trusted me to be their coach and guide. This book is my way of sharing the most powerful insights and lessons I've gathered—personally and professionally—over these years.

I've collected stories that make up more than twenty "Epic Lessons Learned in the Field." They have become the scaffolding of Epic Life. This book contains the eight lessons I consider the most essential. They've been field-tested in my coaching, keynote presentations, leadership workshops, Epic Adventures, and retreats. I've also put them to the test in my own life, again and again.

A Field Guide

I hope this book doesn't read like most self-help books. I don't consider myself an expert, and I don't care for books that preach or promise, "I did it, and you can too—here's how."

I've always been captivated by tales of early explorers—Lewis and Clark, polar adventurers, and those who dared to journey into the unknown. They observed, learned, charted paths, and returned to share what they discovered. That's how I hope this book reads—like a field guide. Most of what I share in these pages are stories and observations.

I hope you'll use this book as a resource, a companion, and a guide for navigating your own epic life. And if you're already living your epic life? Congratulations! I know how hard it is to do, and I hope you're reveling in it.

Who This Book Is For

I wrote this book for those who want to reflect deeply on their life. It's for the seekers. For those who feel a quiet longing for something more. It's for anyone in their 30s, 40s, 50s, or 60s who is at a crossroads, celebrating a milestone, or entering a new season. It's for those who sense something's shifting, or needs to.

I wrote this for leaders, CEOs, and entrepreneurs who value humanity —who want to bring their whole person to their leadership and their organization's culture. This book is for those tasked with guiding others through today's uncharted wilderness. If you're taking stock of your life, craving meaning, or daring to change your path, this field guide is for you.

How to Use This Book

Think of reading this book as a journey. It's structured around eight lessons. Each offers stories, insights, guidance, and reflections from my work, life, and time in the wilderness.

You can read straight through or let one lesson call to you and spend a week (or a month) with it. However you move through it, take this book outside. Bring a journal and a pen. (As part of your book purchase, I'm providing an "Epic Field Study Guide" with many of the reflections & exercises I use in my coaching and Epic programs as a downloadable PDF at YourEpicLife.com/EpicFieldStudyGuide.)

While you can read the lessons in any order, I recommend starting with *Know Your Location*—because you can't live your epic life until you know who you are and how you want to be.

The Eight Lessons

Know Your Location: In the wilderness, not knowing your location is dangerous. You can't chart a course if you don't know where you are. The same is true in life. Without regular self-reflection, you risk following the wrong path. To find your way to an authentic life, you must first know who you are and how you want to be in the world.

Carry the Right Stuff: In a wilderness adventure, every item in your pack matters. Too much, and you're weighed down. Too little, and you're unprepared. To live your epic life, live it thoughtfully. Be intentional about what you carry—in how you show up in the roles and areas of your life.

Dare to Fail: Living your epic life isn't for the faint of heart. It will leave you gasping for air. It will break you open and bring you to your knees. It will steal your breath and demand that you hold onto your hat. But this is where the magic lives—where courage meets vulnerability. When we dare to do hard things, we discover who we are. We go farther than we believed possible. We create meaning. And when we share in challenge, we deepen our relationships. An epic life isn't tidy. It's a hard-earned celebration.

Appreciate Your Setbacks and Failures: Success may be the aim, but it rarely teaches us much. Most of life is lived in the in-between. The journey is full of stumbles and wrong turns. But if you learn to appreciate your failures, they become portals—to insight, growth, and strength. We don't avoid failure on the way to our epic life. We fail our way there.

Take a Load Off: Can you imagine going on an adventure and never stopping to rest or take in the view? What a tragedy—yet we do this all the time. Rest is not a luxury—it's essential. So is joy. So is fun. So is awe.

Cherish Your People: People are what matter most. Ask anyone at the end of their life and they won't speak of accolades. They'll speak of love and connection. No epic journey is made alone. Behind every brave step is someone who believed in us and held us up. Tend to your people like a sacred fire. They are everything.

Tend to the Pebble in Your Shoe: Often, there's a pebble in our shoe—something small but nagging that makes our journey more difficult. We often ignore it; we don't want to slow others down or cause a scene. But left unaddressed, it becomes a blister. Every step becomes painful. And it's not just your pebble anymore. When we neglect our own needs, it affects our relationships and our ability to show up. Tend to the pebble. Before it takes you out.

Be All In: Life isn't meant to be lived halfway. If you want a full, rich, breathtaking life, you must show up—all the way. Commit to your path. Hold nothing back. Life can be a great adventure. But only if you're all in.

A Final Thought

In her poem "Sometimes," the poet Mary Oliver wrote the following as her *Instructions for living a life*:

"Pay attention. / Be astonished. / Tell about it."

For the past fifteen years, I've paid attention. I've been astonished. And now, in these pages, I tell about it.

Welcome to *Breathtaking: A Field Guide to Living Your Epic Life*.

Author's Note

In the pages that follow, I share many stories drawn from my life and experiences, as well as the lives of some of the people I've had the privilege to know, coach, and adventure with. These stories are told to the best of my memory and ability. While I've made every effort to recount events truthfully, some details—dates, sequencing, dialogue—may be imperfect.

Sincerely,
Shelli

Lesson 1
Know Your Location

Your Epic Life

This book is a field guide to living your epic life.

What do I mean by that?

An epic life is *your* life—not the life others expect you to live. An epic life is not an easy life. It is not without hardship and loss. In fact, it's the opposite. A life is epic not despite its challenges but largely as a result of them. Some days, you'll be bent over, gasping for air. At times, your epic life will bring you to your knees. Other times, you'll be holding on to your hat as the wind of life whips around you. In your hardest and most beautiful moments, an epic life will take your breath away.

We all have an epic life. The question is: Are we living it?

I know you're living. But do you *feel alive*?

As humans, we yearn for a life that feels true to us, that we *want* to be alive for. But we exist in a state of striving.

We are all so busy. But a busy life is not the same thing as a full life, and we know this. We feel it deeply inside: a quiet, gnawing hunger for something different. We long for more meaning and a sense of aliveness, but we're not sure how to find it.

So, we look to our devices, staring at screens, scrolling, and searching for something that will make us feel better. We compare our lives to those that are carefully curated and shared online by others only to feel worse and emptier. Meanwhile, it feels like our lives are passing us by.

It doesn't just feel that way. Our lives *are* passing by. According to the 2023 Nielsen Total Audience Report, American adults spend approximately seven to eight hours daily on screens across all devices and activities. This adds up to more than one hundred days—or three and a half months—per year, roughly one third of our waking life.

I am fifty-seven years old. If I live to be eighty and continue with my current device usage and screen time, I'll spend about six and a half years of my remaining life looking at screens. Of course, not all screen time is wasted; much of it is required, worthwhile, and even wonderful.

But still, our time is our life, and I wonder: How much more of it must pass before we turn inward?

One of the greatest lessons I've learned is that living our authentic life—our epic life—is mostly an inside job.

The Wilderness Inside

Yellowstone National Park is the world's original national park and one of the most iconic. It's also immense, spanning more than two million acres—about 3,500 square miles. Every year, it attracts around four million visitors.

Several years ago, while operating my first businesses, *Yellowstone Journal* and YellowstonePark.com, I interviewed Lee Whittlesey, the park's historical archivist at the time, for a story about Yellowstone's record visitation. He told me something I never forgot: Only 2 percent of Yellowstone is developed. Even if you drive the entire Grand Loop Road and see all the major sights and attractions, you'll experience just a sliver of the park. The remaining 98 percent is wild, undeveloped, and largely unfrequented.

Why am I sharing this? Because the same could be said about all of us. Inside each of us is a vast wilderness—an inner life—that goes largely unexplored.

There is so much within us waiting to be discovered, if only we're willing—and daring enough—to go there.

Find Your Way Back to Yourself

"The privilege of a lifetime is to become who you truly are."

—Carl Jung

For more than thirty years, I've been finding my way.

I've never quite felt normal. Since I was a little girl, something about me felt off, different—like I wasn't like everyone else. Maybe that's why I've never wanted to follow someone else's path. For one, I don't think I'd be very good at it. But more importantly, it wouldn't feel true to me.

I spend a lot of time in the wilderness, wandering and moving through vast, rugged landscapes. Nowhere else do I feel so authentically like myself or trust myself so completely. When too much time passes without time in the wilderness, I feel unmoored, as if I've drifted from something essential.

The moment I return, when my feet meet the dirt, I begin to feel oriented again. Sometimes it only takes an hour or two, other times an entire day, but eventually—and always—I find my way back to myself.

There's a Zen meditation called "Find Your Original Face," during which you meditate on who you were before your parents were born. It's an impossible exercise, and that's the point—to challenge us to imagine a time before we were shaped by the expectations, judgments, and influences of our world.

The reality is, over time, we consciously and unconsciously put on masks—and the longer we live, the more these masks accumulate. Some of them we inherit from family, culture, or circumstance; others we craft to fit in, to protect ourselves, to become who we think we should be.

These masks become the roles we assume, personas we project, identities we cling to. It is beneath these masks that our truest and most authentic selves can be found.

One of the greatest lessons I've learned, through both working closely with people to help them find their way and while examining my own life, is that finding your way isn't about following a prescribed route. It's not about adding or acquiring more or climbing some imagined mountain of success. It's not about striving upward; it's about stripping away.

Inner journeys have been described in many ways. Writer and Jungian psychoanalyst Clarissa Pinkola Estés calls it "gathering up the bones." Carl Jung described it as "being with our shadow." Joseph Campbell named it "the hero's journey." I call it a journey through the wilderness inside. When we dare to explore the wilderness inside of us, we don't just discover who we are—we remember who we've always been.

This is important, because only when we truly know and understand ourselves can we discover and live our authentic lives. Only then can we find our way.

We Can't GPS It

"If you can see your path laid out in front of you step by step, you know it's not your path."

—Joseph Campbell

GPS is one of the greatest technological advances in recent history, and I'm grateful for it. When this small-town girl from the frontier rents a car to navigate a big city for work, I'm often more nervous about finding my way than I am about giving the keynote presentation I've been hired to deliver. I need GPS to make it to my destination.

The problem with GPS is that it's made us lazy. We plug in our destination and obediently follow step-by-step directions from point A to point B. We don't even have to pay much attention to our surroundings.

As a result, we miss so much. Imagine all the unexpected beauty, curious side streets, or chance encounters we pass by when our journey is reduced to: "Turn left. Continue for two miles. Turn right." The result? We've become passive. Uninterested. Disengaged.

This won't work when it comes to finding your way. You can't outsource the navigation. You must stay awake. You must stay curious. You must be willing to take a wrong turn, ask questions, try things. If you don't, you'll miss the clues meant only for you—the inner whispers, suggested detours, and invitations that call from your soul.

Your path won't come with turn-by-turn directions. But if you're paying attention—if you stay open, observant, and brave—the way will reveal itself. This could be a great adventure, but only if you're awake for it!

Pay Attention

"Attention is the beginning of devotion."

—Mary Oliver, *Upstream*

If someone were to ask me what I think is the single most important advice for living your authentic life, it would be *Pay Attention.* If you take only one piece of advice from this field guide, I hope that is it.

In the wilderness, paying attention can be a matter of life or death. Fail to look at your surroundings and you risk a surprise encounter with a grizzly bear and her cubs. Fail to look up from the path and you could find yourself above tree line without protection when a storm strikes and lightning flashes all around you. If we're distracted, we could inadvertently wander off course and get lost. Your failure to pay attention could prove fatal. It's the same in life. Are you sleepily passing through, or are you awake and engaged?

So often, we move through our days with our heads down, going through the motions, half asleep and on autopilot yet simultaneously longing to be more interested in our lives. It's only by being present that we're able to notice—let alone *experience*—the wonder, joy, and meaning that's available to all of us, often found in the most ordinary moments of our lives.

Spending time in nature has taught me how to pay attention, to the rustle of leaves, the play of light on a distant ridge, the flicker of movement in my periphery, the crunch of pine needles underfoot, the fresh tracks of a mountain lion, the song of the hermit thrush, or the haunting bugle of a bull elk on a misty September morning.

When you're in the wilderness, there are many potential hazards. There is rugged terrain, heights and exposure, wild animals, and the potential for severe weather. A lot can go wrong, and you're a long way from help. You must be more concerned about things, more deliberate. You must want to stay alive a little more intentionally than when you're in the safety of your home and the front country.

The practice of being fully present in the wild has helped me live more consciously. The more time I spend in the wilderness, the more awake I am in the world. When I pay attention, I feel like I'm alive, like I'm an active participant in my life.

Know Your Location

"To survive, you must find yourself."

—Laurence Gonzales, *Deep Survival*

My pack was heavy, and with each step my feet sank a few inches into the rain-soaked tundra. After two days of lashing rain, the sun finally made an appearance. Its bright light warmed my face as I trudged through the spongy terrain.

I was backpacking in Alaska's Brooks Range, a 700-mile-long mountain range that stretches from west to east across the far north of Alaska and into Canada's Yukon Territory. I was with nine others, and we were part of a fourteen-day National Outdoor Leadership School (NOLS) expedition. During our time in the wilderness, we'd have no contact with our family and friends, or civilization for that matter, and all we'd have with us was the fifty to fifty-five pounds of food and gear we carried on our backs.

The Brooks Range is vast and untamed. There are no roads and no trails. Our final destination—the point at which we'd be picked up at the end of our course fourteen days later—was marked on our map with a large "X." We estimated the distance to be 70-80 miles. Using that X as our primary orienting reference point, each day we studied the maps and terrain and collectively charted our path. It was exciting to get to choose our path, to not be limited to a single route.

At times, the terrain limited or dictated our path—certain conditions were too gnarly, or we predicted a ridge might be impassable—but often, we had freedom and numerous options. We could choose to follow a high (more adventurous) mountainous route, or we could choose to travel a low (safer and more predictable) route that followed a river.

On day two of our expedition, our instructors divided us into two teams and gave us each a topographical map. My four course mates and I studied the map and charted our route, estimating that we had about a seven-mile day ahead of us. After an hour or so of hiking, we all acknowledged that while we didn't necessarily think we were lost, we weren't feeling particularly assured that we were on the right course.

It was already going to be a long day; we didn't want to make it any longer, so we decided to stop and get our bearings. We removed our hefty packs, took out the big, topographical map, unfolded it on the ground and huddled over it. We tried to match the features of the land around us with the features on our map, but the mountains on either side of us looked similar and there were few distinguishing landmarks. We were still rookies and struggled to pinpoint our exact location.

After some time, I grew impatient and rose to my feet. I swung my backpack on, hoping it might influence others to do the same. I was tired of not going anywhere. As I fidgeted and paced back and forth, one of my course mates looked at me and said: "With all due respect, I don't think it's a waste of time to figure out where we are so we can figure out where we're going."

Woods Shock

It turns out my course mate was right. If you're in the wilderness and you think you may be off course or lost, you should *not* keep going. If you do, it likely won't end well.

When our physical surroundings don't match our mental maps, we panic and may experience what psychologists call "woods shock." When someone experiences woods shock, they no longer have their rational abilities. In their distress, the lost person may thrash about, this way and that, frantically trying to correct course and return to familiar ground. But in their desperate attempts, they often become more lost. The consequences can be costly, and even fatal.

According to Laurence Gonzales in his excellent book, *Deep Survival: Who Lives, Who Dies, and Why,* most people who perish in the wilderness after getting lost do so as a result of failure of mind and an inability to respond rationally.

This can happen in life, too. One day we look up only to realize we're somewhere we didn't expect or plan to be, somewhere we wish we weren't.

Somewhere You Didn't Expect to Be

On the night of my fortieth birthday, my husband Jerry and our three sons took me to my favorite local restaurant. When we arrived, I was greeted by a room full of friends, colleagues, and extended family. A dear friend had orchestrated a surprise party for the occasion.

It was a wonderful and meaningful night, and the next morning, my friend emailed me photos from the party. I opened them and began scrolling, searching for myself. At first, I didn't see me. I was in the photos, but I didn't recognize myself. It wasn't just physical; I didn't feel connected to myself.

American philosopher and neuroscientist Sam Harris once told a story on Andrew Huberman's podcast about a woman who was reported lost in Iceland. The woman, who had been part of a bus tour, stepped away from her group during a stop to change her clothes. When she returned, she was unaccounted for and was mistakenly reported missing. A search party was organized, and the woman—unaware she was "missing"—spent hours helping in the search. Several hours later, the search effort ended after the woman realized that she was the missing person they were searching for.

The story describes how I felt the morning following my fortieth birthday. At some point in my life, I had stopped paying attention. I had gone missing—I just hadn't noticed.

When Leaders Ignore Warning Signs

"Rigid people are dangerous people."

—Laurence Gonzales, *Deep Survival*

In the wilderness, where so little is within our control, things seldom (if ever) go exactly as planned. To thrive, and sometimes even to survive, we must be flexible and adaptable.

When we notice conditions are changing, we must be willing to change course. Clinging to a particular path is a dangerous gamble and one that's not limited to the wilderness.

From the 1930s to the 1990s, Kodak dominated the film and photography industry. Few people know this, but in 1975, a Kodak engineer invented the first digital camera. While working for Eastman Kodak, Steven Sasson created a prototype—a clunky, eight-pound machine that recorded grainy black-and-white images onto a cassette tape. It was revolutionary, even if it would be many years before that revolution would take hold.

By the early 2000s, digital photography was rapidly gaining traction. The signs were unmistakable. The world was changing, and so were consumers. They no longer wanted to wait days to see their photos or be limited to twenty-four shots on a roll of film. They craved immediacy, convenience, and control. Kodak had the innovation, the technology, and a head start. But its leaders feared the new technology would cannibalize their profitable film business and refused to pivot.

Well, we all know how that worked out—it didn't. Once the undisputed leader in photography, Kodak struggled to transition and ultimately filed for bankruptcy in 2012. A company that once employed 145,000 people and generated $16 billion in annual revenue is now a fraction of its former size.

In the wilderness, this tendency to remain rigidly attached to a plan can be even more catastrophic. In mountaineering, there is a term known as "summit fever"—the all-consuming drive to reach the top of a mountain at any cost. Many mountaineering accidents occur not because of a single mistake but because of a series of ignored warning signs. Climbers might notice deteriorating weather, exhaustion creeping in, or dwindling daylight, yet they push forward anyway. The summit becomes an obsession, blinding them to signs of dangers.

Experienced climbers understand that reaching the top of a mountain is only the halfway point, and that success lies in making it back down alive. But countless stories exist of experienced mountaineers who refused to turn around when they should have, ignoring their own instincts, their team's advice, and changing conditions. Some have perished within reach of their goal. Others have survived, but perhaps barely.

We see this same rigidity and clinging in our personal and professional lives. Maybe we're in a job that's sucking the life out of us, one that is misaligned with our values or costs us precious time with loved ones. Maybe we're in a high-stress leadership role that is negatively affecting our mental and physical health. Maybe we've outgrown our career path but can't muster the courage to pivot, fearing we'll lose everything we've built. Or maybe we're stuck in unhealthy habits—drinking too much or relying on substances or distractions to numb ourselves in ways we know aren't serving us—but we lack the discipline, or maybe the will, to choose another way.

When we sense something is off and not working, will we have the courage to change course? What's it going to take to summon the courage to make a change? Perhaps the most important question to ask ourselves is, *What will happen if I don't change course?*

Living our epic life requires adaptability. We must be willing to change course when conditions call for it. Whether in leadership, the wilderness, or life itself, the riskiest thing we can do is ignore the danger signs and continue down a path simply because it's the one we started on, and the one that's familiar.

S.T.O.P. (Stop, Think, Observe, and Plan)

If you're in the wilderness and you notice something is off, the conditions are changing, or something doesn't look right, you must STOP, which stands for *Stop, Think, Observe,* and *Plan.* The STOP methodology was developed as a strategy for staying calm and making thoughtful decisions when lost in the wilderness. It encourages us to pause and assess the situation to prevent us from panicking or making irrational decisions.

Continuing while denying your circumstances is not a sound strategy. In the wilderness, we call this behavior "bending the map." To bend the map is to bend the truth, to try to make our circumstances conform to our wishes. We might say things like, "Maybe the mountain wasn't as big as I recalled," or, "Maybe the lake dried up." While bending the map may make us feel better in the moment, denial is not an effective strategy. It's likely to make our circumstances even more dire.

Following STOP in the wilderness keeps you calm and grounded, enabling you to make rational, informed decisions that improve your chances of finding your way or being found.

The same is true in life. We must stay oriented and anchored in ourselves. And we do this by stopping regularly to reflect and take stock. Only when we *know our location*—only when we *know ourselves*—can we live intentionally and find our way to the life that's most true.

Spend Time Alone

"Certain springs are tapped only when we are alone."

—Anne Morrow Lindbergh, *Gift from the Sea*

I didn't always love solitude.

When I was twenty years old, at the start of my junior year of college, I unexpectedly lost my Division I basketball scholarship and, with it, time with my friends. For the first time in my life, I experienced loneliness. Along with the loneliness came a lot of unexpected free time. To fill it, I started hiking.

On the south side of the Mount Sentinel foothill, there's a large, cement "M," and the trail to reach it is easily accessed from the edge of the UM campus. Every day—sometimes twice a day—I would hike by myself to the M and back.

What started out as a lonely experience eventually evolved into something better. My solitary hikes gave me time for self-reflection and provided a spaciousness that allowed my imagination to run wild.

I could examine my life and reflect on the ways I was feeling. I had so many ideas, inspirations, and insights that seemed to come only when I was alone and wandering in the woods or the mountains. The time I spent alone was restorative and helped me heal from disappointment. Soon, I no longer felt sad or lonely, and I looked forward to time alone.

We all know that to deepen a relationship, you must offer it more of your time. Have you ever considered that the same logic applies to the relationship you have with yourself? How much richer would your relationship with yourself be if you were to treat it like you would any other important relationship?

May Sarton writes in *A Journal of a Solitude*, "Loneliness is the poverty of self; solitude is the richness of self." I couldn't agree more. In the last ten years, I've walked many thousands of miles, at least half of them alone—not because I couldn't find anyone to hike with, but because I've come to yearn for solitude. It's common for me to disappear into the wilderness for hours at a time, often from sunrise to sunset.

Recently, a dear friend shared how unusual she thought it was to so frequently hike deep into the wilderness all alone. She wondered, "How are you able to do that?" I shrugged and offered a vague answer, but over the next several days, I thought a lot about her question.

Because so many of the hours I spend walking in the wilderness unfold at sunrise and in the morning, when the sun's angle is still low in the sky, I've grown accustomed to hiking with my shadow. My dark twin stretches long beside me, mirroring my every step. On my longer, all-day treks—from first light to last—I begin my hikes with the long shadow of sunrise beside me and often finish them with that same silhouette returning from the other side, almost as if my shadow is there to walk with me out and back, never letting me go alone. In the quiet company of my shadow, I've come to understand myself more deeply and forged a companionship with myself. *The more I walk—the farther I walk—the closer I get to myself.*

Of course, you don't need to be a hiker or walk thousands of miles alone to find solitude. All you need is space for yourself, time in which you're available to your thoughts. Whether you can take ten minutes before getting out of bed every day or thirty minutes on Sunday evenings, you'll be better for it. Remember, without self-awareness and a deep understanding of yourself, you risk following someone else's path, living a life that others expect you to live instead of the one you aspire to live.

Excuses I hear for not wanting to spend time alone include, "I'm too busy," "It's boring," and "It's uncomfortable."

When I hear "I'm too busy," I'm reminded of the quote, "No one is as busy as someone who is not interested." Usually, when we say we're too busy, it's a priority problem. What we likely mean is that we're not interested. I understand—but what could be more important than taking a little time for yourself?

Time to reflect on your life, assess how you're doing, and imagine what's possible. Solitude is not selfish—it's necessary. In fact, I'd argue that the busier and more stressed you are, the more urgent it becomes to pause and reflect.

In his wonderful book *The Art of Stillness: Adventures in Going Nowhere*, Pico Iyer wrote that Mahatma Gandhi woke up one day and told those around him, "This is going to be a very busy day. I won't be able to meditate for an hour." His friends were taken aback at his rare break from discipline before he added, "I'll have to meditate for two." When we spend time in self-reflection, our life gains more spaciousness.

Many don't spend time alone because they find it to be boring. I don't know if you've noticed, but as a society, we've come to view boredom as a problem to be solved. We'd rather do something mindless—anything other than sitting alone with our thoughts and doing nothing.

According to various reports, on average, adult Americans reach for their phones 50-200 times a day. We can't stand in line at the grocery store, sit in the car while waiting for our child to finish soccer practice, wait at a red light, or make our way through TSA at the airport without reaching for our phones to fill in the empty time and avoid—God forbid—being bored. This is a tragedy, though, because to have new ideas and inspirations, to be creative, our minds must wander, and for them to do so, we must allow for boredom.

Next time you find yourself with a gap in your schedule, whether it's one minute or four hours, I challenge you to resist trying to fill or kill the time with mindless activity. Just sit with yourself and pay attention. What are you thinking? What can you hear? What can you see? What can you smell? How does your body feel? Do you notice tension anywhere in your body? Listen to and feel your breathing. Avoid looking for things to do and tasks that need completing.

Maybe you avoid spending time alone because it feels uncomfortable to sit with your thoughts. I get it. Being with our thoughts—especially when they show up as difficult emotions—is hard, and no one really teaches us how to do it. We aren't always told that sadness, anger, and fear are natural parts of the human experience, so perhaps it's no surprise that many of us instinctively try to avoid our emotions rather than facing them—but suppressing difficult emotions doesn't make them disappear. It buries them, where they can build up as stress, anxiety, or even physical illness, often surfacing in unexpected ways.

This is especially true in midlife, when long-buried memories and emotions often begin to rise uninvited, sometimes triggered by a smell, a moment of stillness, or no obvious cause at all. Psychologists suggest this is a natural part of our developmental arc: As we grow older, our brains become more reflective, drawing us inward to make sense of our story so far.

Psychotherapist Richard Schwartz, founder of Internal Family Systems (IFS) and author of *No Bad Parts*, suggests that these rising emotions often belong to younger, exiled parts of ourselves that are simply seeking attention and care.

Schwartz's work reminds us that healing doesn't come from pushing these parts away but from meeting them with curiosity, compassion, and connection. Experiencing our emotions rather than avoiding them allows us to understand ourselves more deeply, gain insight, and heal while hopefully moving forward with greater self-compassion and resilience.

(If you've experienced trauma or feel particularly tender and afraid to be with your thoughts, I suggest enlisting the help of a therapist, who can help provide loving support and professional guidance.)

While spending time alone can stir up difficult emotions and long-buried memories, that's also part of its power. Solitude and honest self-reflection are some of the most effective ways we can assess our lives, take stock of what's working, and detect what might be missing or calling for attention.

The time after the sale of our Yellowstone business *should* have been one of celebration. I had a loving husband, and we had three healthy sons. We had just sold the company we started from scratch fifteen years earlier to a company we respected. We had financial security, and the sale provided me with an opportunity to take some time to figure out—and feel inspired about—what would come next.

But during some time alone, the first I'd had in years, I realized things weren't as amazing as they looked on the outside. All kinds of alarms were sounding. I was thirty-five pounds overweight. I was eating and sleeping terribly. I wasn't present; I was addicted to my gadgets, email, and devices. I was drinking wine on too many weeknights. Not only were these habits damaging in and of themselves, but I could sense, deep down, that I was on a slippery slope. Despite all my blessings, I struggled with depression, feelings of despair, and occasional bouts of self-loathing.

That was fifteen years ago. I'm happy to report I was able to transform my mental and physical health. But I don't share this to boast. I share it because I honestly don't know where I'd be, or what my life would look like, if not for that time alone and the chance to notice and confront the truths of my life. I am certain, though, that without that reckoning, I wouldn't be living my epic life today.

There's no question that after the sale of our first company, I was devastated to discover the rut I was in. But what bothered me even more was the fact that I had *stopped paying attention* and hadn't even realized it. Since then, I've made it a practice to regularly and consistently reflect on my life.

We must make time to be alone, to take stock, reflect, and reconnect with ourselves. The work isn't always easy or pleasant, but it is necessary. Knowing who you are and how you want to be will ground you. Even during times when you're unsure of the path forward, as long as you know who you are and how you want to be, you will never feel lost.

The Value of Silence

"Before I open my mouth, I consider, will what I say improve the silence?"

—Drew Duncan, priest, Blessed Sacrament,
Fort Washakie, Wyoming

Solitude isn't only about being alone—it's also about learning to listen. I live on the frontier of Wyoming, where the population barely tips over five hundred thousand and the land stretches endlessly in every direction. Out here, silence isn't something you carve out, it's simply a part of life.

Some years ago, I traveled to Cambridge, Massachusetts, to deliver my "Epic Lessons Learned in the Field" keynote during a Girls in Tech event. Following my presentation, a woman raised her hand and asked if I thought living in such a remote place with so much wide-open space affected my thinking and the way I lived. I appreciated the question, and the answer was—and is—a resounding *Yes*.

I have grown to crave silence. I love spending entire days walking alone in the wilderness. There is something about the absence of talking that creates space. Thich Nhat Hanh, a Vietnamese Zen master, poet, peace activist, and renowned teacher of mindfulness, whose wisdom has influenced millions worldwide, said, "Insights don't happen in the *thinking* mind." Perhaps that explains why I often have profound insights, sudden realizations, and deeper understandings about things during my long walks in the mountains.

Some years ago, I was listening to Krista Tippett's *On Being* podcast. Tippett was interviewing acoustic ecologist and "sound tracker" Gordon Hempton. Hempton studies the natural soundscapes of the Earth, especially the rare experience of true silence—or, more precisely, the absence of human-made noise.

He has spent decades traveling the world capturing pristine natural sounds with ultra-sensitive recording equipment. He's especially known for championing the importance of quiet places, not just for the sake of nature but for human well-being, creativity, and inner clarity.

Hempton has said, "Silence is not the absence of something, but the presence of everything." He argues that silence is an endangered species and that if we lose these quiet places, we lose something vital in ourselves too.

In my own experience, I've learned that silence isn't empty. It's where our deepest knowing begins to surface.

Develop Your Internal Compass

"I have lost myself, though I know where I am."

—Rebecca Solnit, *A Field Guide to Getting Lost*

Back in the Brooks Range of Alaska, as my group pored over maps trying to figure out our location, one of my course mates remembered we had a compass in our community gear.

A compass all by itself will not determine your location. You must know how to use it, and thankfully, we did. We were able to determine true north and, from there, identify our location. It turned out we were only a little off course, but had we kept going and not stopped to get our bearings, we could have wandered much farther. The same can happen in our lives if we're not paying attention.

The drift from our authentic life happens gradually and usually inadvertently. It starts when we make a small, seemingly inconsequential deviation. By itself, the diversion may not be significant. But if we do this often, these small diversions compound and can lead us far from the path we meant to follow. When that happens, it can take a long time—and often a great deal of inner work—to find our way back.

The only way to keep from getting off course is to remain oriented. When we take time regularly to pause and reflect on our lives, our self-awareness becomes our internal compass. Over the years, I've developed Epic programs and workshops to help people do just that—pause, reflect, and get oriented.

Programs like *Exploring the Wilderness Inside of You*, *Mining the Lessons Learned in Your Life*, *An Epic Life Review*, *Connecting to Your Younger Self*, *Navigating the Wilds of Midlife*, and *Sorting the Seed from the Dirt* are all designed to inspire deep reflection. This kind of work doesn't just provide insight. It generates meaning and offers powerful direction for whatever comes next.

In a world that pulls us in a thousand directions, clarity is vital. Without it, we drift. Our internal compass provides that clarity. It enables us to stay on course and to find our way back to ourselves, again and again.

Your Time Is Your Life

We have only one life. Our time *is* our life. We ought to be intentional about how we spend it.

The Stoic Seneca wrote in *On the Shortness of Life*: "It is not that we have a short time to live, but that we waste a lot of it."

In 2011, I started viewing the way I use my time as an expense, investment, or experience. I wanted fewer expenses and more investments and experiences. I also learned how to say "no." (If you'd like to feel disconnected from yourself and sidestep your authentic life entirely, just say "yes" to everyone and everything.)

I started living by my calendar. I scheduled everything, including things related to self-care, time in the wilderness, and most importantly, time with the people I love most. One of the mantras I came up with at that time and try to live by still is, "Don't view anything as a waste of time, and it won't be."

That shift in perspective changed everything for me. Now, I try to do one thing at a time. When I'm doing it, I treat it as if it's the most important thing in the world—because it is. The price of anything is the amount of life you exchange for it.

Sorting the Seed from the Dirt

What is it that you want?

Think about that for a moment. And I mean *really* think about it. It's not a simple question, and people seldom ask it.

One of my favorite books is *Women Who Run with the Wolves: Myths and Stories of the Wild Woman Archetype* by Clarissa Pinkola Estés. In it, Estés writes:

> *The way to maintain one's connection to the wild is to ask yourself what it is that you want. This is the sorting of the seed from the dirt. One of the most important discriminations we can make in this matter is the difference between things that beckon to us and things that call from our souls.*

I've learned that "sorting the seed from the dirt" is one of the most important things we can do if we are to live our most authentic lives. But this work takes time. Rushing won't make the seed grow faster, and not everything in the dirt is meant to grow. Some things are meant to be left behind.

If you're in search of a more meaningful and inspired life, if you're wondering what's next, keep sorting. The answer is already there, waiting for you to uncover it. And the patience required is part of the journey. Clarity about who we are and our authentic life doesn't come all at once. It comes in the sifting, the sorting, the willingness to sit with the mess until the answer emerges, if only we'll give it a chance.

I have developed a meditation practice where I stand outside, my face turned toward the sun, eyes closed, arms open and outstretched toward the sky. And then for up to ten minutes, I meditate on this question: *What is it that I want?* This simple ritual reminds me to pause, listen for the call of my soul, and reconnect with the wild in me. I do it daily and any time I'm traveling, hiking, or cross-country skiing.

Because this practice has been so transformative, I often facilitate it during my Epic programs. Seeing my clients standing so peacefully, arms outstretched toward the sky, as they ponder such an important question for themselves is a sight to behold. For some minutes, we feel meaningfully connected to ourselves, to something larger, and to each other.

Try it. I think you'll love it, but most importantly, you'll benefit greatly from such a practice. Connecting with yourself in such a deep and meaningful way will help you know the difference between the things that beckon to you from outside yourself and the things that call from your soul.

It will help you know the difference between someone else's path and your own.

Lesson 2
Carry the Right Stuff

Be Deliberate About What You Choose to Carry

Coaching and leadership clients who are seeking something memorable—and potentially life-changing—often sign up for guided Epic Adventures in the wilderness with me. Before we set foot on the trail, we gather for an orientation where we carefully assess what we'll bring into the wild.

Each client lays out their gear beside an empty backpack and I meet with them individually. We pick up each item and ask a simple but powerful question: "Is this essential for the journey?" If the answer is no, we dare to leave it behind.

This is a time-consuming and tedious exercise, but it's critically important. To be prepared, we must consider all the elements and pack accordingly. What we choose to carry or not carry significantly impacts our experience.

If our pack is unnecessarily heavy or unwieldy, it makes our journey more difficult. The effort required to carry such a heavy load limits the extent to which we're able to enjoy and contribute to the expedition. On the other hand, if we aren't properly prepared—if we don't carry the *right* stuff—our journey is not likely to go well.

If I'm leading an adventure in bear country, it's important to pack essentials such as bear spray and a way to store our food safely and out of bears' reach. If we're heading into the wilderness and the weather forecast calls for precipitation, we need to pack rain gear. If we're traveling over snow, we may need to pack spikes or crampons and ropes.

This "Carry the Right Stuff" exercise isn't just relevant to the clients who come on an Epic Adventure—it should be practiced by everybody. Carrying the right stuff is about being intentional. Just as you put careful thought into what you want to take on your wilderness expedition, you must be deliberate and intentional about how you live, how you lead, and how you show up in all areas of your life.

There are few things in life that we get to choose and over which we have control. Fortunately, our mindset is one of them. This is no small thing. It is one of the greatest opportunities we have, if only we take advantage of it. Our mindset is a set of attitudes and beliefs that shape how we perceive and respond to the world, like the lens through which we see and experience it. From the moment we wake up, the mindset we choose affects every single one of our experiences and interactions.

Your mindset significantly influences your life. When you choose your mindset, you choose your existence.

What Will You Carry?

What we carry or don't carry affects the quality of our lives, the depth of our relationships, and the impact we have on others.

I like to ask the people I coach, "Is there something you're carrying around that you'd like to shed, something that is weighing you down, making your life more difficult, and that could be preventing you from having a more meaningful impact on those around you?" The responses I often hear are complacency, ego, judgment, anxiety or worry, and, above all, need for control.

Conversely, I'll ask, "Is there something you'd like to add? Is there some way of being that you could work toward to make your journey more enjoyable and to help you deepen your relationships?" The most common responses I receive to this question are flexibility, innovation, humility, empathy, and an ability to better manage emotions and instill calm.

The things people want to add are often the opposite of the things they'd like to remove.

Rigid People Are Dangerous People

"The green reed which bends in the wind is stronger than the mighty oak which breaks in a storm."

—Confucius

When we feel a need to be in control, we come across as rigid and closed-minded. Rigidity and control may feel safe or comfortable, but they limit growth, innovation, and resilience, especially in uncertain and rapidly changing environments.

In the wilderness, we often quote Laurence Gonzales: "Rigid people are dangerous people." If I'm leading an expedition and day two of our itinerary calls for climbing a mountain but we wake up that morning and dark clouds fill the sky, implying a storm is imminent, it would be reckless of me to remain rigidly attached to our plan.

Most of my clients report that the thing they most want to shed is their need for control. Organizations suffer when their leaders are rigid—when despite signals and changing conditions, they hold fast to their legacy focus and familiar path.

At the height of its success in the early 2000s, Blockbuster was the undisputed giant of video rentals, with thousands of stores across the country. But technology was evolving, and the landscape was shifting. Consumer behavior was changing. The rise of the internet and on-demand entertainment signaled the beginning of a new era, one in which people wouldn't need to leave their homes to rent a movie.

Netflix saw this shift early.

Founded in 1997, Netflix started as a DVD-by-mail service. It understood that convenience would drive the future of entertainment and quickly adapted to a subscription-based model with no due dates or late fees. Blockbuster, on the other hand, was generating nearly $800 million a year in late fees. Its leaders dismissed the changing conditions and warning signs and refused to consider a different path. A moment of reckoning came in 2000 when Netflix approached Blockbuster with an offer to sell for $50 million. Blockbuster's leaders declined, dismissing Netflix as an insignificant player.

Blockbuster had the opportunity to evolve. It had the brand. It had market dominance. It even launched its own online rental service in 2004, but leadership failed to commit to it. They saw digital as an add-on rather than the future. Meanwhile, Netflix leaned in, embracing the shift with full force. By the time Blockbuster realized its mistake, it was too late. Consumers had moved on. Netflix had built a loyal subscriber base and rapidly expanded its streaming capabilities.

In 2010, Blockbuster filed for bankruptcy with nearly a billion dollars in debt. Today, Netflix is a global powerhouse, valued at over $150 billion, and Blockbuster is a relic—a cautionary tale of what happens when leaders refuse to adapt.

Blockbuster didn't fail because it lacked resources. It didn't fail because people stopped watching movies or because of bad luck. It failed because its leaders were inflexible and refused to adapt to a changing world. They weren't willing to rethink their model, to sacrifice short-term profits for long-term survival. In business, leadership, and life, it's not the strongest who survive—it's the most adaptable.

The antidote to rigidity and control is flexibility. Cognitive flexibility is the ability to adapt our thinking, approach, or perspective in response to new information or changing circumstances. We can be more cognitively flexible by being open to other perspectives, responding to changing conditions with curiosity, or by remaining focused on the big picture.

A leader demonstrates cognitive flexibility when, after introducing a new company-wide workflow system that causes frustration and resistance, he listens to his team, gathers feedback, and adjusts the system to better align with employees' needs. This improves the workflow while building trust and morale, showcasing that adaptability strengthens leadership.

On a personal level, when we're rigid, we create suffering for ourselves and others. I know from experience how hard it is to cede control (just ask my family). I can get so enthusiastic about a particular adventure that I become irrationally intent on sticking to it, even when conditions are unfavorable, especially if it has been months in the making.

When we cling to control, we create unnecessary suffering. Letting go can be painfully hard—even disappointing or frustrating—but it's essential for leading others effectively and for protecting our own well-being.

As the Tao Te Ching says, "The rigid person is a disciple of death. Those who are 'soft and supple' are lovers of life." Fortunately, we have the power to choose which we will be.

This Is a Time for Humility

Humility is one of the most valuable traits in leadership.

I don't know about you, but I'd much rather follow a leader who can release their ego and be honest—one who is willing to say, "I think this is the way, but I'm not 100 percent certain"—than someone trying to convince me they are certain while secretly harboring the same fears and concerns as I am. I admire and respect people who are willing to admit when they don't know the answer and who are humble enough to ask for help.

Most of the leaders I work with admire humility and want to have more of it but find it difficult to practice. They worry that their humility could be mistaken for insecurity, weakness, or timidity. In response, I remind them of the words of British writer and theologian C. S. Lewis: "Humility is not thinking less of yourself but thinking about yourself less."

Empathy: The Most Valuable Skill

Empathy, the ability to imagine and understand what others might be experiencing, is the most valuable skill of them all. Practicing empathy fosters compassion, prevents us from judging, and helps us bridge differences. It also enables us to have a deeper connection with others.

If you'd like to have richer, more meaningful relationships in your life, one of the best ways to achieve this is to learn to be more empathetic. Fortunately, empathy is a skill that can be learned and developed.

Start by practicing active listening. When listening to someone, focus fully on them without mentally preparing your response. To expand your perspective and activate your brain's empathy circuits, seek out conversations or stories from people with different backgrounds. To better understand what others may be feeling beneath the surface, pay attention to subtle emotional cues like tone, pauses, and facial expressions.

Most importantly, remember that empathy isn't about fixing or agreeing but being present enough to truly understand.

Freaking Out Isn't Leadership

Nothing induces worry and anxiety like uncertainty. Almost every person I know and work with would like to be better at responding amid uncertainty and remaining calm in a crisis. Our emotions are contagious; our mental state impacts others. I like to say, "Freaking out isn't leadership."

To be an effective leader (or teacher or parent), we must be able to manage our emotions. Freaking out during a crisis makes it difficult to act rationally, and losing our composure doesn't exactly inspire confidence among those we're leading or surrounded by. Thankfully, modern research has given us the tools we need to improve how we manage our emotions, including self-reflection, mindfulness and meditation practices, breathing exercises, and journaling.

When it comes to getting better at managing our emotions, it's critical we practice these skills ahead of time so that when we find ourselves in high-stress situations, we'll have the wherewithal and ability to compose ourselves and respond thoughtfully instead of reacting emotionally.

Choose Optimism

In a time of rapid change and uncertainty, optimism is more than a nice-to-have quality—it's critical. An optimistic mindset equips us to see opportunities where others see obstacles and to foster the resilience and creativity that are essential for adaptation and growth. No person I know would wish to work for or follow a leader who says at the outset of a challenge, "We're never going to make it through this."

That is not to say that we must declare everything's great when it isn't. That would be toxic positivity. An optimistic leader acknowledges the harsh reality of challenging conditions while maintaining a hopeful outlook. This kind of optimism looks something like this:

> *"This is a challenging time, and we're facing real uncertainty. There's a lot we don't know and can't know right now. So let's stay focused on what we can control. Let's take the next step, then the one after that. We'll adjust as needed—whether that means backtracking, rerouting, or changing course. We'll be in this together, and we will find a way forward."*

Optimism isn't only essential for effective leadership; it's a competitive advantage. It fuels creativity, leadership, and the ability to navigate uncertainty. Yet too many people dismiss it as naive, failing to recognize that optimism is deeply wired into the brain as a tool for innovation and adaptability.

When we take an optimistic view of the world—when we see the glass as half full—it sparks activity in a key area of the brain: the rostral anterior cingulate cortex (rACC). This region is involved in emotional regulation, self-reflection, and forward thinking. In other words, when we're optimistic, our brains literally orient us toward the future, helping us imagine possibilities and solutions that others miss.

This is why some of the greatest breakthroughs in history didn't come from people who feared failure and played it safe. They came from inventors, artists, and leaders who were optimistic and believed in what wasn't yet visible, from those who dared to see beyond obstacles. On the other hand, when we view the world through a pessimistic lens, our brains shift into a different mode.

Pessimism encourages caution and analytical thinking—useful in some cases but limiting when it comes to creativity. Instead of exploring new ideas, we focus on avoiding failure. Instead of seeing possibilities, we search for reasons something won't work. This kind of narrow thinking limits our problem-solving abilities and makes us less likely to take the risks that innovation requires. It's also not a lot of fun to be around (think "Debbie Downer" of *SNL* fame).

This doesn't mean pessimists can't be creative—some use defensive pessimism to anticipate problems and refine their ideas—but optimism broadens cognitive flexibility, which is critical for adapting and innovating in an unpredictable world. Today, leaders who cultivate optimism aren't just more inspiring, they're also more adaptable. They see potential where others see dead ends. They generate ideas instead of excuses. They don't just react to change; they shape it. Those who believe in a better future are the ones who create it.

If you struggle to be optimistic—which is understandable in highly uncertain and difficult times—try practicing gratitude, journaling to process your emotions, exercising and moving your body, and doing breathing exercises to shift your mindset from being negative and limited to optimistic and more expansive. When I'm feeling pessimistic or down about my circumstances, I often ask myself, "What can I make of this?" Doing so shifts my mindset into a more constructive state.

Beyond asking ourselves this question, there are numerous other tools we can look to for shifting our mindset from negative and pessimistic to positive and optimistic.

Shift Your State: Tools to Shift from Negative to Positive

Even the most grounded among us find ourselves stuck in a negative spiral from time to time—overwhelmed, emotionally contracted, or steeped in pessimism. But we can shift our state from survival mode to something more constructive. The following are a few tools I have tried and tested that can help shift your mood in the moment.

1. Utilize Breathing Exercises

Try box breathing: Inhale for four seconds, hold for four, exhale for four, hold for four—and repeat. This practice helps calm the nervous system and restore mental clarity. Or try the *physiological sigh*, recommended by neuroscientist Andrew Huberman: take one big inhale through your nose, then a second small sip of air right after, followed by a slow exhale through the mouth. Just a few of these can bring your nervous system back from fight-or-flight to a neutral state.

2. Shift Your View—Literally

When you're feeling emotionally contracted—trapped in stress or rumination—look up and out. Huberman's research shows that expanding your visual field (by gazing at the horizon or a wide landscape) can signal to your brain that you're safe, shifting you from a sympathetic (stress) to a parasympathetic (rest-and-digest) state.

3. Practice Gratitude

Gratitude isn't just a feel-good idea; it's an orientation tool. When you're feeling stuck, list three things you're grateful for—either in a journal or aloud. Don't worry if they feel small or obvious. Gratitude shifts our focus from what's wrong to what's also true. Science shows that even just asking the question, "What am I grateful for?" can shift our brain chemistry.

4. Journal It Out

Writing helps us to process our emotions. If you're overwhelmed, sad, angry, or anxious, try writing for ten minutes. Just write it out; don't worry about quality or form. Simply express your feelings on the page.

5. Write a "Hot Letter"

President Abe Lincoln used to write letters to those he was furious with but not send them. He called these "hot letters," and they're an excellent way to express strong emotions without doing harm. You can try this too. Write the letter, let it burn onto the page, then don't send it. The clarity and release you gain are often all you need.

These practices will help you to shift from a negative mindset to a more positive, optimistic, and constructive one.

Survival Starts Before the Accident

Trigger warning: The following story contains vivid descriptions of a traumatic accident involving a child, including graphic injuries, blood, potential spinal trauma, and emotional distress. Read with care.

It was March 30, 2017, and my husband Jerry, our three sons, and I were exploring the hoodoos known as the "goblins" of Utah's Goblin Valley State Park when we heard a scream followed by a loud yell. We quickly descended and bolted toward where the yell came from, and that was how we came to meet Ivy, who, just moments before, had been having the time of her life exploring with her little sister and uncle.

We found her crumpled under the cliff, her face bloodied and her right eye blue and swollen shut. Her right cheekbone and nose appeared to be fractured. Her face, beneath the blood, was pale. Although she was screaming and trembling, her body wasn't moving. A man was with her, cradling her feet in his hands, and a younger girl sat nearby, crying.

As I took my first steps toward the girl, I was an emotional wreck. I knew I had to act fast to do something to help the girl, but I was finding it hard to breathe, let alone concentrate, in my panic. I reminded myself, *Freaking out isn't leadership.* I had to get it together, and quickly.

Years earlier, when I started Epic Life Inc. and planned to start guiding clients on adventures in the wilderness, I became a certified Wilderness First Responder. If something were to go wrong for my family, friends, clients, myself, or anyone I encountered in the wilderness, I wanted to have the skills to effectively respond. I needed to know what to do in situations like this one and, if necessary, how to save a life. Until that morning in Goblin Valley, except for blisters, altitude symptoms, and minor injuries, my first responder skills had never been put to the test. I had hoped it would stay that way.

Since my sons were toddlers, Goblin Valley has been one of our family's favorite destinations. It's a natural jungle gym made up of thousands of hoodoos ("goblins") that beg to be climbed and explored. A child's natural instinct is to climb, so it was unreasonable to take our sons to Goblin Valley and expect them not to explore the endless mazes of hoodoos.

When our boys were little, I spent most of my time yelling and worrying as I tried my best to keep them on a short leash. As they got older, I gave them more freedom and yelled less, but my worry remained and "what ifs" ran rampant through my mind.

What happened to Ivy was any guardian's worst nightmare. She had taken a big fall from a "goblin" towering above us.

My heart was racing, the beat thumping in my chest. My breathing was fast, and I worried I might start hyperventilating. The mom in me was in hysterics, and I wanted to scream and cry and run straight for the injured girl. At the same time, I felt paralyzed, unable to leap into action.

As the weight of responsibility pressed heavily on me, and I felt stuck in place. But then I remembered the advice from my most recent Wilderness First Responder (WFR) recertification class: "Go slow to go fast." I took some deep breaths, trying to compose myself and hopefully transform from crazy into capable. I did a quick recall of the first steps of the Wilderness First Responder protocol. "Size up the scene," I told myself, and I quickly scanned for immediate dangers.

I determined Ivy had fallen. I learned that it was her uncle who was with her and that she had been exploring with her younger sister, who was nearby, scared and sobbing.

"Did anyone see her fall?" I asked.

Her younger sister pointed to where Ivy had fallen. I craned my neck to see the goblin. I estimated she fell one hundred to one hundred fifty feet.

"Did you see how Ivy landed?" I asked.

She shook her head.

I couldn't get Ivy to calm down enough to talk to me directly. She was in excruciating pain, moaning and crying loudly, and at times, screaming. She trembled in pain.

I asked her uncle if she had been unconscious when he got to her after the fall. "I think she was," he said, visibly rattled. "For a minute, maybe."

When someone suffers a fall from a height, there is a significant risk of spine and head injuries. Ivy was not on level ground, which made it hard to assess her condition. Still, we made sure not to move her. I quickly went through what is known as ABCDE.

Airway: I checked for obstruction. Her mouth was full of blood, and I couldn't tell if her teeth had been knocked around, but as far as I could see, there was nothing obstructing her airway.

Breathing: I looked, listened, and felt her chest and throat. This was hard given Ivy's screaming and pain. My anxiety and concerns for her were great, and it took a Herculean effort for me to manage my emotions.

Circulation: I checked her pulse and examined her for any bleeding other than what I could see on her face. I expected she was in shock.

Disability: I prepared for a possible spine injury, cautioning anyone who could hear me to not move her.

And, last, *Environment/Exposure*: I assessed environmental threats and any serious exposed wounds. There appeared to be fractures to her face and nose. I wondered if her left arm or wrist might be broken, and I worried about her back being broken, or at least severely injured.

Next, I did a head-to-toe exam. She had sensation in her toes and fingers. "Good news there," I told myself. I tried repeatedly to discern from Ivy what hurt the most but couldn't make out what she was saying. She was in tremendous distress and couldn't talk. I recalled from WFR training that it was important to keep her awake and alert, so her uncle and I continued talking softly to her, trying to calm her down.

We asked her if there was a song she liked that she could sing. It was no use; she was in extreme pain and couldn't compose herself. But we did keep bringing up that idea. It would help her, and us, if we could calm her down even a little bit so we could learn more about her injuries.

Then, to my great relief, a man appeared who identified himself as a family doctor who happened to be in the area and had a trauma kit with him. I moved aside to let him take over the medical care. I remained in the background, focusing my attention on calming Ivy down. A moment later, another doctor arrived on the scene.

"I know it's hard, but try to take some slow, deep breaths. It's going to be okay, Ivy," I told her, rubbing her left arm lightly. Now that there were doctors on the scene, the mother in me took over. "Help is here, and more is coming. You're going to be okay. We're right here with you," I told her over and over again, while also trying to make myself believe it.

In the meantime, the doctor managing Ivy's care wondered out loud if there was something we could lay Ivy on to at least transport her to more level ground without compromising her spine. The uncle mentioned he had a cot in his trunk and gave the key to my sons Hayden and Wolf. My boys ran as fast as they could to the parking lot, while other tourists started showing up and lending a hand.

Another man, who I think was a friend in the group, went to get help from the ranger station. The rangers arrived carrying a stretcher, oxygen, and other supplies just as Hayden and Wolf returned. Several minutes passed while the head ranger and doctors worked on Ivy, and not long after that, we started hearing Ivy mumbling what sounded like "Jingle Bells."

As the group tended to Ivy, my son Wolf worked to comfort Ivy's sister, who was in great distress. The rangers and doctors completed their assessments, and a handful of people were able to move Ivy to a board, then put her on the stretcher. The crew administered oxygen to Ivy, and the group, including our oldest sons, took turns carrying the stretcher with Ivy in it. Once in the parking lot, Ivy was put in the bed of the ranger's truck and accompanied by the doctor, her uncle, and the rangers to meet an inbound helicopter. As we parted ways with Ivy's uncle and sister and the others who had helped in the rescue effort, Ivy's uncle grasped my hand. He thanked us, and before we parted ways, I told him we'd pray for Ivy.

During our one-mile hike back to our camp, my family was mostly quiet. It had been a sobering experience, and we were all a little traumatized. One of our sons spoke up, recalling that, coincidentally, the uncle and Ivy and her sister had been camped in the spot right next to ours in the Goblin Valley State Campground the night before, which felt like a lifetime ago in that moment. We had marveled at the beautiful sliver of a moon and the thousands of twinkling stars. It was one of those brilliant and unforgettable nights, and as we ate s'mores, the boys' excitement about getting to explore their beloved "goblins" the next day was palpable. Later, as we lay in our tent before falling asleep, we could hear the man (whom we now knew to be Ivy's uncle) and the girls' voices laughing and talking, presumably by their own campfire. By all indications, it had been a blessed night for them. We had commented that the uncle looked like one of our favorite comedians, Jim Gaffigan. We had no idea that we'd meet the way we did the next day, or that we'd be involved in saving Ivy's life.

For a day or two following the experience, we were so traumatized that we felt like it had been bad luck for us to have been part of such a terrifying and serious experience. But soon after, we began to view our role in the experience as more of a blessing. We felt grateful to have been nearby and able to help.

After returning home, I tried to hunt Ivy and her family down. My family continued to talk about the experience and pray for Ivy, and we all desperately wanted to know if she was going to be okay. She had been life-flighted by helicopter from Goblin Valley to St. Mary's Hospital in Grand Junction, Colorado, but because Ivy was a minor and we didn't know her last name, we were limited in our quest. I searched Facebook extensively and shared about the experience with all my friends in Grand Junction and Salt Lake City (where her uncle, during the rescue, had told me she was from) in hopes that someone who knew her might respond. But we never heard anything.

Although I will probably never be completely confident in my Wilderness First Responder capabilities, I am grateful for them. Thanks to my training, I was able to know the very basics of what to do when I met Ivy on that spring day in Goblin Valley. We have not returned to our beloved Goblin Valley since. I have confidence that someday we will, but for now, we haven't felt ready. In the meantime, during every Christmas season, when we hear "Jingle Bells," we think of Ivy.

Like many experiences, this one was a great teacher. I learned so much, including how quickly one's life can go from feeling full to seemingly fragile. One minute you're playing, feeling so alive, and the next, your life could be hanging in the balance. A lot can go wrong in the wilderness, and when it does, you're a long way from help. You're also likely to be a long way from a reliable cell signal.

Worrying and trying to keep your kids on a short leash in the wilderness is a good start (and better than having a cavalier attitude), but in the wilderness, worrying is not enough. What happens when someone falls or gets injured? We all need to consider this question before going to a place like Goblin Valley. A first aid kit is of no value if we don't know what to do when we need to use it. At the very least, I recommend taking a CPR class. If you spend a lot of time outdoors, are a parent, or lead groups on adventures, consider taking a Wilderness First Aid or Wilderness First Responder course.

Time spent outdoors is important, fun, and invaluable for children—for all of us. Most of the time, things don't go wrong. For years now, my family and I have spent significant time outdoors, and we have never suffered from any serious injuries. Until that day in Goblin Valley, we had never been involved in a rescue or evacuation. Incidents like Ivy's, although serious and sobering, should not be a deterrent from spending time exploring the outdoors, but they should serve to inform us.

When I arrived on the scene that day, I came close to freaking out. My spiraling thoughts and panicked breathing may have overwhelmed me had I not spent time practicing the skills that such a high-stress situation required. It's imperative that we practice the necessary mental and practical skills long before an accident happens. Most of us are well trained in worrying about worst-case scenarios, and while it's important that we reflect on what could go wrong, it's equally important to reflect on how we'll respond—what steps we will take—if and when the worst-case scenario happens.

Leaders Aren't Made Under Blue Skies

As an adventurer and adventure guide, there's nothing I love more than a favorable weather forecast. Nothing says possibility like a clear, blue sky. It usually means we can climb the mountain or do whatever we hope to do. There likely won't be a great need for leadership. Conversely, if there's an 80- or 90-percent chance of a storm, or there are torrential rains and lightning when we wake up at camp in the morning, it's clear what we can and cannot do. But when it's cloudy and the weather is notably variable and uncertain, it's a different story.

When I open my weather app and see a 50-percent chance of rain, my stress increases. There is nothing as uncertain as a 40-, 50-, or 60-percent chance of a storm. These conditions are what I call "cloudy with a 100-percent chance of leadership."

Some years ago, I was in Wyoming's Wind River Range leading my Epic Women program. We were on a five-day expedition that included two mountain climbs. On day two, we planned to climb a mountain.

I always opted for an alpine start to provide the biggest window of opportunity to reach the summit and be down before the weather changes and storms are likely. We woke up at 3 a.m., and after quaffing some cowboy coffee, we left camp, a line of bobbing headlamps as we navigated the terrain under a star-filled sky. We made our way toward Temple Pass, a one-thousand-foot pile of loose rock piled on top of more loose rock. Ascending the pass in the dark was slow going, but eventually we crested the pass and were greeted by a sunrise that set the surrounding peaks ablaze with light.

The women were doing great. I could tell they'd trained hard. As we ascended the boulder-strewn alpine tundra toward the summit of our mountain, the women's determination showed on their faces. Meanwhile, I had begun taking notice of the changing weather conditions. Darkness was quickly filling the once-clear sky. I continued to lead us higher, but I worried. The dark clouds signaled trouble, and I could smell moisture in the air. The summit was just six hundred vertical feet above us, but the mountaintop would be only the halfway point. We'd still have to descend the steep, rugged terrain. If we were caught in a storm during our descent, conditions could turn deadly.

I stopped and removed my backpack. One by one, the women reached me, their faces glowing with anticipation. One of them pointed up, her voice full of excitement: "It's right there! We've got this!" But I knew better. I could feel the shift in the air, the way the mountain seemed to hold its breath. Even though we were close—so close—I had to turn us around.

"Ladies," I began, "you're not going to want to hear this." I paused, feeling the weight of my words. "We're turning around. The summit may be right there, but it's not worth the risk. A storm's coming, and I'm not willing to put us in harm's way."

Their disappointment was immediate. Their faces fell. Some blinked back tears. They had worked so hard. They had wanted so badly to climb this mountain, and here I was telling them that their goal—our goal—was no longer within reach.

I explained that the summit was only the halfway point and reminded them of the treacherous terrain we'd have to descend. It would take some time to safely navigate down, even without a storm; lightning is common with storms in the high country, and we'd have no protection for hours.

Leadership is hard. But we can make it a little less hard when we take time to reflect deeply about the kind of leader we wish to be. It's important to gain clarity about our values and ethos, and how we will lead when the going gets tough, *before* the going gets tough.

It was so hard to have to turn my clients around, to witness their disappointment when we were so close to the summit. But it would have been harder if I hadn't established my ethos ahead of time—if I had had to make such a decision in real time when emotions were high, especially given my people-pleasing tendencies. And it would have been even harder to get them down safely over exposed and treacherous terrain in a storm.

We Are A Leader When We Choose to Be One

One time, following my keynote presentation to a leadership team in Chicago, a woman raised her hand and asked:

"Do you ever work with non-leaders?"

The question bothered me then and still bothers me today, because I view all of us as potential leaders. If you don't have a leadership role or title, it doesn't mean you aren't a leader or that you don't lead. In fact, most of us know high-level "leaders" who don't always lead or act like a leader, while people who have positions that are lower in the organization's ranks are often stellar leaders. We are a leader when we choose to be one.

Mind over Mosquitoes

"Everything can be taken from a man but one thing: the last of the human freedoms—to choose one's attitude in any given set of circumstances . . ."

—Viktor Frankl, *Man's Search for Meaning*

The date was July 6, 2014. After a two-hour drive, my friends Joel and Alan and I arrived at the trailhead. It was 5:30 a.m. and the sun was just beginning to rise over the horizon. The moment we slid open the truck door, we were under siege by millions of mosquitoes.

While cursing the mosquitoes, we took turns dousing ourselves with mosquito repellent, putting on our long-sleeve shirts, and scrambling to locate our bug head nets.

I recalled warning them months earlier when we had settled on this date that the mosquitoes "could be horrendous." Alan had responded with a chuckle and said something to the effect of, "I'm not scared; I'm from New Jersey where mosquitoes are huge." I couldn't help but wonder if he still felt the same way.

As our driver disappeared out of sight, I almost cried. The mosquitoes were so bad. I had never seen so many. If this were Jerry, the boys, and I, it would be a no go. But it was Joel and Alan, and we had been planning this for six months. It was a go.

As we entered the forest and started up the trail, Joel and Alan continued to curse the mosquitoes and swat at their bodies in attempts to keep the pesky insects away. I did the same, although I kept my cursing to myself. I thought, in anger, *Are you kidding me? These mosquitoes are going to ruin this trip before it even starts.*

I was still in my early years of operating Epic Life, and I had already been feeling nervous, determined to provide an unforgettable, hopefully transformational experience for my friends. It would serve as a "test drive" for one of my prospective programs. But now, the mosquitoes threatened to hijack our adventure. I was so stressed about the situation that despite it being only thirty-five degrees out, I felt sweat pooling behind my neck and in my armpits.

As I led us through the thick cloud of insects, I remembered all the whiskey the guys had packed. I had tried to reason with them to leave some of it behind, reminding them that a little went a long way at high altitude. But now, I was glad they had ignored me and hoped they might share.

As Joel and Alan continued cursing and swatting, I watched and listened as the swarms hovered in front of my face and all around me. Mosquitoes filled the air, part of the view, and their buzzing was loud and constant, but none of them were getting in. Our head nets, repellant, and clothing kept them out. As annoying as the mosquitoes were, they posed no danger to us. We were protected.

It was then that I realized how I responded to the mosquitoes might influence how Joel and Alan would respond to them. As we walked, in my mind, I strategized about how I was going to lead us through the hardship of mosquitoes for five days and remembered the words of Viktor Frankl.

Frankl was a Holocaust survivor who spent three years in Nazi concentration camps. He later wrote *Man's Search for Meaning*, and in it, he suggested a now well-known idea: "Between stimulus and response, there is a space, and in that space, we have the power to choose our response."

If Viktor Frankl could endure the unimaginable hardships of a Nazi concentration camp and still choose his response, surely we could do the same with these mosquitoes.

In that moment, I made a decision and resolved: *These mosquitoes will not hijack our adventure.* Choosing that mindset made all the difference. (Remember, when we choose our mindset, we choose our existence.) Despite the mosquitoes' constant presence, we still managed to have an inspiring and an unforgettable experience.

That is not to say that choosing or changing our mindset is easy work. It's not like flipping a switch. It's not a one-and-done exercise. We may have to choose a particular mindset several times in a day, which is what I did during my adventure with Joel and Alan. I probably chose the mindset *These mosquitoes will not hijack this adventure* hundreds of times a day.

By the time I was leading Joel and Alan on our adventure, I had spent every day for the previous two years practicing mindfulness every morning for ten to thirty minutes. Before I regularly practiced mindfulness, I didn't have the space that Frankl referenced between stimulus and response. I had to learn how to become an observer of my thoughts and acquire the ability to create a pause during which I could choose my response. (I may still freak out, but at least it's a choice.)

Adopting the mindset of *These mosquitoes will not hijack our adventure* enabled us to have an incredible experience. If not for changing and choosing my mindset, our experience could have been a miserable, five-day, complaint-filled one. Instead, it was an adventure of a lifetime. And not only that, the greatest gift of all to come from the experience was the deepening of our friendship—three people, bonded not just by time in the wilderness but by enduring the challenge together.

I already knew how much I valued Joel as a friend—he's one of the most creative people and original thinkers I've ever known. He's been in my corner since 2005, helping shape both of my businesses—first designing the Webby Award–winning websites for my Yellowstone company, and later becoming one of my first coaching clients when I reinvented myself and launched Epic Life. We've shared many adventures, and he's been a steady, generous presence on my journey ever since. I trust his perspective and appreciate his friendship so much. And it was Joel who introduced me to Alan, whose friendship has become another gift, one I now treasure deeply.

The mosquitoes were relentless—but so were we.

Reappraise Your Emotions: "I'm Not Nervous, I'm Excited!"

Emotional reappraisal is a form of cognitive reframing where you change a negative emotional experience into a more positive one. This has several benefits, but the biggest is that it reduces negative emotions. For example, if your belief is, "I'm not good enough," reappraising it as, "I'm learning and improving every day," changes the emotional tone of your self-perception and can rewire how you respond to setbacks.

Even though I've been a keynote presenter and public speaker for twelve years, there is nothing that makes me more nervous than the moment right before I walk onto the stage.

My first in-person presentation after the COVID-19 pandemic was for an organization in Atlanta, Georgia. Arrow Exterminators had hired me to be the keynote presenter at their Fiscal Year Kickoff, and I was simultaneously excited and terrified. It had been two years since I'd given a live presentation, and because this was a particularly beloved and important client, I wanted to hit it out of the park.

The event was a major production. Spotlights illuminated the stage while booming, energetic music blared from the speakers. Hundreds of leaders sat in the audience, their faces alert and expectant, waiting for me to share what I'd been hired to deliver. I peered at them through a slit in the curtain from behind the stage while the president of the organization read my bio. I worried and felt paralyzed by my nerves.

The instinctive thing to do in this kind of situation is to try to calm yourself down. But good luck with that. It's not likely to work. According to Alison Wood Brooks, a prominent researcher and professor at Harvard Business School who has contributed significantly to the field of emotional regulation, being nervous is a high arousal state and being calm is a low arousal state. This means closing the gap between the two is difficult, if not impossible. While there are breathing exercises and other tools to help, the reality is that most of us won't be able to calm down in short order when we're feeling so nervous.

According to Wood Brooks, it's more effective to try to go from nervous to excited than from nervous to calm because, like anxiety, excitement is a high arousal state. I remembered this and started telling myself over and over, *I'm not nervous. I'm excited.* And the difference it made was remarkable. As I stepped onto the stage, instead of feeling small, contracted, and paralyzed, I felt energized and expansive.

While leading my Epic Adventure programs in Zion National Park, I often guide clients on a hike called Angels Landing. It's a bucket-list hike that people travel from all over the world to experience, and it's not for the faint of heart. The last half mile follows a narrow ridge with 1,500-foot drop-offs on either side and only chains to hold onto. I love guiding this hike because it provides a unique opportunity for my clients to operate beyond their comfort zones and practice being courageous. Before we begin our ascent, I huddle with my clients and remind them that they'll need to pay close attention.

"When we do something that's hard—something we're not sure we can do—we must remember to focus on one step at a time," I tell them. "If and when you feel nervous, pause and take some deep breaths, and then say, 'I'm not nervous, I'm excited.' And see what happens." It always helps, so much so that "I'm not nervous, I'm excited" has become a mantra for many of my Epic clients when they dare to do hard things.

Record New Tracks

We all experience—or have experienced—what it's like to have negative and limiting beliefs about ourselves. Insecurity and self-doubt are part of the human experience, after all. These negative stories and limiting beliefs tend to enter our minds whenever we're feeling nervous. Most of these stories have been with us since we were young, and they hold us back. These limiting beliefs work to protect the status quo, to keep us safe from risk, but consequently they keep us from growing.

Fortunately, we can rewrite these stories we tell ourselves. Our brains are adaptable. Neuroplasticity is the brain's ability to reorganize itself by forming new neural connections throughout life. By adopting and practicing new and more constructive thought patterns, we can "rewire" our brains, creating new neural pathways that better serve us.

Do you remember cassette tapes? When I was in junior high, I would listen to Casey Kasem's Top 40 hits every Sunday. Provided I didn't pull out the plastic tabs on the cassette, I could record each week's Top 40 songs over the previous week's hits. I always think of these when I think of our limiting beliefs and our negative self-talk. They are just like old songs on a cassette tape—we can record new tracks over them.

Most of us can identify and name our "tracks" pretty quickly because they tend to be the same few things we hear again and again whenever we experience self-doubt. Currently, when I'm doubting myself, my top track is, "Don't get too excited, because the other shoe's going to drop." This is a real limiter for me because it prevents me from ever fully celebrating my achievements. Another negative belief I hear my brain repeat often is, "You're from Wyoming. You don't have anything to say that hasn't been said before."

I have worked to record new tracks over these that are more positive and constructive. When I hear the first one, I simply restate, "Congratulations! Allow yourself this moment of celebration. It was hard-earned and is worthy of celebration." For the second one, I respond with, "That may be true, but the way I say it is original." By doing this, I'm creating new neural pathways that support healthier, more positive, more effective ways of thinking and being.

To do this work, grab a journal and list the negative stories and limiting beliefs you often hear from your inner critic. Next to each, write a new, more constructive belief to replace it with. Then, after you've done this reflecting, do the work. Every time you hear one of these negative stories, respond by telling yourself the new one. Eventually, these new constructive stories will become the norm, and you'll hear the limiting stories less frequently. Soon, you'll notice your wings will no longer feel clipped, and you'll finally be able to soar.

Change Your View

"We don't see things as they are. We see them as we are."

—Anaïs Nin

Every year or so, I commit to an experience that's unfamiliar where I'm not the leader, I don't know the people, and I'm challenged in new ways. In 2017, I joined a group with Jackson Hole Mountain Guides to climb Wyoming's tallest mountain, Gannett Peak. I didn't sign up because it was the state high point. I signed up because I wanted to cross some of the last remaining glaciers in the Lower 48.

On the first day, after hiking thirteen miles to reach our camp, we were setting up our tents when Nate, our guide, warned us to hurry. There was a storm coming—the skies were already darkening, and thunder had begun echoing through the surrounding granite mountains. Nate and the other two climbers, Rick and Robert, dove into their tents. I followed, scrambling to get inside before the rain hit.

What followed was two solid hours of intensity. Thunder cracked and reverberated off the canyon walls like a war drum. Lightning flashed, lighting up my tent. I felt completely exposed, just a small dot in a vast, wild place, above tree line and surrounded by lakes and tall mountains.

I'd read extensively about lightning and the dangers of being in the high country during electrical storms. I'd experienced wilderness storms before. Intellectually, I knew we were probably safe. I knew, logically, that we'd likely be okay—but still, I was afraid for my life. It didn't help that I had recently read *A Bolt from the Blue* by Jennifer Woodlief, a book about a harrowing rescue in Wyoming's Teton Range after lightning struck a group of thirteen climbers.

As thunder boomed and echoed off the granite and lightning flashed far too frequently, I remembered reading that lightning can strike from as far as ten miles away. My mind spiraled. I felt vulnerable. Mortal. Eventually—after what felt like an eternity but was probably only a couple of hours—the thunder stopped, the lightning faded, and silence settled in. I unzipped my tent door and saw a clear, blue sky.

When I'd crawled into my tent, I was forty-nine years old. When I crawled out, I felt like I was one hundred.

"What a spectacular storm!" Nate exclaimed as we emerged. *I wish I'd received that memo,* I thought. Nate and I had experienced the same storm, but our perspectives couldn't have been more different. He saw wild beauty. I saw a death threat. He was awestruck. I was panicked.

Just as we have the power to choose our mindset, we also have the power to shift our perspective. Every time the lightning lit up my tent, I repeated a fear-driven story: *I'm going to die!* If I'd known Nate's perspective, I might have had the wherewithal to replace that story with: *What a spectacular storm!* And what a difference it could have made.

The Stoic philosopher Seneca famously said, "We suffer more often in imagination than in reality." My work often involves challenging and helping people change their perspectives, especially as it relates to their perceived struggles. Think of a difficult experience, relationship, or task that drains you, that generates negative energy and dread. Now, reflect on two or three different ways you could view it and write them down. Even if the reframe feels like a stretch, do it anyway. Because when we change our view, we change our experience.

The Stonecutters

One hundred years ago, a traveler came upon a scene where several individuals were working with stone in a big, quarry-like area. Curious, the traveler approached one of them and asked, "Excuse me, could you tell me what it is you're doing?"

The worker's movements were stiff and robotic as he cut the stone in front of him, and he replied, "I am a stonecutter, and I am cutting stones. I do it to feed my family. I'll be done working at dusk, and it won't come soon enough."

Walking along and still curious, the traveler noticed a second stone worker. This stone worker was measuring his stone and comparing its quality to the stone he had cut before it. The traveler politely interrupted him to ask, "Excuse me, would you mind explaining what you're doing?"

The worker thought for a moment, glanced at the traveler, and explained, "I am a stonecutter, and I want to be the best stonecutter in the world."

Soon after, the traveler approached a third stone worker. This stone worker was completely absorbed by his work. He cut a stone, stood back to admire it, then worked on it some more. He wasn't even aware of the traveler's presence.

The traveler asked the worker, "Sorry to interrupt you, but would you mind telling me what you're doing?"

Stopping for a moment, the worker stared at the stone in his hand and the stones he had cut on the ground. Then, he turned to the traveler and said, "I am building a cathedral!"

These three men were all working at the same site, performing the same task over and over. They had the same job description and role, yet each had a very different perspective about their work. The first saw his work as nothing more than a job—a way to pay the bills. The second saw his work as a career. He took great pride in it and wanted to be the best in the world at his craft. The third saw his work as being a part of something bigger—a calling. Since I first heard this parable years ago, I've made it a habit to ask myself, *What is my cathedral?*

In all that I do, I consider, *What is the greater purpose?* Doing so adds more meaning and creates more purpose in my life. Do you view your work as a job, a career, or a calling? What is the cathedral you're building? I invite you to reflect on these questions. Doing so will help you find and create more meaning in your work and in your life.

Develop a Growth Mindset

"Whether you think you can or can't, you're right."

—Henry Ford

Early in her career, world-renowned psychologist Carol Dweck set out to determine the consequences of believing that our intelligence, personality, and abilities are fixed versus believing that they can be developed. She found that the consequences are significant. The mindset we choose has a significant impact on how we think of ourselves and on what we're able to achieve.

In her book, *Mindset: The New Psychology of Success*, Dweck refers to these mindsets as "fixed" and "growth." A fixed mindset is the belief that our abilities and intelligence are static traits. Individuals with this mindset tend to avoid challenges, give up easily, view effort as something to avoid, take feedback personally, and tie their value and worth to their accomplishments and outcomes.

A growth mindset is the belief that our abilities and intelligence can be developed through effort, learning, and persistence. Individuals with a growth mindset embrace effort and are more likely to persist through challenges, ask for and value feedback, and view setbacks as learning opportunities and stepping stones, part of their personal development and growth.

Dweck believes that our mindsets tend to fall on a continuum, that we don't operate with entirely one or the other. We may be growth mindset–oriented when it comes to learning and new skill development, but we may be fixed mindset–oriented when it comes to how we view failures and setbacks.

The good news is we can all work to foster a growth mindset by changing the way we view learning, challenges, effort, feedback, and setbacks and failures. We can remind ourselves that skills can be learned and developed, that challenges are something to be embraced, and that improving and realizing our potential requires effort. We can ask for, and even value, feedback. And, most importantly, we can praise our efforts rather than the outcome. To foster a growth mindset, we must acknowledge and accept that we will experience setbacks and failures. It's not a matter of if, but when and how often, setbacks arise. And when they do, we must learn from them.

When it comes to mindset, words matter. Fourteen years ago, when I was first starting Epic Life Inc., I wanted to offer leadership development facilitation. A prospective client who was in the market for a facilitator for her organization's annual leadership meeting asked me, "Can you provide a workshop about deep listening?"

I was so appreciative that she didn't ask, "*Have you ever* provided a workshop for deep listening?" but rather, "*Can you?*" It was a subtle but important difference. One would have left me feeling limited and may have resulted in me not being offered the work. But the other gave me the opportunity to believe in my abilities and respond with an emphatic "yes." The workshop went wonderfully, and I've since facilitated numerous leadership workshops that cover a wide range of topics.

All of this just goes to prove that the way we view ourselves—whether we think we can learn, grow, and change or not—impacts what we are able to achieve or not achieve, how meaningful and fulfilling our lives will be, and how impactful we'll be as a person and leader.

Inspire a Culture of Growth

It turns out that the biggest influence on whether we operate from a fixed mindset or a growth mindset is outside of us.

As Mary Murphy, author of *Cultures of Growth: How the New Science of Mindset Can Transform Individuals, Teams, and Organizations*, explains, a culture is like an unseen force shaping the attitudes, behaviors, and potential of everyone within it. A tree's growth doesn't depend only on its seed—it depends on the forest it's in. Is there sunlight? Rich soil? Enough space to grow? Or is the tree competing for light, surrounded by shallow roots?

Just like that tree, our mindset is shaped by the conditions around us and the ecosystem we're in, not just what's inside us. The cultures we create—in our workplaces, communities, families, or any groups we're a part of—have a profound influence on whether individuals feel empowered to grow, supported to try, and encouraged to reach for new possibilities, or they feel constrained by fixed expectations and fear of failure.

Murphy describes two types of cultures. A "culture of genius" believes that talent and success are innate, reserved for a select few. In such environments, people are often afraid to make mistakes, reluctant to take risks, and hesitant to try new things for fear of being seen as incompetent.

In contrast, a "culture of growth" is grounded in the belief that abilities and potential can be developed through effort, learning, and support. Growth cultures celebrate progress over perfection, view mistakes as essential steps toward mastery, and provide opportunities to stretch and grow. In growth cultures, leaders actively signal confidence in others, provide constructive feedback, and encourage learning through challenges.

To cultivate a culture of growth, Murphy suggests we ask and reflect on the following questions:

Do I believe in the potential of those around me and actively communicate that belief?

Do I create opportunities that challenge and inspire growth?

How do I frame mistakes—as evidence of failure or as critical learning moments?

Our homes are one of the best places to work to foster a culture of growth, especially if you have children. When my husband and I were raising our sons, we often asked each other during dinner, "What have you failed at lately?" and "What did you learn today?" and "What lesson did you learn the hard way?" By fostering environments that support learning, effort, and development, we can help unlock the potential in everyone—at work, at home, and in our communities—and inspire transformation that uplifts our entire group.

The Journey Is for the Soul, the Summit Is for the Ego

Several years ago, I was a member of a mountain-climbing expedition, but due to a storm, we couldn't reach the summit. In fact, the conditions were so severe that we didn't even make it to the base of the mountain. Knowing from the weather forecast that our chances of summiting would be slim, as we were heading to the trailhead at the start of our adventure, my partner guide told us: "Just remember, the journey is for the soul, and the summit is for the ego."

This simple yet profound statement is an important one to remember for anyone striving for a growth mindset, anyone interested in finding or reclaiming their authentic life. Because most of life isn't spent on the peaks—it's lived in the journey, in the lessons, challenges, and resilience we build along the way.

Life is also where we reconnect with ourselves. By embracing the process and journey rather than the outcome or the destination, we're forced to let go of our ego's expectations and listen to the quiet call of our soul. It is on the journey that we find or reclaim our epic life, one that feels true, vital, and fully ours. And it all starts with our mindset and being intentional about what we carry and don't carry on our journey.

Lesson 3
Dare to Fail

An Epic Life Is Not an Easy Life

Life brings challenges and hardships—some we choose, and others we'd never choose but must face anyway.

When we choose to do hard things, to push ourselves beyond comfort and convenience, we grow. We build strength, resilience, and inner clarity—qualities that will carry us through the devastating experiences we can't predict or control.

To dare to fail is to evolve. Every time we stretch beyond what we thought possible, we enter a process that reveals and reshapes us. These moments—often painful, always transformative—draw us closer to who we really are. And it is only by truly knowing yourself that you can begin to live your most authentic, meaningful, and epic life.

I've come to believe that a life is epic not despite its struggles and losses but because of them. When I share this truth, I sometimes worry it might not land the way I intend. What I mean by this is that our challenges, including our greatest losses, don't diminish our lives, they deepen them. They give our lives meaning.

And this is why I return again and again to one of my favorite poems, "Kindness" by Naomi Shihab Nye.

To me, it isn't just about kindness; it's about what it truly means to live a deeply felt, epic life:

Before you know kindness as the deepest thing inside you must know sorrow as the other deepest thing.

This, to me, is the paradox at the heart of an epic life: the very things we wish we could avoid are often the ones that make our lives meaningful and most worth living.

We Can Go Farther than We Think We Can

"Are you breathing just a little and calling it a life?"

—Mary Oliver, *West Wind*

We can go further than we think we can, if only we dare to.

Mariah, Jenni, Jackie, Vicki, Diana, Wendy, and Roxanne had signed up for my Epic Women program and traveled from near and far to embark on a six-day backpacking expedition in Wyoming's Wind River Range. As we left the trailhead, I was trembling with both nerves and excitement. This was the first official implementation of a program I had spent the past two years imagining and refining during my wilderness wanderings.

I wasn't interested in offering a "guided tour." I wanted to provide an experience that would push my clients beyond their perceived limits and take them to new heights. My own transformational experiences had come from pushing myself to do things I wasn't sure I could do, and I wanted to provide my clients with a similar opportunity. They hoped to have a transformational experience, and I would do my best to facilitate one for them.

Part of my vision was to introduce an audacious challenge early in our expedition, so I planned for a mountain climb on day two. Most of the women had traveled from urban areas at sea level, and our expedition would start at 9,000 feet and reach 12,500 feet. As such, the altitude could be a limiting factor for some of the women, especially in the beginning of the adventure as their bodies worked to acclimatize. As a result, my plan for us to climb a mountain on day two instead of waiting to do it later in the adventure was ambitious.

But there was a method to my madness. When a group of people embarks on something challenging together, it requires them to let their guards down. They must be brave and vulnerable. I predicted that such an experience would generate a close, meaningful bond among the women. Sharing such an experience early in the expedition would mean—if all went as I hoped and planned—our group would emerge as a stronger, more deeply connected team, ready to face the remaining days in the wilderness with greater resilience and trust.

Day two arrived, and we planned an "alpine start." We woke up at 3 a.m., and after a quick breakfast of oatmeal and coffee, we left camp at 4 a.m. with our headlamps on.

We would climb one of my favorite mountains, one adjacent to a group of dramatic granite spires and towering peaks called the Cirque of the Towers. From our mountain's summit, the women would get to enjoy panoramic, jaw-dropping views in all directions. I couldn't wait for them to experience such grandeur. Most of these women had never slept in a tent in such a remote wilderness, let alone climbed a mountain.

Our route up Mitchell Peak would not be technical, but the ascent would be steep, and at times, it would require scrambling over fields of boulders. At the beginning of our climb, the women chatted with each other, but it wasn't long before my clients grew quiet. It's hard to carry on a conversation while huffing and puffing up a tall mountain at altitude. I have come to love this part of a mountain climb—a time when everyone turns inward, and the only sounds are our collective hard breathing and the occasional clicking of our trekking poles.

Climbing the mountain took several hours, and throughout the climb, I made sure to spend time hiking with each of the women. Sometimes, I was in the front, other times in the middle of the pack, and, occasionally, in the back.

Every single step the women took was out of their comfort zones. Their apprehension was palpable. This is how it is for any of us when we do something we don't know how to do, anything we're not sure we *can* do. At some point in the struggle, we reach what I call the "end of our self"—a point when we do not have the necessary skills. When this happens, we may feel like we're in over our heads and may ask ourselves, *Whose idea was this?* The women's courage as they ascended the tall mountain was inspiring to witness. I don't know about you, but I am more inspired by someone's willingness to be brave and vulnerable than I am by their greatness.

It's in the crux of such a hard struggle that most of us consider quitting. This is one of the most important points in a journey; it is in this moment that we are faced with a powerful choice. Will we trust the inspired version of ourselves who thought this challenge was a good idea, or will we give in to our short-term pain and quit? Will we choose discovery, growth, and transformation, or will we choose safety?

When we dare to step forward into growth, we won't be breathing just a little. At times, we'll be bent over, gasping for air, but we'll also have our breath taken away.

Self-Actualization: Stepping into Growth

Self-actualization is the process of realizing and fulfilling one's unique potential, talents, and purpose in pursuit of becoming the best and most authentic version of oneself.

Pioneering American psychologist Abraham Maslow is renowned for his "hierarchy of needs," a concept that identifies self-actualization as the pinnacle of human aspiration. Maslow's work promotes stepping out of one's comfort zone and pursuing growth to achieve a more fulfilling life. Maslow wrote, "At any given moment, we have the opportunity to step forward into growth or back into safety." Self-actualization requires effort. (If it were easy, everyone would do it.)

Some years ago, I was coaching a man who had terminal cancer. It was meaningful work, and I want to do more of it, but at the time I felt ill-equipped. Often during our coaching calls, I'd think, *I don't know how to do this.* At times, both the logical and emotional sides of my brain struggled to know what to say. It was so hard. But by staying the course, I acquired the needed skills and was able to give Joe my best.

Some years back, two dear friends asked me to be the officiant for their wedding. I was touched and said yes, but I was scared out of my mind about it. Given it was such a special occasion and they were dear friends of mine, the stakes felt high. I had never planned on being an officiant and wasn't sure about my abilities. For the next several months, I worried.

Just two days before their wedding, as if the stress level wasn't high enough—or maybe *because* it was—I lost my voice. (Apparently, stress can cause a condition called "psychogenic dysphonia.") After some research and soliciting advice from friends, I learned that gargling apple cider vinegar could help me get my voice back.

The day before the wedding, during our twelve-hour road trip from Wyoming to Iowa, Jerry drove while I gargled apple cider vinegar like it was my job. Fortunately, when the time came for me to officiate the wedding, I had just enough voice to do my part. My friends' wedding was spectacularly beautiful, and officiating it was truly an honor. The experience was also a teacher. Losing my voice reminded me that daring to fail doesn't mean things will go smoothly—it means showing up anyway, even when your voice is shaky.

When I first started Epic Life and planned to provide guided adventures in the wilderness, I lacked skills and confidence when it came to crossing rivers. One of the reasons I chose the Brooks Range of Alaska for my NOLS course was that I knew it would mean spending a lot of time in and crossing rivers. I was out of my comfort zone for most of the fourteen-day expedition, but by the end, I had developed the necessary skills.

There was also a time fifteen years ago when I decided I wanted to learn how to skate ski. I knew how to cross country (classic) ski, but skate skiing, which is more explosive and involves pushing off the inside edges of alternating skis to propel forward, looked like more fun.

I decided to teach myself; let me tell you, it wasn't pretty. It was humiliating and painful. During my first attempt, I fell at least thirty times within a mile. But, eventually, after repeatedly falling—and failing—something clicked. I became a skate skier, and now it's one of my favorite sports.

I also can't help but think of our first business and entrepreneurial journey when considering stepping out of my comfort zone. It was so challenging so much of the time, especially in the early years. There were many times I was tempted to give up and quit. The journey was full of ups and downs, setbacks and failures, before reaching its peak and becoming profitable and award-winning. All the lessons I learned the hard way during my first journey have benefitted me while operating Epic Life Inc.

To struggle is to learn. And to learn is to grow. Or, as I like to say, it's hard because it's hard. When you're in the crux of any struggle in your life and you're tempted to quit, ask yourself: *Do I choose my higher self or my smaller self? If I fast-forward ahead a few years and look back at this time, what do I hope I will see?* Will you choose what you are yearning to do, or will you choose to retreat and leave it for later?

These are important questions, and how you respond to them will determine a lot. I'm not saying there isn't a time to quit. Sometimes it is best to quit. In those cases, quitting can require more daring and courage than staying. But, to live an epic life, we must make it a deliberate practice to turn toward our authenticity again and again, even—perhaps *especially*—when it requires us to do hard things.

When we choose to live authentically, we'll experience moments that will leave us breathless or move us to tears. Such moments transform us. Living an epic life is one of the hardest things any of us can do. But it's even harder to *not* live it. One of the most valuable things I've learned is that we risk our lives when we don't truly live them.

Making It Through

When we make it through something challenging, especially something we didn't know how to do and weren't even sure we could do when we began, we feel inspired. We are transformed by the experience.

Mariah, Jenni, Jackie, Vicki, Diana, Wendy, and Roxanne are each more than they were before, and we, as a team, are more than we were before. While standing on the summit, we can look back and down to see how far we've come. We look around at other, taller mountains and wonder, *If I did this, what else can I do?* When we accomplish something challenging, it can feel like anything is possible. And what a great perspective from which to live and lead.

Dare to Fail

"And the day came when the risk to remain tight in a bud was more painful than the risk it took to blossom."

—commonly attributed to Anaïs Nin

Living our authentic lives requires daring to fail, or what I sometimes jokingly refer to as "shitting our pants." This seems to be a universal sensation that arises right before we dare to do a hard thing—it "scares the crap out of us."

In everyday life, daring to fail might look like pursuing a creative passion, such as learning to paint or writing a book, even if you're unsure of the outcome. It might be signing up for an adventure you don't know how to do with a group of people you've never met. It might be volunteering to speak at an event when public speaking terrifies you. Daring to fail might mean navigating vulnerability in your relationships—initiating a difficult conversation, apologizing, asking for forgiveness, or admitting feelings of fear or love. It could mean stepping into parenthood despite feeling ill-equipped and unsure of how to be the parent your child needs you to be.

In the workplace, leaders dare to fail when they take bold, innovative steps despite the risk of failure. This might involve championing an untested idea that could redefine their business or pivoting the organization in response to changing markets. It's also seen in leaders who are transparent, openly admitting mistakes to their teams and seeking critical feedback to improve.

Daring to fail could be choosing to be a servant leader. Servant leadership prioritizes serving others—empowering and uplifting individuals and the organization—before focusing on personal power or advancement. While widely admired, servant leadership is relatively uncommon in practice, as traditional leadership models often place a higher value on authority, control, and bottom-line results and less value on the people-first approach that servant leadership embodies.

Reflect on your life. Is there something you're yearning to do, but you're hesitating because you're afraid?

If so, you're not alone. In fact, I'm willing to bet that every single one of us has something we want to do that we're not doing because we're afraid.

What Are You Afraid Of?

When I ask people, "What are you afraid of?" I usually hear one or more of the following: "I'm afraid I'll fail, or it will fail, and I won't be able to recover;" "I'm afraid I'll disappoint others;" "I'm afraid I'll let myself down;" "I'm afraid I'll look bad and I'll make a fool out of myself."

Occasionally there's a fifth response—one that isn't as common. It's one I usually coax out of a client after I've gotten to know them well, and that is: "I'm afraid of my success and the way it could affect or change my life."

The Value of Doing Hard Things

"Discomfort is the price of admission for a meaningful life."

—Susan David, *Emotional Agility*

My most transformational experiences have involved doing hard things. "Hard" doesn't always mean physically demanding, but it does require one to step into discomfort, uncertainty, or vulnerability. When we choose to do hard things—what psychologist Paul Bloom calls "chosen suffering"—it helps us expand our tolerance for adversity, builds resilience, and inspires self-confidence. But that's not all.

In his book *The Sweet Spot: The Pleasures of Suffering and the Search for Meaning*, Bloom writes that engaging in chosen suffering enables us to learn new skills, deepen our self-understanding, and create more meaning in our lives.

So, don't shy away from tackling challenges. In fact, go after them, because they are great opportunities to grow and to create more meaning in your life.

"Peak Experiences"

A peak experience is a profound, transcendent moment of intense joy, connection, and fulfillment that causes us to feel more fully alive and aligned with our true selves.

Described by Abraham Maslow as a hallmark of self-actualization, "peak experiences" provide a sense of clarity, purpose, and unity with the world, often leaving a lasting impression of awe and gratitude. They also elevate our sense of meaning, increase our resilience, and provide us with a deeper understanding of life's possibilities.

Scott Barry Kaufman is a prominent psychologist, author, and researcher known for his work in human potential, creativity, and self-actualization. In his book *Transcend: The New Science of Self-Actualization*, Kaufman uncovers Maslow's unfinished theory of transcendence, arguing that true fulfillment comes not just from self-actualization but from experiencing transcendence: going beyond the self to connect deeply with others and the greater whole.

What makes the pursuit of peak experiences and transcendent states so compelling is their transformative impact. Such experiences provide clarity, deep satisfaction, and a sense of purpose. In addition, they can inspire creativity and new insights, resilience, and a profound sense of belonging, making life feel more meaningful and inspired.

Ultimately, they challenge us to grow, connect, and contribute in ways that not only elevate our own lives but also positively influence the world around us. To experience more peak moments and to achieve transcendence, Kaufman emphasizes the importance of stepping beyond our comfort zones and embracing meaningful challenges. By doing so, we cultivate the ideal conditions for these transformative states of growth, connection, and fulfillment.

Into the Depths of the Grand Canyon—and Myself

"What hurts you, blesses you. Darkness is your candle."

—Rumi

It's May 20, 2010, and I'm standing on the South Rim of the Grand Canyon, waiting for my friend Jon to arrive. I'm looking across the great abyss to the distant North Rim, trying not to shit my pants. *What was I thinking?*

When my husband and I sold our Yellowstone business in September 2008 to Active Interest Media, a company that—at the time—owned *Backpacker,* Jon was the magazine's editor. Kindred spirits, we became fast friends and soon realized we shared a goal to hike a Rim-to-Rim-to-Rim of the Grand Canyon in a day. I'd spent the previous thirteen months transforming my health—losing fat and weight and gaining strength. I was in the best shape of my life, and part of my incentive was to be ready should a Rim-to-Rim-to-Rim opportunity present itself.

That opportunity finally arrived eight days earlier when I received a voicemail from Jon that said, "Can you call me? It's urgent." Upon connecting, he told me he was going to be at the Grand Canyon for a meeting and invited me to join him and give the Rim-to-Rim-to-Rim goal a go.

And here we are. Or rather, here I am.

The Grand Canyon has always been a special place to me. I had hiked into its depths during a memorable trip in 1999 with my husband Jerry, which first introduced me to the canyon's grandeur, and later trips with our sons and my parents.

Our plan was ambitious: a forty-five-mile round trip with twenty-three thousand feet of elevation change through one of Earth's most spectacular landscapes in a single day.

We descended the South Kaibab Trail, where geology tells us a two-billion-year story in layers of limestone, sandstone, and shale. The descent took us through an array of formations—from the pale Kaibab limestone at the rim, through deep reds and oranges, to bright yellows and whites. Prickly pear cacti dotted the terrain, their bright-pink blossoms a stark contrast to the rugged landscape. Yucca plants and cacti speckled the landscape, and towering century plants stood like sentinels in the blazing sun. As we descended deeper into the canyon, the heat intensified.

After reaching and crossing the green waters of the Colorado River, my journey transformed from challenging to torturous as blisters formed between my toes and across the balls of my feet. As we hiked through "the box"—a corridor of towering Redwall formations that make up Bright Angel Canyon—each step became increasingly excruciating.

Nine miles in, the reality of my situation became brutally clear. The blisters had torn open, causing each step to feel like glass was breaking under my feet. My raw, inflamed skin pulsed with every impact, and the pain radiated upward into my calves and thighs. I sat on a rock, considering my options: retrace our steps in defeat or continue forward for another thirty-six excruciating miles?

Jon looked at my ravaged feet and suggested we turn back. I was moved. We were still fairly new friends, yet he was willing to give up his own bucket list adventure just to make sure I got back safely. The physical pain would be intense either way, but turning back would add disappointment to the mix. After careful consideration and determining that continuing would not do any permanent damage to my feet, I made my choice.

"I don't want to turn back," I said simply, and Jon smiled supportively. I had originally set out on this epic hike to push my physical limits. Now, it would be something much harder.

After doctoring my blisters, we continued up the trail. My body was drenched in sweat, and dirt coated my legs. The heat had been sweltering, but now night was falling. I was a little uneasy about hiking through the dark, but I welcomed the cooler air ahead. We dug out our headlamps and kept moving.

Meanwhile, every step I took sent pain screaming through my feet. At Cottonwood Canyon, we stopped to refill our water bottles and use the restrooms and started what would be a significant and sustained ascent to the North Rim, 7.2 miles and 4,200 feet. Lunging up the trail, bats occasionally fluttered by our ears, and every now and then we spied a scorpion.

I was purposeful as I hiked up the seemingly endless, steep switchbacks of the North Rim. Then, as if out of nowhere, just off the trail, we spotted a cluster of bright, white flowers. The trumpet-shaped blooms seemed to glow in the dark. I had never seen anything like them.

Jon explained we were looking at moonflowers—*Datura wrightii*, also known as sacred datura. This desert plant only blooms at night, its flowers unfurling in the dark to release a sweet, intoxicating fragrance before closing by morning. As I crouched to take a closer look, Jon cautioned me not to touch them. He told me the plant is toxic; ingesting it can cause delirium, vivid hallucinations, and, in some cases, even death. We lingered for a moment, quietly admiring their ghostly beauty, before continuing up the trail.

My feet were throbbing masses of agony—each step unleashing a fresh wave of searing pain. Just days earlier, I'd read a hiker's account of his Rim-to-Rim-to-Rim, where he estimated there were fifty to sixty switchbacks between this point and the North Rim. I've always been a strong uphill hiker and even prefer hiking uphill. I reminded myself of this as I blinked back tears. The pain was relentless. Finally, as if by some miracle, there was no more "up." We had arrived at the North Rim.

Jon was stoked and, for a moment, his enthusiasm lifted my spirits. He shared some peanut-butter-stuffed pretzels and jalapeño-stuffed green olives. I could only eat a few before my lips blew up into bright flames, but the sodium hit the spot, and I chased the food down with large gulps of water.

Jon asked about my feet, and I didn't lie, but I also didn't go into great detail about the level of pain and suffering I had endured to reach the "halfway point." After capturing a celebratory selfie of us in front of the North Rim sign, I suggested to Jon that he go on ahead and I would catch up. I watched as he hiked away, the light of his headlamp growing smaller and fainter with each step, then I tilted my head back and looked at the sky.

The quarter moon was bright, and millions of stars sparkled like white diamonds across the black vastness. I thought of my dad and the constellations he had taught me how to find. I spied the Big Dipper, Cassiopeia, and Boötes. The sight was breathtaking, and tears began to well up in my eyes. I whispered a prayer, asking God—or any higher power that might be listening—for strength and fortitude to carry on.

I removed my socks to survey the damage. My feet were in ruins—blood-soaked wounds stung between my toes, blisters covered my heels, and fluid-filled bubbles spattered numerous places on both feet. Even though I knew it would be of little help, I cleaned and dressed the blisters and wounds as best I could. The physical torture of descending back into the canyon would be unimaginable. My trekking poles would help, and I planned to rely and lean on them heavily, but there would be no way to avoid the pain of friction caused by what would be thousands and thousands of sliding steps down the steep trail.

As I carefully navigated the steep switchbacks in the dark, taking soft, deliberate steps, bats occasionally darted past my ears, their sudden movements startling me. The jagged terrain demanded precision, but as my legs weakened and my focus blurred under the weight of unrelenting pain and fatigue, my movements grew increasingly clumsy.

Silent screams echoed in my mind as I cursed the trail and my plight. The pain became a merciless metronome, its rhythm marking each agonizing step forward. I had to summon every ounce of focus to navigate the switchbacks through the Redwall Limestone leading to Roaring Springs. I recalled that there were significant drop-offs here from my ascent hours earlier. A single misstep would send me plunging into the vast abyss of the canyon. *At least I'd be out of my misery.*

I had begun to hear Roaring Springs in the distance when, finally, I reached Redwall Bridge. I could see Jon's headlamp. He was waiting at the end of the bridge. I worked to compose myself. I didn't want Jon to see how much I was suffering. He laid on his back on the bridge and encouraged me to do the same. "Turn off your headlamp and check out the sky," he said. I was happy for the break and did as he suggested. The sky was a black canvas full of blinking stars. I was struck by the vastness and for a moment forgot about my throbbing feet.

After starting again, I followed Jon, but at a distance. I was really struggling and needed to dig deep. I wanted to be alone. With every step, it was becoming harder and harder to avoid falling apart, and the last thing I wanted was to negatively impact Jon's experience. Finally, after what seemed like an eternity, we reached "the Box"—the winding section of Bright Angel Canyon and the innermost canyon. The sun was just starting to show its first light, and I felt like collapsing. I encouraged Jon to go ahead again, and we agreed to meet at Phantom Ranch, which was about four and a half miles away.

I waited for Jon to disappear before I let my tears fall. I dropped to my hands and knees in the middle of the trail and my crying turned to sobbing. Although I was relieved the steep descent was behind me, my body was battered and depleted. I had reached my end. I had nothing left. I was done. That's what I was thinking as I remained on my hands and knees on the trail for some minutes.

But then, as if out of nowhere, thoughts and visuals of my beautiful mother—diagnosed with multiple sclerosis twenty-seven years earlier—appeared. She had endured constant pain yet somehow refused to be bitter. Memories of her enthusiastic spirit flashed through my mind like a slideshow.

I remembered the words of Viktor Frankl, a Holocaust survivor who endured three years in brutal Nazi concentration camps, in *Man's Search for Meaning*, "Everything can be taken from a man but one thing: the last of the human freedoms—to choose one's attitude in any given set of circumstances, to choose one's own way."

After moving myself to a rock, I sat, slumped, and promised myself I would remember Frankl's words. Dawn was about to break. The first rays of sunlight ignited the cliff faces like a rim of fire and painted the canyon walls in gold and pastel pink. I thought of my mom again: how she had managed to live a full life, and do so joyfully, despite the almost constant pain she endured. How tough and resilient she was!

And then, something extraordinary happened. In the depths of my despair, I felt as though I had been untethered from my body—lifted up, so that I could look down over myself. It was strange yet profoundly calming. I could feel, viscerally, the presence of God—or some higher power—surrounding me. I felt held, and the canyon, with its sheer immensity, seemed vivid and alive. My elation that I had miraculously made it through the night overwhelmed me.

My throbbing feet pulsed, and I noticed blood on my shoes from where it had seeped through. I was covered in dirt, and my tears had dried, making the skin on my face feel tight. I watched as the sun's first rays lit up the scene. The sun's painting of the rugged terrain was gradual—like a timelapse video—and it was breathtaking. I started crying again. The scene was so unreal that it took my breath away. For a moment, I wondered if I was leaving this life and entering another realm.

The moment seemed to last a long time before I returned to thoughts of my mom again. I felt a profound sense of connection to my own strength, to my mom's enduring spirit, and to the divine presence. I was overwhelmed with gratitude and felt so alive. It was as if I had been resuscitated.

As I sat there, I wondered, *What will I make of this?* I pondered this for a time and decided it would be my mantra. I forced myself to eat a Snickers and took several gulps of water, then I talked myself up and off the rock and continued down the trail.

As I staggered through the otherworldly landscape of deep-red cliffs whose rims were ablaze in the sun, I resolved to remember my mom's resilience and her joyful spirit and to recite the mantra, *What will I make of this?* a million times, if necessary, to get me out of these depths and to the South Rim.

The strategy was helping and, before I knew it, I arrived at Phantom Ranch, where Jon had just woken up from a nap. We caught up briefly before continuing toward the Colorado River and connecting to the Bright Angel Trail, which would mark the start of the final stretch of this adventure, the 9.5-mile, 4,300-foot ascent to the South Rim.

With every single steep and lunging step uphill, my feet protested. Despite the fact that they were throbbing and on fire, somehow I was still able to enjoy the experience. I could see the South Rim, still far above me, and people, who looked tiny like ants, walking along its rim.

I walked slowly and tried not to stop. (I was afraid I might not be able to get going again.) As I ascended the steep trail, I captured hundreds of photos of the dramatic views all around me and engaged in several short but meaningful conversations with fellow hikers, and the South Rim grew closer.

Finally, I reached the finish.

I was beyond exhausted, and my feet were bloody stumps. I didn't have another step left in me and plopped down on the freshly watered lawn near the rim to call Jerry and the boys. I cried so hard when I heard their voices—I was so overwhelmed I could hardly talk. I felt so blessed, and I was so grateful to have found a way out of the depths.

As I hung up the phone and struggled to get back on my feet to walk to my car, I asked a visitor how far it was to the Backcountry Information Center parking lot, where I had parked my car twenty-three hours earlier.

"About one mile," he said.

I just about died—and just then, a gust of wind caught my cowboy hat and lifted it from my head. I watched, helpless, unwilling and unable to chase after it, as the winds carried it to the rim, and it dropped into the depths and out of sight.

In the days following my return from the Grand Canyon, the experience was all I could think about. My friends and family wanted to hear all about it, and I was happy to oblige. Among other things, everyone wanted to know what went wrong.

How and why had I suffered such extreme blisters? I analyzed this question myself ad nauseam, and in the end, I was unable to offer any logical explanation other than I had started the long hike in the afternoon, in high heat. That combined with the friction caused while hiking a steep and sliding downhill grade for the first seven miles was most likely the culprit.

A few friends asked if I wanted a do-over of the experience. Did I want to go back and try it again, without blisters? The answer was no, but the question perplexed me. It was as if they assumed that since it had not gone as originally planned, I would want to do it again to get a different result. But I had no interest in having a different version of my experience.

My Rim-to-Rim-to-Rim endeavor was one of the most transformative experiences of my life. I didn't view it as a failure or a "bad" experience. Even though every step—for thirty-six of the forty-five miles—was filled with pain and suffering, I was still moved by the scenery, and somehow, by some miracle, I still found joy in the experience.

Upon my return, a friend asked if I had experienced a "dark night of the soul." The phrase, first coined by the 16th-century Spanish mystic and poet Saint John of the Cross, describes a stage in the spiritual journey marked by profound emptiness, desolation, and a feeling of abandonment by God. It is said to be a necessary passage, a deep and painful stripping away that clears the way for union, awakening, transformation.

The term has since been used more broadly to describe any period of intense suffering, confusion, or spiritual crisis. A time when everything familiar falls away, and something essential is reshaped in the darkness.

I didn't know if that's what had happened to me. But it seemed plausible. All I knew for certain was this: I was not the same person who had entered the canyon. Something in me had shifted. Something had broken open.

I think of the moonflowers and their glowing radiance in the dark. The flower needs extreme heat, a full day of scorching sun, to gather the strength to open itself to the night. In some traditions, the moonflower symbolizes spiritual enlightenment or the awakening of the soul. I love that. Whatever I experienced, something bloomed inside of me, and I was more than I was before.

Becoming Often Requires Suffering

"One does not become enlightened by imagining figures of light, but by making the darkness conscious."

—Carl Jung, *Alchemical Studies*

We are always in the process of becoming. Life itself is a continuous transformation. One of the most profound lessons I've learned—both firsthand and through the people I've worked with—is that becoming is not about accumulation. It's about peeling away the layers and the masks so we can uncover and return to who we are at our most authentic core.

This is not easy work. Transformation demands discomfort, and suffering in some form is often part of the process. It requires us to shed old identities, confront painful truths, and walk through uncertainty.

Carl Jung, the pioneering Swiss psychiatrist and founder of analytical psychology, developed concepts that continue to shape modern thought, including archetypes (universal symbols in the collective unconscious), the collective unconscious (a shared human reservoir of knowledge and experience), and individuation (the journey toward becoming one's authentic, whole self). Central to Jung's philosophy was the belief that we cannot grow unless and until we spend time with our shadow—the hidden, repressed parts of ourselves that often remain buried beneath discomfort, fear, or denial.

Jung argued that embracing the shadow is essential to living authentically. Such work often requires suffering, as it involves confronting the parts of ourselves we'd rather avoid: our fears, weaknesses, and impulses that don't conform to societal expectations. Yet, this inner work is transformative.

By integrating both light and dark, we gain wholeness, meaning, and alignment with our true nature. Without it, the shadow can unconsciously dictate our lives, keeping us from being fully ourselves. Through courage and self-examination, we can transform suffering into growth and unlock a deeper connection with ourselves and the world.

Personally, my most profound transformational experiences have included moments of awe, immersion in stunning natural beauty, physically pushing myself beyond what I believed possible, emotional vulnerability, and time spent with my shadow. These experiences—while extremely challenging—have been catalysts for my deepest growth.

These elements aren't a prescription but rather a reflection of what I've witnessed to be the raw ingredients of transformation. I'm profoundly grateful for them and for what they've revealed and awakened in me.

Add "Type 2 Fun" to Make Your Life More Epic

"Life is either a daring adventure or nothing at all."

—Helen Keller

The "fun scale" was first articulated by climbers to categorize the nature of their adventures.

Type 1 fun describes activities that are enjoyable while you're doing them, such as flying a kite, eating ice cream, or going for a leisurely bike ride.

Type 2 fun refers to activities that may not feel enjoyable or pleasant while you're doing them but are deeply rewarding and memorable in hindsight. These experiences often involve challenging and uncomfortable moments.

Type 3 fun describes activities that are miserable while you're doing them and remain miserable in hindsight, such as an expedition gone awry or enduring a dangerous or traumatic event.

Inserting more Type 2 fun into your life will make it more meaningful and memorable.

The Path to Meaning

"It hurts just as much as it's worth."

—Zadie Smith, quoting from a condolence letter
in "Joy," *New York Review of Books*

In literature and movies, an "inciting incident" is a pivotal event in a story that sets the protagonist on their journey or disrupts the status quo, propelling the narrative forward. This concept mirrors the human experience. Life often changes direction due to an event—an unexpected letter, a loss, a chance meeting, an opportunity to answer a call of some kind that promises to take us out of the ordinary and into the unknown—that transforms us and changes the trajectory of our lives.

My Rim-to-Rim-to-Rim of the Grand Canyon in 2010 was an inciting incident. It changed the trajectory of my life.

Before that experience, I had accomplished plenty of challenging adventures, including fifty-kilometer trail runs and epic backpacking adventures and mountain climbs, but these "epics" were not a regular staple of my life. They were things I did on occasion when I needed an adventure to break me out of the monotony of my day-to-day routine. My Grand Canyon experience awakened something in me. Despite the severe pain and despair, I felt enlivened. I met parts of myself I hadn't met before, and I wanted more.

My new passion for long-distance day hikes—what I came to call "epic hikes"—meant I got to spend more time in the places I loved most: nature and the wilderness. In the years following the Grand Canyon experience, I started going on weekly treks throughout my backyard—in my beloved Wind River Range—choosing routes I had never traveled before and linking favorite trails while challenging myself to go farther than I thought I could.

During my reinvention, I recruited my closest girlfriends to join me for many hikes, and they helped me "test drive" concepts for Epic Life Inc. in its early days. I partnered with our local community college for two years and offered a hiking course that included teaching the essentials of hiking and guiding women on easy and intermediate hikes before the program culminated with a longer "epic" hike.

I climbed the Grand Teton and several peaks in the Wind River Range, embarked on a fifty-mile day hike traverse of Zion National Park, completed a fourteen-day NOLS course, and climbed Mount Whitney (the tallest mountain in the Lower 48). Every time I experienced one of these epic hikes, I returned re-inspired about my life and clearer than ever about who and what were most important in my life.

Type 2 fun hasn't been just a solo endeavor. Jerry and I have been drawn to it since we met in 1990. Over the years, we've enjoyed hiking, backpacking, ultra trail running, climbing mountains, biking, snowshoeing, skiing, and snowboarding. These adventures not only tested us physically and mentally, but they also created meaningful memories for us and became a staple in our relationship.

One of our longest-standing traditions has been to commemorate our wedding anniversary each year by going on an epic hike that is as long in miles as our marriage is in years. Most recently, we celebrated our thirty-second anniversary by spending a long day—from sunrise to sunset—hiking a thirty-two-mile traverse of the Wind River Range.

Jerry and I wanted to instill the same sense of adventure in our three sons. We raised Wolf, Hayden, and Fin largely in the outdoors, spending evenings, weekends, spring breaks, and other vacations adventuring.

Some of our most memorable family experiences include our hiking, backpacking, and llama trips in Wyoming's Wind River Range and Red Desert; our countless and unforgettable Yellowstone trips and adventures; our family's epic hike and climb of Mitchell Peak to commemorate Jerry's and my thirtieth anniversary (and soon after, getting tattoos of the mountain's coordinates to commemorate the occasion and a favorite mountain); our backpacking pilgrimage on the Camino de Santiago in northern Spain; epic twenty-four-mile day hikes through Switzerland; and exploring Iceland, including a 3,000-foot ascent of a 700,000-year-old, glacier-covered volcano in a whiteout. I know—our poor sons!

I'm sure there have been many times when they have wished they had been born into a different family. But while some of these experiences may not have been what our boys would have picked, these Type 2 endeavors have developed resilience and grit in each of us, brought us closer as a family, and created cherished memories.

The Unexpected Gift of Type 2 Fun: Meaningful Connection

There's something about sweating together, weathering discomfort, getting lost and finding our way back—whether as family, partners, friends, or teammates—that forges connection like nothing else can. Experiencing Type 2 fun with others has deepened many of the most meaningful relationships in my life.

Adventuring has strengthened my bond with Jerry, drawn me closer to each of my sons, deepened our family connection, and sparked some of my most treasured friendships.

My dear friend Kathy—trail name "Fremont"—has hiked hundreds of miles with me over the last fifteen years. She joined me for an eighteen-miler in 2010, got hooked, and the rest is history. We've shared countless hikes in our beloved Wind Rivers, including a memorable 56-mile fastpack where we witnessed two bull elk bugling across a misty canyon, each guarding herds of thirty or more cows. Kathy is the friend who has climbed mountains she didn't necessarily want to climb just to experience astonishing beauty and to spend time with me. From the Tetons to the Grand Canyon to an unforgettable forty-mile day hike across Zion, our friendship was forged in deep wilderness and built on meaningful conversations, support through struggle, and, of course, plenty of misadventures that still make us laugh until we cry.

Then there's Jon, who invited me to join him on the Grand Canyon Rim-to-Rim-to-Rim. His companionship during that grueling challenge sparked a lasting friendship and many more epic hikes. (The next year, he invited me on a fifty-mile traverse of Zion, and the year after, he and some of the same crew joined me for a Wind River traverse.)

Kathy Browning—trail name "SoX"—was a kindred spirit and beloved friend for almost two decades. Among other things, we shared long hikes, fifty-mile ski days in West Yellowstone, and a deep connection through it all. She died while mountain biking July 4, 2024, and her tragic passing devastated me. (I've written more about SoX in *Lesson 6: Cherish Your People*.)

In the early years of my reinvention and when I was discovering my love of long-distance day hiking, Barb and Leann—both a little older than I— offered not only their example of badassery but also friendship grounded in wisdom and lived experience, which I especially appreciated during my early years of parenting. They were the two I called to join me on my initial challenges. I fondly recall a time when all three of us were hiking—more like sliding—down a steep hill of loose rock on top of loose rock. We giggled most of the way down and it was a miracle we did so without injury.

Barb's presence in my life during that time was meaningful. I valued her strength and insights. For years, Leann was a constant companion, joining me on backyard epics, including some of the early hikes that pushed me further than I thought I could go. Her friendship brought comfort, perspective, and so much joy. She also joined me (along with Kathy S.) for a Rim-to-Rim in the Grand Canyon and an unforgettable hike in Zion.

Joel and Alan, whose story is told in *Mind over Mosquitoes*, became dear friends and trusted confidantes through that shared hardship. That trip cemented a bond I now hold close.

One of the most unexpected and beautiful gifts of guiding clients on Epic Adventures is witnessing the friendships formed on the trail, connections that often run deep, forged by shared challenge and wonder. The trail has introduced me to remarkable people I might never have otherwise met, and sharing those hard and beautiful miles has opened the door to relationships I now treasure.

Your Mountain May Be *Not* to Climb the Mountain

Most of the people I work with are somewhere in their midlife. They are highly accomplished achievers, so much so that they've grown weary from a lifetime of striving. They're experts at scaling figurative peaks and powering through challenges. For these people, their mountain to climb— their real work and path to transformation—may be to choose *not* to climb the mountain, to work on *being* rather than *doing*.

I'll never forget a moment during my 2016 Epic Women expedition. Among the group of seven clients were Monica and Cheri, who were fifty-four and sixty years old at the time. They had come from urban areas at sea level and trained hard to prepare for our journey. Along with the rest of the group, they were looking forward to climbing mountains.

On the morning we set out to climb our second mountain, everyone was doing great. But when we reached the top of the pass where the rugged alpine terrain toward the summit began, Monica and Cheri each informed me that, while they felt strong and capable enough to climb the mountain, they'd prefer not to. Instead, they wished to use their time taking in the views and enjoying the fruits of their labor. Their decision was unexpected and deeply inspiring. I knew as I witnessed their choice that it held a wisdom I would one day benefit from.

Both Monica and Cheri had full lives and had been hard-working and impactful leaders. They had experienced years of powering through and climbing mountains in their lives. Why climb another if they didn't have to, and if it was up to them?

I will always love climbing mountains, but I've also grown weary from all the striving I've done in my life. When I catch myself swept up in the familiar frenetic energy of striving, I ask myself: What am I striving for? While I still have things I hope to accomplish, I've come to value meaning more than achievement. Asking this question holds my feet to the fire. It helps me recalibrate and brings clarity to how I want to proceed.

Managing Your Inner Critic

The only thing that's harder for my clients than climbing a mountain or rappelling over a cliff into a slot canyon is having to deal with the unrelenting criticism from their inner critics.

Writer Steven Pressfield calls this critic "the Resistance." Coaches often refer to it as our saboteur. Whatever the name, it's the voice of self-doubt that shows up whenever we're struggling, learning, doubting ourselves, or experiencing a hardship that we feel ill-equipped for.

It's the inner voice that says: *What were you thinking? You don't know how to do this. You're holding others up. You've got to quit. You're going to die. You're never going to be able to do this. You're making a fool out of yourself.*

I've learned we can never defeat our inner critic, even if we spend our entire lives trying to. Well, I suppose there is one way you could make your inner critic visit you less often: avoid doing anything hard. Just don't do anything that requires courage.

My inner critic shows up often, so I've come up with a strategy to help me manage and deal with it. When it appears, I say (not out loud because I don't want my clients to think I'm crazy), *Oh, it's you again. Thanks for stopping by. I appreciate your concern.* And I mean it; I'm not being sarcastic. I have come to appreciate my inner critic because its presence reminds me that the stakes are high and that I better pay close attention.

Then, I imagine strapping my inner critic into the backseat. I can't get rid of it, and it's a helluva backseat driver, but at least I'm in the driver's seat.

Feeling Like a Fraud

Fidgeting in the backseat of an Uber one December morning, I stared out at the towering Atlanta skyline. I was on my way to deliver my keynote "Epic Lessons Learned in the Field" to a group of women leaders from the Arthur M. Blank family of businesses. The event was being held at the Mercedes-Benz Stadium, and my Uber driver and I were trying to figure out at which entrance he should drop me off.

I had been up for hours rehearsing my presentation to ensure it was polished. Yet, as we circled the stadium, my mind wasn't focused on the content—it was fixated on my outfit. Jeans, a blouse, and cowboy boots were my standard keynote attire, but I worried it might not measure up to the corporate world's expectations. These were high-powered women living in the city and working for a prestigious organization. Would they see me as too casual?

Recalling Brené Brown's story in her wonderful book *Braving the Wilderness: The Quest for True Belonging and the Courage to Stand Alone* about a time she changed from the outfit she thought she should wear into the outfit she wanted to wear right before a big presentation provided little comfort. But as we inched closer to the venue, I started to sweat—both figuratively and literally. Turner Networks was my second presentation that day, and the name alone triggered waves of panic. What could I—someone who lived out on the frontier of Wyoming and worked almost as far from the corporate world as you could get—possibly have to offer these audiences?

The fraud police had arrived.

Psychologists Dr. Pauline Rose Clance and Suzanne Imes coined the term "imposter syndrome" to describe the persistent self-doubt many high-achieving individuals feel, despite clear evidence of their accomplishments. Symptoms include downplaying successes, attributing achievements to luck, and fearing exposure as a fraud. Originally identified in professional women, research now shows that impostor syndrome can affect anyone, regardless of gender or background.

I've worked with hundreds of high-achieving leaders, many of whom battle impostor syndrome. Yet, despite knowing how universal these feelings are, I still found myself trapped by them that morning. My brain dismissed years of hard-earned success: past speaking gigs, positive feedback, and the countless hours of preparation. None of it seemed to matter.

Years earlier, when I started Epic Life Inc., a friend offered to host a brunch in San Francisco where I could test-drive my presentation for women leaders. It was a dream opportunity, but as the event approached, panic set in. I locked myself in a guest room moments before my talk, paralyzed by doubt. *What if I can't do it? What if they're not interested in what I have to say? What if they've heard it all before?*

Whether I'm coaching clients, leading Epic Adventures in the wilderness, or delivering a keynote, the fraud police are always nearby, whispering doubts: *Who do you think you are? What do you have to say that hasn't already been said?*

Even icons struggle with impostor syndrome. Nobel laureate John Steinbeck once wrote, "I am not a writer. I've been fooling myself and other people." Meryl Streep, a twenty-one-time Oscar nominee, questioned why anyone would want to see her act again, doubting her talent.

Adam Grant, in his book *Hidden Potential: The Science of Achieving Greater Things*, reframes impostor syndrome as a signal of growth, not failure. Doubting yourself, he suggests, means you're tackling a new challenge, learning, and stretching beyond your comfort zone. It's a sign others see potential in you that you may not yet see in yourself.

As I stepped out of my Uber in Atlanta on that cold December morning, I asked the driver to meet me in two hours to take me to my next event at Turner Networks, where I knew the fraud police would be waiting for me all over again.

Try Some Self-Compassion

One of the most common excuses I hear from clients for not doing a hard thing they really want to do is that they don't want to risk disappointing themselves. They can't bear the thought of having to endure the self-induced criticism should the outcome not meet their high expectations. This doesn't surprise me.

Many of the people I work with are high achievers. They work exceptionally hard and experience a lot of success. They are also known to set the bar impossibly high for themselves, often at perfection. Unfortunately, I'm a veteran when it comes to self-criticism. When I don't meet my personal expectations, I can unleash an internal storm of self-criticism so brutal I wouldn't wish it on anybody.

Kristin Neff is a pioneering psychologist and researcher renowned for her expertise in self-compassion. In a podcast conversation several years ago, Neff described self-criticism as being like a coal-powered steam engine. She said something to the effect of, "It will get you up the hill, but not without a lot of black smoke." If you tend toward self-criticism, pay attention: science shows that we achieve more when we are self-compassionate than we do when we're self-critical, not to mention it's a much more pleasant experience!

One of my favorite aspects of leading Epic programs in the wilderness is witnessing the incredible empathy, support, and encouragement my clients show each other. Even as someone is struggling up a mountain or facing their fears while rappelling down a tall cliff into a slot canyon, they still find the kindness and generosity to uplift those around them.

"You're doing awesome!"

"Way to go!"

"You've got this!"

These moments of collective encouragement foster a profound sense of connection and shared triumph that's so beautiful to witness. Yet, all too often, the person offering support to others isn't extending the same grace to themselves. Internally, they may be battling harsh self-criticism, berating themselves.

The good news is that all of us already know how to be kind and compassionate to others. It's a skill we all possess. The challenge is to start practicing it on ourselves. If we can do this, we'll have a more enjoyable experience *and* we'll be more likely to succeed. The next time you find yourself in a struggle, remember this simple yet powerful reminder: "Treat yourself the way you would treat others."

Leave Your Ego Behind

The philosopher Friedrich Nietzsche is often credited with the sentiment, "Whenever I climb, I am followed by a dog named Ego." Whether or not he said those exact words, the image is unforgettable—and true.

Whenever we do something that requires vulnerability—something we've never done before, don't know how to do, or aren't sure we can do—we are not being led by ego. In fact, ego often disappears in these moments of raw becoming. When we're stretching and struggling, we are anything but egotistical.

My clients, whether they're daring to ascend an exposed ridge on a hike, climb a tall mountain, rappel into a slot canyon, learn a new skill at work, step into a higher level of leadership, speak publicly for the first time, have a difficult conversation with someone they love, or find their way through a painful transition or other crisis, are anything but egotistical.

What they are is vulnerable.

Transformation Isn't Pretty

Transformation isn't pretty. A caterpillar doesn't instantly (and magically) turn into a butterfly. There are many stages of decay along the way. In fact, at one point during its transformation, the caterpillar digests itself. Transforming oneself requires vulnerability, and to be vulnerable is to be uncomfortable. And who *wants* to be uncomfortable?

To be vulnerable means peeling away the layers we rely on for armor—pride, fear, pretense, or control—and revealing the raw and unfiltered truth of who we are. It's the daring act of showing up fully, without the comfort of our usual "masks" and defenses.

One woman I was guiding up Angels Landing in Zion National Park, who is an accomplished leader and overall badass, was trembling, and at times crying, as we navigated the narrow ridge, gripping the chains for support. Concerned, I asked, "Are you sure you want to keep going?"

She sniffed, steadied herself, and said, "Yes. Sometimes I cry when I'm scared. But I want to continue."

I was witnessing vulnerability—growth in action—and I've never forgotten it. I've had the privilege of witnessing hundreds of such personal transformations, and I haven't forgotten any of them. They inspire me to no end.

Transformation has a ripple effect. When one person dares to be vulnerable, it gives others permission to do the same.

For much of history, society has viewed vulnerability as weakness. But thanks in large part to the work of social scientist, professor, author, and thought leader Dr. Brené Brown, vulnerability is no longer viewed as weakness but as strength.

Brené Brown's 2010 TED Talk "The Power of Vulnerability" was a groundbreaking moment in reshaping the conversation around vulnerability. The TED Talk, which has since been viewed 65 million times on the TED platform plus 22 million times on YouTube, brought vulnerability out of the shadows of perceived weakness and into the spotlight as a cornerstone of courage, connection, and authenticity Brown's work has challenged cultural norms, showing that vulnerability is not about exposing weakness but about embracing uncertainty, risk, and emotional honesty.

It is now clear that vulnerability is essential for meaningful relationships, creativity, and leadership. As a result, many individuals and organizations have fundamentally shifted how they approach the concept of vulnerability.

When was the last time you had to be vulnerable? Can you remember what it felt like? And what growth did it facilitate?

Courage Can Be Cultivated

"Life shrinks or expands in proportion to one's courage."

—Anaïs Nin

Vulnerability and courage are inseparable; one cannot exist without the other. To be vulnerable is to open ourselves to uncertainty, risk, and emotional exposure—whether it's sharing our true feelings, pursuing a dream, doing something we don't how to do, or admitting we need help. These acts require courage, as they involve stepping into the unknown and confronting the fear of judgment, rejection, or failure.

Vulnerability demands that we show up authentically, without the armor of perfection or control, trusting that we are enough. It is not easy to risk revealing ourselves. To allow others to see us authentically requires courage.

Just about every person I know would like to be more courageous. Since I first became a mother twenty-five years ago, I decided I wanted to be courageous. I admire people who are courageous and who choose to do hard things. I wished to model bravery to my sons and in my roles as a coach, facilitator, presenter, writer, and guide.

One of the adventures I include in my Epic Zion programs is a canyoneering adventure. The adventure includes some rock climbing, scrambling, and rappels over steep cliffs into slot canyons. Most of my clients feel nervous about this adventure, and that's no accident. It's one of the reasons I include it—to inspire people to do hard things despite their nerves. Such adventures give my clients a chance to practice shitting their pants—er, I mean, to practice being courageous, to face their fears and move forward anyway.

On several occasions during the canyoneering adventure, clients have told me that while they wouldn't normally choose to rock climb and rappel, they signed up for it because they aspire to be the kind of person who would have the courage to do it. Have I mentioned lately how much my clients inspire me? The courage they display, whether on an Epic Adventure or in our coaching work as they navigate life's challenges and level up in countless ways, is one of my greatest sources of inspiration.

Courage is a skill that can be cultivated.

Start small. Take tiny steps outside your comfort zone. Do hard things that don't come with high stakes. Each small act of bravery forces you to face your fears. Acknowledge that courage feels uncomfortable, because growth requires discomfort.

Focus on your why. Connect your actions to something deeper—a purpose, a goal, a dream. A strong why will carry you through fear. Reflect on past moments when you were brave. What did you learn? What did it change?

And most importantly, surround yourself with people who inspire you. Lean on them when your courage wavers. Because courage, like fire, burns brighter in community.

~~Fearless~~

We often think the people who inspire us and who are most impactful are special. We think they must be fearless. But they're not. They are afraid, just like the rest of us. The difference is, they are more afraid of not trying than they are of failure.

Are You More Afraid of Failure or Regret?

"Of all the words of mice and men, the saddest are, 'It might have been.'"

—Kurt Vonnegut, *Cat's Cradle*

Regret is a feeling of sadness, disappointment, or remorse over something that has happened, something that has been done, a missed opportunity, or a poor decision. It is a reflection on past choices or actions (or inactions).

It's that heavy, silent companion that whispers, "What if?" in the quiet moments of our lives. It has a unique sting because it carries the weight of things undone, words unsaid, and chances not taken. According to psychologist Daniel Pink in his book *The Power of Regret*, regret is a universal and fundamentally human emotion, and while the concept often has negative connotations, Pink suggests that regret is a valuable tool for learning and growth.

If we're open to it, our regrets have the power to provide insights about what we care about most and can lead to better decision-making. Research shows that as we grow older, we're likely to regret our inactions more than our actions. Missed opportunities, unspoken words, or risks not taken often weigh heavier on us over time, as their potential remains forever unrealized. I recall listening to Tim Ferriss on a podcast conversation some years back with designer, author, and thought leader Debbie Millman. They were discussing the fear of failure, and Millman asked Ferriss, "Are you more afraid of failure or regret?" I never forgot that question, and I've since used it as a filter whenever I find myself hesitating or not doing something I want or need to do because I'm afraid.

Personally, I'm more afraid of regret than failure. I'm motivated to live my life without regrets, not because doing so will mean my life is full of nothing but bucket-list adventures, but because it will mean that I am living my life thoughtfully and courageously. According to Pink, some of our greatest regrets are due to a failure of courage. Remember this if you aspire to live a meaningful life.

Lesson 4
Appreciate Your Setbacks and Failures

"The birds make great sky-circles of their freedom. How do they learn it? They fall, and falling, they're given wings."

—Rumi

When Things Don't Go as Planned

Sometimes things don't go as planned. Even though, in our disappointment, a situation may feel like a failure or even a disaster, it isn't all bad. A lot of learning and development can come as a result of things not going according to plan. I've never learned anything while standing on top of a mountain under a clear sky or when making a champagne toast following an accomplishment.

In April 2013, I had the opportunity to join a *Backpacker* magazine team on a Mount Whitney expedition. Mount Whitney is in California's Sierra Nevada and it's the tallest mountain in the contiguous United States. Our expedition would take four days and follow the Mountaineer's Route. In the wilderness, things seldom go exactly as planned, but this Mount Whitney expedition was an exception.

The weather was impeccable—so stellar that we were able to linger on Mount Whitney's summit for more than an hour, something that's uncommon in the high country, where afternoon storms are a regular occurrence. The adventure was so amazing that even before the expedition had come to an end, I decided I would offer an Epic program the next year that would follow the same itinerary. As soon as I returned home, I got to work, and in short order, recruited and signed up ten people for my 2014 Epic Mount Whitney Expedition.

I picked the same dates, the same itinerary, and partnered with the same outfitting company. I planned for it to be an exact replication of my experience the year before.

If only it were so simple. As the dates of our Mount Whitney Epic Adventure approached, the weather forecast for our time in the mountains turned unfavorable. A major storm was predicted to strike during our second day in the mountains that would bring with it significant snow and high winds. It was disappointing to know before we even entered the wilderness that our chances of summiting Mount Whitney were slim.

On our first day, we backpacked under a clear, blue sky to our first camp. The stoke and camaraderie were high. After setting up camp, we lounged and enjoyed the mild air and took photos of Mount Whitney, which we could see perfectly from camp. It was a stunning sight, and our anticipation was palpable. After eating an early dinner and dispersing to our tents for a good night's sleep, I tossed restlessly. I spent the night worrying and hoping the weather forecast was wrong.

Morning came and we woke up with hopes to advance higher, to our next camp, so we would be positioned to summit Mount Whitney the next day. However, as we ate breakfast, the weather changed, and by 9 a.m., Mount Whitney and its surrounding peaks were obscured by a curtain of white.

I hoped we could stick to plan A and move to our next camp before the brunt of the storm hit, but our guides said we'd be going nowhere. The dangers of advancing, setting up camp, and living exposed at twelve thousand feet in gale-force winds during a blizzard for the next several hours were too great.

As snow began falling and a biting-cold wind penetrated our camp, we battened down the hatches. Our new plan—plan B—was to try for a summit attempt from our current camp in the wee hours of the morning, weather permitting. It wasn't ideal; it would make for a very long summit day. But we wanted to climb Mount Whitney, and it was our best hope. As the morning wore on, wind blew through our camp and a blizzard turned it into a winter wonderland.

We spent most of the morning hunkered down in our tents. For lunch, we chewed on frozen energy bars and jerky and focused on staying hydrated. In the early afternoon, our guides lured us from our tents. We bundled up, and they taught us skills that would help us during our mountain climb, including how to hike with crampons on, how to use an ice axe as a hiking stick on steep, snowy terrain, and how to self-arrest.

We put it all to practice on an uphill hike in high winds and blowing snow. It felt good to move, even if it was a miserable experience. My fingers and toes were numb, and pebbles of snow blasted my face. I did my best to remain enthusiastic and optimistic, but internally, I was cursing our plight.

After the training hike, everyone seemed invigorated. We quaffed soup and hot beverages as our guides discussed what we needed to have ready for our summit climb. Despite the unfavorable conditions, we ate dinner and tried to remain hopeful. Our guides indicated they'd wake up at 2 a.m. to assess the weather. If all was clear, they'd wake us up, and we'd start our long trek toward Mount Whitney and, eventually, its summit. If the guides found the weather wasn't favorable, plan C would be a later start for the summit trek. As leader of the group, I wanted my people to be comfortable and warm and rested and for them to get a shot at Mount Whitney's summit. I was encouraged when everyone wore bright, optimistic smiles as we returned to our shelters in the storm.

It was another sleepless and restless night for me. High winds hammered our tents, carrying and dumping more snow on our camp. Every hour or so we'd shake it from our tents, but the snow persisted, and the result was cold condensation that dripped on our tired faces and made us shiver. As I lay there, trying to be strong and hopeful, 2 a.m. (and plan B) came and went. The wind howled, causing our tent to violently shake and flap. When we woke up that morning, it was so cold that one client's contact lenses were stuck to her eyeballs.

After using a key to chip the ice free from the zipper of our tent door so I could open it, I poked my head out to get a look-see. Our camp was buried in snow—a complete winter wonderland—but the sky was clear and blue. Mount Whitney beckoned, in all its glory. *Could plan C be possible?* I wondered and prayed that it would be.

It was a spectacularly beautiful morning. We huddled close together around our guides as they made us coffee and tea, and I waited impatiently for what I hoped would be instructions for starting the long trek and summit attempt. A few minutes passed before our guides explained that they had hiked a distance above our camp earlier to assess the conditions. The snow was deep but not impassable, but they predicted the snow and conditions up high were unstable. To add to that, high winds were predicted up top. Plan C was out.

With one day remaining in our expedition, we had exhausted plans A, B, and C. I looked at my clients and saw the disappointment on their faces. They were physically and emotionally exhausted. They had signed up to climb Mount Whitney and had instead spent two days and two nights in blizzard conditions, going nowhere. I wanted to cry.

Two sleepless nights, endless shivering, and the Herculean effort it took to manage my emotions while trying to be a good leader for my clients had taken a toll. When we'd entered the wilderness three days earlier, I had been forty-four years old. Now, I felt like I was one hundred.

As a consolation, the guides rallied to take us on a hike toward Mount Whitney, under a bright-blue sky and through a blanket of fresh, deep snow. It was a spectacular scene and a worthwhile experience even if it felt like child's play compared to what we had hoped to achieve.

After the short hike, our guides proposed that we leave the wilderness and spend our final day rock climbing in nearby Alabama Hills. We made the best of it, and we had fun, but I couldn't help but feel like our expedition had been a failure. But which Mount Whitney expedition developed me more? It's no contest.

Those few days of setbacks, hardship, disappointment, and discomfort turned out to be a masterclass in leadership. Can I really call our Mount Whitney expedition a failure if it strengthened my leadership, revealed truths about myself I couldn't have learned otherwise, and, let's be honest, if I can't control the weather?

At the start of our expedition, during the van ride to the trailhead, one of the guides had said to us, "Just remember: the journey's for the soul, the summit's for the ego."

Now, I understood.

Sometimes We'll Fail

"Fall down seven times, get up eight."

—Japanese proverb

Failure is not the opposite of success—it's the foundation for learning and growth. It shouldn't be referred to as "win or lose" but "win or learn." It's through a process of repeatedly failing that we learn or master most skills.

Rock climbers learn to conquer harder routes by falling again and again, each slip teaching them what is required to hang onto the cliff and continue up the route. Alpine skiers master black diamond slopes and moguls only after they've endured countless tumbles honing their skills. Writers produce several rounds of rough drafts that fall flat before crafting something they're proud of, and musicians hit wrong notes again and again before mastering a piece. Even seasoned adventurers who expertly navigate vast wildernesses must get lost a few times before learning how to effectively find their way. Each stumble helps build the skills and resilience required for achievement, success, and mastery.

In the workplace, failure is essential to growth. A manager who mishandles a challenging conversation with a team member will hopefully learn, through feedback and/or the experience, to communicate with more empathy and clarity next time. A keynote speaker who stumbles through early presentations discovers through trial and error how to captivate an audience and deliver an impactful message.

Entrepreneurs whose initial ventures falter gain hard-earned insights that fuel future success. When I was operating our first company, a business I started in 1994, we failed over and over before eventually finding our way and doing our best work. Leaders who take bold risks will occasionally fail, but it is only through that process that they become better and more skilled at innovating, risk-taking, and leading.

It's how they learn to know when it's time to pivot. It's how they become good at strategy. Each failure is a stepping stone toward learning and, eventually, mastery. Failing is an inevitable and invaluable part of living one's authentic life—of becoming, and being, the person we aspire to be.

Innovating Requires Failing

"I have not failed. I've just found ten thousand ways that don't work."

—Thomas Edison

We're in a time of great uncertainty and change.

Never before in human history have we found ourselves in such a "wilderness" as we do today. The reality is a lot could go wrong. It's natural to want to avoid failure, but that would be the wrong approach. Organizations whose leaders fail to innovate will not thrive and are not likely to survive. The slogan for organizations and leaders today should be "innovate or die."

This is a time to be creative and resourceful—to be innovative—and that will require risk-taking and periodic failure. It's how we learn. It's how we improve our companies, products, and services. Astro Teller, the cofounder of Moonshots and the X lab, said, "I don't want to fail, but if we avoid failure, we avoid learning. You don't learn when you're right." Reshma Saujani, the founder of Girls Who Code, said, "We need to stop being ashamed of failure and start being proud of it. It is the way we learn; it is the way we grow, and it is the way we lead."

Thomas Edison was one of the greatest inventors in the world. He had 1,093 patents to his name. He brought us the light bulb, the phonograph, the motion picture, and the camera. He improved the telegraph and telephone. He gave us some of the most established and valued inventions, but only as a result of many failures. When Edison was working to invent a storage battery, his experiments kept failing. A lab assistant sympathetically expressed his dismay about the repeated failures. In response, Edison famously said, "I have not failed. I've just found ten thousand ways that don't work."

Consider the story of Howard Schultz, who tried multiple times to convince investors to fund his vision for Starbucks as an upscale coffee experience. Schultz was rejected by more than two hundred potential investors, many of whom failed to see the potential in his idea. Despite these rejections, he persisted, refined his pitch, and ultimately transformed Starbucks into one of the most recognized global brands in the world.

Or take Dyson, the company known for its innovative vacuum cleaners and other technologies. Founder James Dyson spent fifteen years creating 5,126 prototypes before developing the bagless vacuum cleaner that would revolutionize the industry. Each of those prototypes represented a failure, but also a step closer to his breakthrough.

The best ideas come to fruition only after trial and error, several iterations and corrections, and repeated failures. We must value and reward leaders and employees who are willing to do things differently and take risks. They dare to fail, and sometimes, they actually *do* fail.

A high-level leader of a global organization said on a podcast, when talking about failure being part of innovation, that if he was tasked with laying people off, he would start with the leaders who never made a mistake. This is no time to play it safe. In a world where innovation is the key to survival and growth, failure is not optional. It's required.

Psychological Safety Required

Psychological safety is the belief that you can speak up, take risks, and express ideas, questions, or concerns without fear of punishment, humiliation, or negative consequences. It creates an environment where people feel safe to be themselves, contribute, and learn from mistakes. When psychological safety is present, leaders and group members feel as though they have permission to make mistakes—to fail.

What does this look like in practice? Imagine you have an idea to transform your company's product or service. In a workplace that lacks psychological safety, you might keep it to yourself, fearing negative consequences such as ridicule, punishment, or rejection. In a psychologically safe workplace, however, you feel wholeheartedly comfortable expressing your thoughts to the team, and they are equally able to raise any questions or concerns without judgement. This environment not only enhances individual well-being, but also supports organizational learning, adaptation, and innovation.

Harvard Business School professor Amy Edmondson, who has studied failure for three decades, coined the term "psychological safety" and literally wrote the book on it. In her book *The Fearless Organization: Creating Psychological Safety in the Workplace for Learning, Innovation, and Growth*, Edmondson explores the many ways psychological safety leads to improved team performance, innovation, and organizational resilience.

In her research to determine what made teams most effective, Edmondson discovered that the key to the most effective teams was not intelligence, education, or experience, but psychological safety. Her findings were reinforced by Google's Project Aristotle, which identified psychological safety as the most important element of high-performing teams.

To foster psychological safety, Edmondson recommends modeling humility, being open about your own mistakes, communicating clearly, collaborating, and encouraging and inspiring innovation. But psychological safety shouldn't be limited to our work cultures, environments, and teams.

As parents, we can foster psychological safety in our families and homes. Around the kitchen table during meals, we might ask our children and each other, "What is something you've failed at recently?" When we openly talk about these things, we do our children a tremendous favor.

Many kids today are afraid to fail. The expectations placed on them, either knowingly or unknowingly, can induce a fear of failure. This can create a huge challenge for them when they're on their own and living and working in a world that requires daring to fail, and where failing occasionally is to be expected. Fostering psychological safety within a team, organization, group, or family requires that we lead by example, demonstrate vulnerability, and admit our mistakes.

It requires that we encourage open communication and create regular opportunities for discussions where everyone's input is valued. It requires active listening, showing genuine interest in what others have to say, and responding without judgment. Finally, to foster psychological safety we must recognize and reward behaviors that demonstrate courage, innovation, and constructive feedback.

By consistently implementing these strategies and fostering a culture of trust and openness, we can create an environment where psychological safety leads to enhanced collaboration, creativity, and overall team performance.

Fail Well (Not All Failures Are Created Equal)

This is not to say we should recklessly set out to fail. Not all failures are created equal, after all. According to Amy Edmondson, who also authored the excellent book *Right Kind of Wrong: The Science of Failing Well*, there are three kinds of failures: basic, complex, and intelligent.

A basic failure is exactly what it sounds like—a simple, preventable mistake. They're the kind of mistakes we kick ourselves for making, like setting our alarm for the wrong time or showing up to a meeting on the wrong date. We should aim to avoid such basic failures, but they're not life changing.

A complex failure is also preventable, but it includes and involves several failures that add to its complexity. This kind of failure follows a series of mistakes. For an example of a complex failure, look to July 2024, when cyber security company CrowdStrike released a faulty update to its Falcon security software. The action caused widespread problems, including those that lead to the crashing of approximately eight and a half million Windows computers.

This massive failure disrupted critical sectors, including airlines, banks, hospitals, and emergency services, leading to grounded flights, financial transaction halts, and compromised patient care. Obviously, we should work to have systems in place to prevent such complex failures. Finally, there are intelligent failures, and this is the type of failure that Edmondson says is valuable and a key part of innovation.

According to Edmondson, the criteria for an intelligent failure include: the failure provides an opportunity for learning, innovation, and improved quality; it explores new territory (there's no recipe or playbook); key assumptions are communicated; cost and scope are kept as small as possible; and most importantly, we learn from it.

Scientific research, an inherently unpredictable field where breakthroughs can be rare, is full of intelligent failures. Major advancements are usually the result of many small, incremental steps, most of which involve experiments that don't yield the desired outcome and results.

Robert J. Lefkowitz, winner of the 2012 Nobel Prize in chemistry, is a renowned physician and biochemist whose groundbreaking work on G-protein-coupled receptors transformed our understanding of how cells communicate with each other.

His discoveries had profound implications for the development of medicines and treatments for countless diseases, yet his journey was marked by countless failed experiments. In various interviews and articles, Lefkowitz has said, "Science is 99 percent failure." He would know, as he speaks from a lifetime of experience navigating trial and error in the highly complex and uncertain world of biomedical research.

His insight underscores that every failure is a building block for eventual success. The iterative process of refining hypotheses, running experiments, and interpreting unexpected results is not only essential to scientific breakthroughs but a microcosm of how progress happens in any field.

The "Debrief"

As a leader, coach, adventurer, adventure guide, and parent, I feel strongly about having a process in place to review and learn from mistakes, setbacks, and failures.

I call such a practice a "debrief," and I first learned of the concept during my 2011 NOLS course. Whenever something major happens—if something goes wrong, or something unexpected occurs—as soon as we're safely able to, we huddle and have a debrief. During the debrief, everyone shares their perspective about what happened, and then we spend time capturing what we can learn from the experience so we can prevent it from happening again in the future and be better prepared and equipped should it happen again.

Mine Your Failures

In my coaching and leadership work, I often ask my clients to reflect on their failures. This exercise isn't always met with enthusiasm, and I get it. Who wants to relive a failure or a mistake? Wasn't it miserable enough the first time? I understand, but hear me out.

I'll ask someone to reflect on what they consider to be their greatest failure, mistake, or setback in their life. I want them to write about it in their journal and to reflect on things they learned from the experience and if and how the experience changed them. So often, we are ashamed of our failures. We're not proud of them and wish they wouldn't have happened. They leave scars, and sometimes open wounds, that reside deep inside of us. But when we have the courage to revisit our failures, mistakes, and setbacks, we often find all kinds of ways in which the experience positively informs our lives.

If we're open to it, we may glean some of our greatest lessons from our failures. Mining our failures like this benefits us in two significant ways. For one, it changes the flavor of the failure. Realizing how we learned from it and how the experience caused us to improve changes our view of the experience from a failure and something bad into something more constructive. But also—and this is very important and the reason I value the exercise so much—revisiting and learning from our failures makes us less afraid to fail in the future. To live our lives out of fear is to stay small, and this smallness and tendency to play it safe is a recipe for an unlived life.

Failing and Flying

One of the most inspiring and resonant books I've read in recent years is *Bittersweet: How Sorrow and Longing Make Us Whole* by Susan Cain. In a social media post she made following the publication of her book, Cain shared a poem called "Failing and Flying" by Jack Gilbert.

"Failing and Flying" explores the idea that although we may take an action that ultimately results in failure, something that doesn't work out the way we hoped, the process of arriving at that point may not be a failure but a triumph. Gilbert draws upon the tale of Icarus, pointing out that although he did indeed fall, he also achieved his goal of flying.

The poem's first line is, "Everyone forgets that Icarus also flew." And the poem's last line, which I find profound, is, "I believe Icarus was not failing as he fell, / but just coming to the end of his triumph."

I often work with people who are divorced, and although most of them, often years after the experience, acknowledge it was the right choice, many still view it as a personal failure. Others I know and work with have grappled with the decision of whether to get a divorce. Even when their hearts tell them it's the best path forward, they may hesitate for years. They remain paralyzed by the fear that others will label them a failure.

When working with someone who is experiencing such fear and shame, I almost always share Gilbert's poem with them, and it helps. Something shifts, and eventually they're able to reframe the narrative of failure into a necessary and courageous act.

Examining our failures is hard but worthwhile work. Mining them for meaning, learning, healing, and, often, self-forgiveness, can be transformative. The process can set us free.

In her post, Cain wrote that Gilbert's poem contains "one of the most beautifully expressed, life-altering ideas I know." I couldn't agree more. What if we all worked to see our failures this way, as the end of a triumph instead of a failure?

One of My Most Spectacular Failures

"The years teach much which the days never knew."

—Ralph Waldo Emerson, "Experience"

In 1989, I stood outside the Adams Center, the University of Montana's fieldhouse, with my head in my hands and tears burning the backs of my eyes. I could never have anticipated this moment of devastation, sadness, and loss.

Just one day earlier, I had been excited to start my junior year of college—I was attending UM on a full-ride, Division I basketball scholarship. As a member of the Lady Griz, coached by the legendary Robin Selvig, I had worked hard to make a comeback after a freshman-year ACL injury that red-shirted me, and I was making progress. Or so I thought.

Coach Selvig contacted me and requested a meeting. As I entered his office, we exchanged friendly hellos. As I sat down, however, the seriousness in the air intensified. I folded my hands and nodded at Coach, indicating I was eager to hear why he wanted to meet. He hesitated for a moment and then explained that another player—a walk-on—had been performing well. He thought she deserved a scholarship. *My* scholarship.

Coach's words landed like a punch, and I was stunned. My heart sank. I could barely hear a word of what he said next. I wanted to argue my case. *But I've been doing well. I've come back from the injury.* But before I could find the power to voice my thoughts, something stopped me. I knew it was no use. The decision had been made.

I felt a pit in my stomach, and my eyes filled with tears. *How will I explain this to my parents? What will I tell my teammates?* I was stunned, heartbroken, and humiliated. Coach encouraged me to stay on the team, but I left the building and never returned. I quit.

Fast forward to 2015. I was hired by the YMCA to facilitate a leadership development program in Missoula. Twenty-three years had passed since the last time I was in Missoula. Planning the trip stirred memories I had long since buried. When I'd first seen Missoula, I had fallen in love with it. I had come of age there. I had received my degree, gotten married, and started my career there. During my reflection, I realized how profoundly the loss of my scholarship had shaped my life.

Failure is often a seed of transformation. Losing my scholarship is what led me to discover and fall in love with hiking. It inspired me to start hiking to the "M" on Mount Sentinel. It led me to spend time alone and to find and realize the value of solitude. It also led me to fall in love with books and reading. After losing my scholarship, a journalism professor who knew I was struggling recommended I read *Man's Search for Meaning* by Viktor Frankl. I wasn't much of a reader at the time, but the book inspired me to no end.

Frankl's story about surviving the Holocaust and three years of brutal Nazi concentration camps inspired me that I didn't have to be a victim to my circumstances, that I could choose to be a survivor. I could choose my existence. The insight changed my life, and reading that book turned me into a lover of reading.

Today, I'm a voracious reader who reads fifty to seventy-five books every year, and books are a tremendous source of inspiration for me. Hiking, solitude, and reading—three of my greatest joys and regular staples of my life and my work—all grew from that single, painful "failure" of losing my scholarship.

During that work trip to Missoula, I got up at sunrise and hiked to the top of Mount Sentinel. Retracing the thousands of steps I had taken twenty-six years earlier while healing from the disappointment and failure in basketball was profoundly moving. I experienced a full-circle moment, a reminder of how far I had come. I'm so glad I failed at basketball.

Consider Writing a "Failure Resume"

When we think of people who are successful, impactful, and inspiring, we tend to think they're special, that they always succeed. But we're missing a significant part of their story. What about the jobs and grants they didn't get, the teams they didn't make, the things that didn't go their way?

In 2010, neuroscientist Melanie Stefan publicly shared her "failure CV"—a resume listing all the rejections, missed opportunities, and setbacks she had faced in her academic career. She did this in an effort to normalize failure and to show that even the most accomplished, "successful" people suffer disappointments and failures on their way to achievement. In fact, failure is a necessary part of achievement.

The concept resonated widely and went viral, inspiring others to share their own stories of failure as a counterbalance to the polished narratives so often portrayed publicly and in professional circles. Today, many leaders and organizations use the exercise of writing a "failure resume" to foster transparency, encourage resilience, and promote learning from setbacks as an essential part of growth and innovation.

I incorporate the exercise in my coaching and leadership workshops and programs. To fail is human. When we share about our mistakes, setbacks, and failures, it humanizes us. Our sharing inspires others to be less afraid of failure.

We Only Have to Try

I recently took Aaron Sorkin's screenwriting class on Masterclass.com. Sorkin is an acclaimed screenwriter, playwright, and director known for his masterful dialogue and compelling storytelling. His most celebrated works include *A Few Good Men*, the innovative baseball film *Moneyball*, and the Oscar-winning *The Social Network*.

I didn't take the class because I have plans to write a screenplay. I took it because I hoped Sorkin would share some nuggets about what makes an interesting and compelling story. And—no surprise—he did. In the masterclass, Sorkin explains that for a story to be a good one, there must be an obstacle, or obstacles, for the protagonist to have to confront and work to overcome. This was all useful and interesting, but it was what Sorkin said next that stayed with me.

"It's not required that your protagonist—your hero—overcome the obstacle," he said. "They don't have to win. They just have to try."

The same is true in our lives. We don't have to overcome all the obstacles and challenges for life to be meaningful or for us to be happy and successful. We only have to try.

Lesson 5
Take a Load Off

"You can't pour from an empty cup."

—Unknown

Can you imagine going on an adventure and never stopping to rest or take in the scenery? What a tragedy, not to mention a lost opportunity. And yet, we do this all the time—in work and in life. Despite the sometimes-debilitating weight of our heavy loads—our ambitions, responsibilities, and expectations—we tend to remain heads-down and refuse to stop.

In a world that glorifies busyness and relentless productivity, the idea of taking a break can feel counterintuitive. Faced with uncertainty and rapid change, many leaders worry that pausing and allowing their teams to take breaks could look like, or lead to, complacency. Yet, it's precisely during times like these, when levels of stress and uncertainty are at their highest, that we must take a load off.

In the Brooks Range of Alaska, my course mates and I took off our backpacks and cheered. We had made it to the summit of the fourth and final mountain we would climb during our NOLS course. We were ecstatic, not only because we were done climbing mountains, but because the next day we'd get to return to civilization where we'd reconnect with loved ones, get to enjoy a warm shower, and sleep on a bed.

But first, we had to descend the mountain.

To do so, we would have to follow a path of loose rock piled on top of more loose rock. Almost as soon as we set foot on the unstable terrain, we began to slip, and a few of us fell. The hike was treacherous, especially on our tired, unsteady legs. After half an hour or so, our leader of the day suggested we just sit and slide down the mountain.

We all had rain pants on, which we had rented, so we decided to "ride them like rentals" and slide our way down. We giggled as we slid, and although our behinds were covered in mud and other debris when we finally reached the bottom, there was no damage to our pants, and our spirits had been significantly lifted. We had turned what was a potentially dangerous pursuit into a fun exercise, one that became one of my favorite memories from the adventure.

Looking for opportunities to take a load off and lighten up, even if it's just for a little while, should be a top priority for all of us. Our health and well-being, performance, and happiness all depend on it.

Beware of Burnout

Burnout is a state of emotional, mental, and often physical exhaustion caused by prolonged or repeated stress, typically arising from work-related pressures. It manifests through symptoms such as chronic fatigue, cynicism toward job responsibilities, and a sense of reduced professional efficacy. But burnout isn't limited to work; it can also occur in other areas of life, including parenting and caretaking.

Burnout is not only a miserable condition, it can also require a lot of time and effort to recover from. Following the COVID-19 pandemic, I knew five people who had suffered serious health setbacks and were experiencing disabling burnout. They had powered through for so long that their mental and physical health began to protest in significant ways. Two of these leaders were forced to take a medical leave of absence so they could tend to their health, and the other three started going to therapy before eventually landing new jobs that were less stressful and more meaningful, even if they paid less.

This tendency to never stop—to wait until we're exhausted or unwell before we pause and get some rest—is what leads to burnout. According to a 2023 survey, 57 percent of people in the United States reported experiencing symptoms of burnout. A LinkedIn survey of sixteen thousand US workers revealed that 40 percent experienced burnout at work.

I want to inspire you to take a load off, slow down a bit, look up and take in the sights, and enjoy the fruits of your labor. I want to inspire you to experience more joy, have fun, laugh, celebrate more, feel inspired and be struck by awe.

Doing these things will create more aliveness in your life.

We Need a Respite from Our Burdens

If you're like most people I know, you're going so hard you may feel as if you're bent over, gasping for air, about to collapse as you try to catch your breath.

This is exactly when you need to stop—when you think you can't afford to. We must train ourselves to take breaks when our tank still has fuel in it. If we wait until our tank is empty, which is our tendency, it will be too late. Making time to rest rejuvenates us and makes our journey feel less burdensome and more manageable. Besides, life can't be all struggle and daring to fail. If it is, what's the point?

Breaks Are a Biological Necessity

Taking breaks or time off is not a sign of laziness but a biological necessity. Growing research indicates that intentional pauses—both short microbreaks and extended rests—are vital for improving our health, happiness, and cognitive performance.

The human brain is not designed for prolonged, continuous focus. According to Dr. Andrew Huberman, a professor of neuroscience at Stanford University and host of the *Huberman Lab Podcast*, our brains operate optimally in cycles of focused effort and recovery. Mental fatigue can set in as early as twenty-five minutes into a task. When fatigue accumulates, it impairs decision-making, creativity, and memory. Taking breaks allows the brain to "reset" and replenishes glucose and oxygen levels that are essential for peak cognitive function.

Overcome the "Forgetting Curve"

The "forgetting curve," a concept introduced by German psychologist Hermann Ebbinghaus, illustrates how rapidly we lose newly learned information over time. Within the first hour, we forget up to fifty percent of what we learn, and within twenty-four hours, this rises to seventy percent. How can we counteract this decline when it is so steep and inevitable?

The answer lies in everything I've mentioned in this lesson so far: by taking regular breaks. In one experiment, taking just a ten-minute break after learning improved recall by as much as thirty percent. Dr. Barbara Oakley is a professor of engineering and an expert in the science of learning. She is best known for her massively popular online course "Learning How to Learn," which has reached millions of learners worldwide.

Her work synthesizes insights from neuroscience and psychology to explain how rest enhances learning and cognitive performance. Dr. Oakley emphasizes the importance of "diffuse thinking" periods—when the brain is at rest or engaged in unrelated, low-effort tasks—to foster creativity and problem-solving. She contrasts this with "focused thinking," which requires intense concentration.

To put this to the test, try focusing for fifty minutes on whatever you're reading, listening to, or trying to learn, and then give yourself ten minutes for diffuse thinking. You can spend this time looking out the window and daydreaming, walking around the block, folding a load of laundry, taking a shower, petting your dog or cat, listening to music, working on a jigsaw puzzle, meditating, or setting your timer and taking a short nap. You'll be surprised at how it improves your recall while keeping your energy levels high.

One popular way to implement more regular breaks is to practice the "Pomodoro Technique." The Pomodoro Technique is a time management method developed by Francesco Cirillo that enhances productivity and focus by breaking work into intervals. It involves working on a task for twenty-five uninterrupted minutes followed by a five-minute break.

Each twenty-five-minute session is called a "Pomodoro" (Italian for "tomato," inspired by Cirillo's tomato-shaped kitchen timer). After completing four Pomodoros, you can take a longer break of fifteen to thirty minutes. This technique is effective because it leverages the brain's natural rhythms to prevent mental fatigue, improve concentration, and maintain consistent productivity throughout the day.

Rest to Recharge

Microbreaks are short breaks that last one to five minutes each. Such brief pauses interrupt the buildup of cognitive fatigue, allowing the brain to recharge and regain clarity.

Getting in the habit of taking microbreaks will improve your recall, ability to focus, and performance in all areas of your life.

The Tale of Two Lumberjacks

Two lumberjacks were competing to see who could chop down the most trees in a day. The first lumberjack was confident he would win because he worked nonstop from morning to night.

The second lumberjack, however, took breaks throughout the day. At the end of the day, the first lumberjack was surprised to find that the second lumberjack had cut down more trees. He asked the second lumberjack how he managed to chop down more trees despite taking so many breaks.

"During my breaks, I was sharpening my axe," the second lumberjack replied.

Invite Joy into Your Life

I often ask my coaching clients, "On a scale of one to ten, with one being awful and ten being perfect, what score would you give your life today?" After getting their number, I'll follow up by asking, "What is keeping you from giving it a higher score?"

The answer to the second question that I often hear—from high-achieving leaders, in particular—is, "I want to experience more joy in my life."

Joy is a deep and often spiritual or emotional sense of fulfillment, contentment, or connection. It arises from within and is not dependent on external circumstances. Unlike happiness or fun, joy is more enduring and profound, often arising from experiences of connection, growth, or transcendence. Most of us could afford to experience more joy.

One of my earliest coaching clients was a high-achieving corporate leader. While she found her role to be fulfilling, her workdays were long and stressful. She didn't have a lot of free time. She couldn't remember the last time she felt joy, and she was determined to change that. She wanted to consciously create more joyful moments in her daily life.

I asked her what she used to do that brought her joy when she was a young girl, and she remembered her childhood love of swinging on swing sets in parks and playgrounds. I asked her if there was a park near her home or work, and there was. For "homework," she agreed that occasionally she'd make time to stop and spend a few minutes swinging. She gave it a try and loved it so much that even when she was required to travel for work, she would locate a park with a swing set and spend five to ten minutes swinging as high and as fast as she could.

She sent me occasional texts with photos of her swinging high in the air. The expression on her face was one of childlike joy. Seeing her like that delighted me to no end. It turns out that joy is a kind of emotional wildfire: when you share it, others often catch it and pass it on. This phenomenon is called "emotional contagion." When we see someone light up, smile, or share something uplifting, our own brain tends to mirror that emotional state, prompting us to feel these feelings with others.

Joy can arise just from being present in the world. There is so much joy to be experienced, in the ordinary moments of our daily lives, if only we're paying attention.

Have More Fun

Having fun is no trivial matter. When we make an intentional effort to incorporate more fun into our lives, it can make a difficult life worth living. Engaging in forms of play, whatever that looks like to you, will reduce your stress, enrich your relationships, make you more empathetic, foster feelings of belonging, and inspire creativity.

For the last fifteen years, I've consciously pushed myself to have more fun in my life, my work, and my relationships. When I was reinventing myself in 2010, I came up with an exercise that required me to come up with five ways I wanted to be. One of them was "fun." Although I was already having some fun in my life, I wanted to have more of it.

At the time, my sons were young, and I wanted to be the kind of parent who would get down on the ground to play and engage with them, to run and jump alongside them, and even to participate in their "crusher" wrestling matches. I also wanted to insert more fun into my relationship with Jerry.

To have more of something in your life, you must be intentional. It won't just magically happen, and it most certainly won't magically happen consistently. My husband and I started going on "happy hour golden hour" bike rides, walks around town, trips to the park or rodeo grounds, or drives up Sinks Canyon to our favorite sites by the river where we love laying in a hammock or having a picnic. We'd pack our cribbage game and a bottle of wine, and it turned into a regular tradition.

Now, all these years later, we play one hundred cribbage games a year; we keep score of course, which adds to the fun. We've been married for thirty-two years, and doing things like this has made a huge difference in keeping the fire in our relationship stoked. Around the same time, I started a weekly ice cream tradition for my three sons and me. Every Friday after school, we'd go for ice cream, then spend time chasing each other around the parks and on the merry-go-rounds and monkey bars on the playgrounds we passed on our walk home.

During family dinners, to this day, we often play gin rummy or other card and board games. Doing this enables time together as a family when we don't have the bandwidth for a lot of conversation at the end of a day full of school and work. Playing games during mealtimes can open us all up in unexpected ways. It's informal and fun. We've also had a tradition of pizza on Friday nights that we started as soon as the boys were old enough to eat solid food.

During the pandemic, a time when my parents were in the "vulnerable" category, we started a tradition of playing cornhole with them every Sunday afternoon. Again, this has helped us do something other than just sit around a table and have the same conversations over and over again. Adding cornhole, Scrabble, and jigsaw puzzles to our time together has enriched our relationships and made our time together more memorable.

When I lead my Epic Adventures, I schedule some time for fun and play, and it's always appreciated. It's valuable to lose our seriousness and bring out our childlike qualities from time to time, and there's no better way to do that than having fun together. I often ask people, "Do you know who said, 'I regret having so much fun?'"

Everyone guesses correctly: no one. No one ever said that, and in fact, when you talk to people who are approaching the end of their lives, almost all of them say they wish they would have lightened up and had more fun. They wish they wouldn't have taken life so very seriously all the time.

Laugh a Little

Laughing is one of the most enjoyable human experiences. I love to laugh, and there's nothing better than laughing so hard with a friend or family member that your stomach hurts the next day. If you ask me, *that* is living. Laughter triggers the release of dopamine, the brain's "feel-good" chemical. That's why we love to laugh. For a moment, we are able to forget any pain or suffering we might be experiencing.

Babies and kids laugh hundreds of times a day, but for adults, it's not so frequent. In fact, some publications have reported that kids laugh an average of three hundred times a day, and adults only laugh seventeen times a day, if they're lucky. Several years ago, when I first learned of this statistic, I shared it with my family at dinner. Our sons cleverly saw it as an opportunity to do some research, so we watched one of our favorite funny movies, and one of the sons recorded how many times I laughed during it. The movie was one hour and forty-five minutes long, and according to their record of tally marks, I laughed 171 times. Can you guess what movie it was?

Why do kids laugh so much more frequently than adults? It's most likely because children have an innate curiosity, joy, and playful nature. Unfortunately, as we grow up, we seem to lose these natural tendencies.

When we laugh, we activate the brain's mesolimbic reward system: a network involved in motivation and pleasure. This system reinforces its own behavior, making us naturally inclined to seek out humorous situations. But laughter is more than just a social or emotional response—it's a complex physiological and psychological process that offers numerous benefits. Laughter has been shown to reduce our stress and blood pressure, strengthen our immune system, improve our pain tolerance, and enrich our connection with others.

Laughter is a universal language. Studies show that we are thirty times more likely to laugh in social situations than we are when we are alone. Laughter promotes the release of oxytocin, often called the "love hormone," which deepens feelings of trust, empathy, and closeness with others.

This is why shared laughter can bring people together and strengthen relationships. Laughter is contagious. When we observe someone else laughing, mirror neurons in our brains are activated, and we can't help but laugh too. If you don't believe this, just watch a "baby laughing" video on YouTube.

Laughing is also good for our hearts. Literally. A study conducted by Stanford University revealed the remarkable health benefits of laughter, particularly deep belly laughter. Just thirty seconds of deep laughter provides the same cardiovascular benefits as ten minutes of strenuous rowing, improving our heart health. I don't know if you've ever rowed for ten minutes, but I have, and I wouldn't categorize it as easy *or* fun. I'll pick belly laughing every time.

Laughter also plays a powerful role in emotional resilience, helping us navigate setbacks, failures, and challenges with a lighter heart and a more optimistic mindset. The ability to laugh easily has been shown to improve our relationships by making us more approachable and fun to be around. It also makes us more likely to think outside the box and take risks. It strengthens our immune systems by increasing the production of natural killer cells and antibodies, which help fight infections. When we laugh, endorphins are released that act as natural painkillers, reducing our perception of pain.

Finally, laughter contributes to a more positive outlook on life, leading to greater satisfaction and more joy. To make your life more epic, find more opportunities to laugh.

Be Willing to Laugh at Yourself

Being willing and able to be silly and laugh at ourselves is more than a good habit to have—it's a skill. When we do so with others, it creates an immediate atmosphere of connection, lightness, and joy. It dissolves tension, invites vulnerability, and reminds us that we're all perfectly imperfect.

In a group or family setting, such silliness and shared laughter fosters a sense of belonging. It breaks down the walls of self-consciousness and encourages genuine interactions. This is fun on more than just the surface level; it allows us to let go of the pressure to appear flawless and lets us tap into a childlike and playful energy that's both liberating and contagious.

Today, my sons are eighteen, twenty-three, and twenty-five years old, but when they were young boys, we often did things that caused us to be in stitches from laughing so hard. One of the most notable examples of this was the two years we recorded and produced videos in a series we created called "Stalking Bigfoot in Wyoming." We recorded eight episodes, and we laughed our guts out during the entire process. (Email me if you'd like the links, or you can find them on my YouTube.com/HaveMedia channel.)

As a family, we'd brainstorm the plot of each episode, which was always a hilarious process in its own right. In one episode, Big Foot steals one of the boys' iPods; in another, he steals one of the boys' Nikes; in another, the boys stalk him by following a trail of "cheeseball dust." We'd often be rolling on the ground laughing during brainstorm sessions before we even headed into the field for recording. Once we had the plot lined out, we'd head outdoors and locate a unique setting.

My husband would dress up in the Big Foot costume, and our sons, who wore helmets and life jackets (to be prepared for all possible scenarios), transformed into official Big Foot stalkers. Capturing and directing the episodes in various outdoor locations always generated a lot of laughter, and by the time we returned home to do the editing—another hilarious stage—our faces and stomachs would ache from all the fits of laughter.

We must have laughed thousands of times over the course of thinking up, acting out, recording, and editing a single episode. Not only was it priceless in the moment, revisiting those videos all these years later still causes us to laugh until we cry.

What could you do with your family, friend group, or work team that would generate some silliness and laughter? I challenge you to follow through with your ideas, because you will benefit from the aliveness it adds to your life. And in the process, it may even bring you all closer together.

Celebrate More Often

To savor something is to intentionally pause, reflect on, and appreciate an experience. Celebrating helps us to savor our accomplishments and the good things in life. Whether it's a success, something in your life or work that's going well, an unexpected opportunity, or a relationship that feels like it's blossoming in new ways, it ought to be celebrated.

Celebration strengthens our emotional connection to the moment, experience, or accomplishment. And yet, most of us don't adequately celebrate our achievements, which is a big mistake. Studies in social psychology indicate that sharing achievements with others strengthens our relationships with one another. When we celebrate together, we experience stronger social bonds, mutual support, and feelings of belonging.

When I was operating my first business, I didn't allow for enough celebration. I had an amazing team, and we accomplished a lot, but looking back, I wish I would have paused along the way to appreciate how far we had come.

We were small and nimble and innovating at a fast pace, and I think I was afraid of slowing down or stopping because I feared it would cause us to lose our edge. I regret that I didn't know better and didn't do a better job of celebrating with my exceptional team.

Research in positive psychology, including the work of Dr. Barbara Fredrickson, shows that when we take the time to celebrate our achievements, we generate positive emotions such as pride and gratitude. These emotions broaden our thought-action repertoire, making us more creative, resourceful, and resilient. Celebrations are a way of signaling value and recognition to others, whether in a workplace or personal context. Publicly acknowledging someone's achievement fosters trust and camaraderie.

For the past five years, I've had the privilege of working with Arrow Exterminators and its exceptional leaders. Arrow Exterminators is a family-owned-and-operated company headquartered in Atlanta, Georgia. It is one of the largest and most respected pest control companies in the United States.

Operating across twelve states with more than 170 service centers and more than three thousand dedicated team members, Arrow has consistently earned recognition, both nationally and regionally, as a "Best Place to Work." This recognition is a direct reflection of the company's unwavering commitment to its people and its remarkable, people-first culture.

Since its founding in 1964, Arrow Exterminators has built its success on a foundation of celebrating its people and fostering a culture of connection, care, and purpose. Over the years, I've had the privilege of working closely with more than fifty of Arrow's leaders, and what stands out, without exception, is their genuine love for their people.

They don't just *talk* about valuing their people—they live it. A prime example of this is Arrow's Pinnacle Club and Premier Club, programs tied to revenue goals which recognize and reward top-performing team members. When goals are achieved, members are celebrated on an epic scale with unforgettable experiences such as luxury trips and exclusive events, showing just how deeply Arrow invests in its people.

In addition, Arrow's leaders show their commitment to the professional development and career growth of their people by providing training academies and career pathing. The organization is a stellar example of what it looks like to foster a thriving culture that celebrates its people every day.

To date, I've taken several of Arrow Exterminators' leadership teams, including more than fifty leaders, through my eight-month virtual leadership program, and I can tell you they all love working at Arrow. When asked why, they all point to the organization's people-first culture.

Promote Progress and Small Wins

It's also important to acknowledge and celebrate the "small wins" that are achieved while in pursuit of a greater goal. Small wins act as incremental reinforcements, and they count for a lot.

Teresa Amabile, a professor at Harvard Business School, has conducted extensive research on workplace motivation, culminating in the "Progress Principle." In her study of twelve thousand daily work diaries from employees, Amabile found that small, incremental progress in meaningful work leads to higher levels of motivation, engagement, and happiness.

When we acknowledge and celebrate small steps forward, it boosts our self-confidence and reinforces our sense of competence. This creates a psychological snowball effect, encouraging continued effort and perseverance toward larger goals. When I'm leading my Epic clients up a steep trail or a tall mountain, we take frequent one-minute standing breaks during which we don't remove our backpacks or sit down. We simply catch our breath and compose ourselves while enjoying the views, including glimpses of how far we've come and the progress we're making.

Planned microbreaks inspire efficiency, acknowledge progress, and can turn an arduous journey into a more manageable and enjoyable one. Celebrating small wins also reinforces a growth mindset (which I wrote about in Lesson 2). To live an epic life and find a way through the uncertain and rapidly changing time we're living in, we must foster and operate with a growth mindset. When we focus on our progress rather than the outcome, we are more likely to view challenges as opportunities to grow rather than insurmountable obstacles.

We must view the journey as more than just a means to an end, as something that, in itself, is worth appreciating. Celebrating our small wins is a great way to do that.

When We're Inspired, We Live More

Joel and Alan, two leaders and friends, were looking to do something epic, to be physically and mentally challenged, and to experience awe-inspiring scenery in a remote wilderness. I designed a five-day itinerary that included mountain climbing and traveling some of my favorite trails. After three days of mountain-climbing and enduring clouds of millions of mosquitoes, we broke camp and set off on a spectacular route that would lead us to our final camp. Our path took us over a rugged mountain pass that reached eleven thousand feet.

After a lot of uphill hiking, Joel, Alan, and I reached the middle of the pass. Towering granite mountains appeared, jutting out of the alpine tundra. The views were breathtaking and left Joel and Alan speechless. (Watching people's reactions when they see such views during an Epic Adventure is one of the reasons I love taking people into the wilderness.)

After several attempts to capture a photo of the three of us jumping so that it looked like we were jumping over the nearby cirque, I suggested that we take a load off and linger in the beautiful spot for an hour or two. The guys were delighted at the prospect of dwelling in such a stunningly beautiful place. I watched as Joel and Alan each found slabs to perch on before finding my own slab and plunking down.

About one hundred yards in front of me, Alan was a tiny speck, engulfed by the astounding natural beauty. I watched him for a time as he sat there. One of the biggest values for my Epic Adventure clients is being able to get away and to not be needed for a few days. At the time, Alan was a leader of people at a purpose-driven company. He took pride in being available to his people and their needs, and that was a tall order since there were many of them and they worked around the globe.

But here, there was no cell signal—no phone calls, emails, or notifications dinging in the background. As I watched him, lost in his thoughts and taking in the scenery, I wondered what the experience felt like for him.

Two weeks after the expedition, Alan sent me a text that indicated he had been experiencing a lot of tears. Concerned, I texted him back,

"Is everything okay?" to which he replied, "Yes, everything's great." He explained that his tears were tears of gratitude, adding, "The space for me to grow is so much bigger than I thought it was."

At the time of our expedition, Alan was fifty, happily married, and the father of two adult children. He was content with his life and loved his work. He wasn't unhappy or struggling with anything in particular. Still, his experience in the wilderness had transformed him in unexpected ways.

Alan's words resonated with me so much, and that's why I've never forgotten them. When we're inspired, the space for us to grow *is* bigger. When I wake up feeling flat and uninspired, I feel like I'm just going through the motions, flying under the radar, merely existing. We all experience these sorts of days.

But when I wake up feeling inspired, I not only have more belief in myself, but I have more enthusiasm for my life. I play bigger, and I participate more fully in all areas of my life.

This reminds me of a favorite passage from Jack London's "Credo." They are words I wish to live by:

> *I would rather be ashes than dust! I would rather that my spark should burn out in a brilliant blaze than it should be stifled by dry rot. I would rather be a superb meteor, every atom of me in magnificent glow, than a sleepy and permanent planet. The proper function of man is to live, not to exist. I shall not waste my days in trying to prolong them. I shall use my time.*

To be inspired is to use our time. It is to live *more*.

Get Awe-Struck

Did you know there are an estimated one hundred billion to four hundred billion stars in the Milky Way? Think about that for a moment. Once that fact sinks in, consider this: according to the latest respected, peer-reviewed estimates, scientists believe there are at least two trillion galaxies in the observable universe.

These numbers are so vast, so staggering, that they defy comprehension. This is the essence of awe: when the mind can't quite hold it, but the heart feels it.

Dacher Keltner, a psychology professor at the University of California, Berkeley, and author of *Awe: The New Science of Everyday Wonder and How It Can Transform Your Life*, has spent years studying this powerful emotion. He describes awe as a profound experience that evokes wonder, shifts our perspective, and connects us to something greater than ourselves. Awe pulls our attention away from our daily worries and redirects it toward the vastness and beauty that surround us. Research shows that experiencing awe can make us more generous, more cooperative, and even healthier.

It may trigger the release of oxytocin, the so-called "love hormone," which strengthens trust and deepens social bonds. It may even reduce inflammation, the root cause of many chronic illnesses. I don't know about you, but I'm all in for awe. I want more of it. The good news is that awe is available to all of us, and it isn't limited to once-in-a-lifetime or grand experiences. You don't have to hike deep into the wilderness or visit the Grand Canyon or see the Northern Lights to experience awe.

Through his research, Keltner identifies eight common sources of awe: nature (grand landscapes, powerful storms), music (moving compositions, powerful performances), visual art (paintings, architecture), spiritual and religious experiences (such as prayer, meditation, or sacred rituals), collective effervescence (group experiences like concerts, sporting events, or protests), acts of moral beauty (witnessing kindness, courage, or generosity), big ideas (scientific discoveries, philosophical insights), and birth and death (the profound transitions of life).

A few years ago, my family capped off a three-week Iceland adventure by summiting Snæfellsjökull, a 700,000-year-old volcano that required the three-thousand-foot ascent of a glacier. We were swallowed in the shifting clouds, so our visibility was limited. We could barely see each other. But occasionally, the fog would dissipate just long enough for us to get a glimpse of Faxaflói Bay below. When we got to the top, we couldn't see the abyss below, but we could sure feel it.

Post-adventure, after returning to level ground, I noticed a white bird with black feathers on the top of its head. Its head moved jerkily as its beady eyes scanned the ground for food. I asked our guide what kind of bird it was, and he responded, "Arctic tern." I snapped a quick photo, and later that night, while writing a blog post about the day's adventure, I Googled "Arctic tern." And I'm so glad I did.

It turns out this rather ordinary-looking bird is renowned for its extraordinary migratory journey, covering more distance annually than any other animal. These small seabirds embark on a round-trip migration from their Arctic breeding grounds to the Antarctic and then back again, traveling approximately forty-four thousand miles in a single year! Over their lifetime, Arctic terns will travel 1.5 million miles—the equivalent of flying to the moon and back three times! You don't have to have an interest in birds for facts like these to inspire awe.

We can be struck by awe during profound experiences. I'll never forget the feeling when I saw and met each of my sons for the first time at their births—or the time Jerry and I, on our first backpacking adventure in 1991, looked up while stargazing and were stunned by an epic aurora borealis display stretching across the sky. Often, though, we can be struck by awe in the ordinary moments of our day.

I'm a sunrise and sunset junkie—I try to witness as many as I can. Still, I'm struck every time by how the rising and setting sun paints the mountains and their ridgelines in bright pink. Awe shows up watching the sun rise over the ocean, hearing the unbridled laughter of a child in an airport, or standing before a field of wildflowers nodding toward the morning light. It's in the smell of Wyoming sagebrush after a (rare) rain shower, hearing the roar of a waterfall before seeing it, finding a perfect heart-shaped rock in the middle of the trail.

I felt awestruck when we spotted a mama moose and her baby beside the trail on a family hike, or the time Jerry and I hiked through a dark forest just before dawn, beginning a thirty-four-mile day hike and mountain climb, when the silence was cracked open at 5:01 a.m. by a full chorus of birds that erupted. I remember locking eyes with a wolf in Yellowstone, and the time I watched as a grizzly bear, fresh out of hibernation, plucked pocket gophers from the ground and ate them whole.

I'll never forget the morning our family was up early walking the Camino de Santiago, and for two full hours, we had the path completely to ourselves—just the five of us, held by the quiet, the cool air, and the sacredness of being alone on that ancient trail. I could go on and name hundreds more moments like these that have blessed me with awe.

As I remember all of these, I'm reminded of how lucky I am to get to spend so much of my life outdoors and in beautiful places. (It's also a compelling pitch for everyone to spend more time outside.)

When we experience awe, it often transcends our understanding of the world. It reminds us of the vastness of life—its mysteries, its wonders—and our small but significant place in it. One of the things I love most about awe is that it's visceral: the prickling of goosebumps, tears welling in our eyes, the sense of being held by something greater. It grips us, mesmerizes us, and has the power to change us.

Best of all, awe invites us to be present—to pause, to marvel. If you want to experience it, try looking at the night sky or watching a sunset, spending time near water, taking a walk to listen to birdsong, learning something new and astonishing while chasing your curiosity, or engaging with a work of art—a book, a song, an image—that moves you.

Awe brings with it a pulse of aliveness, a vivid reminder that we are here, awake, and part of something wondrous. The world is waiting to remind us of its beauty. And when we notice it, our lives become richer, fuller, and far more meaningful.

Saying "Hell Yeah" to More Aliveness

"What does it feel like to be alive? Living, you stand under a waterfall. You leave the sleeping shore deliberately; you shed your dusty clothes, pick your barefoot way over the high, slippery rocks, hold your breath, choose your footing, and step into the waterfall. The hard water pelts your skull, bangs in bits on your shoulders and arms. . . . You could learn to live like this."

—Annie Dillard, *An American Childhood*

Every year, I choose a word to guide the way I live.

Ever since I started this practice, I've found that doing so helps me live intentionally. For several years now, my word has been "Hell Yeah." (I know that's actually two words, but hey, I make my own rules.)

I chose "Hell Yeah" to challenge myself to say yes to experiences that my reasonable, cautious self might otherwise decline. "Hell Yeah" has an enthusiasm and gusto to it that reminds me to embrace bold experiences and to say yes to things I might normally be quick to reject. Don't get me wrong, my goal isn't to live recklessly—it's just about not living so *reasonably*. It's about living *more*.

One afternoon in August 2013, I sat on the shore of a high-altitude lake and watched as seven women on my Epic Adventure dared to plunge in the icy-cold waters. I thought they were crazy and said as much, but then something happened. I saw myself from a distance, sitting on the lakeshore watching the fun and not participating in it, and I found the image disappointing.

I had led these brave women up a tall mountain only to sit and watch from the sidelines as they splashed, swam, laughed, and celebrated. Their energy was ecstatic, and I was envious. I wanted to have what they were having.

I stood up and announced I would give it a try. One of my partner guides encouraged me and held my hand as we walked into the frigid waters. I took a breath, then dared to take the plunge. I gasped as the freezing water enveloped me. It was invigorating and electrifying! That feeling was my baptism into "Hell Yeah," and I was hooked.

Over the course of the following years, I slid down a waterfall with my three sons—something I hadn't done since I was eighteen years old. I talked my husband into taking our family on a thirty-day trip of a lifetime in Europe. The next year we planned a month-long van trip from Vancouver, B.C., to Los Angeles, stopping and adventuring on beaches and in beautiful natural destinations along the way. We followed it up with a backpacking pilgrimage on Spain's Camino de Santiago and an epic trip to Iceland.

We went on even more road trips and family adventures and, when we stayed at hotels, instead of sitting and watching Jerry and the boys, I dove into the swimming pools with them. I joined in their basketball games and even participated in our family's "crusher" wrestling matches. I raced them down ski slopes and sand dunes; when we went to amusement parks, I dared to go on bigger roller coasters and scarier rides.

But to me, saying "Hell Yeah" wasn't just about doing exhilarating things. I made a habit of rising early to watch the sun rise. I chased sunsets with Jerry and the boys and set the alarm at all hours of the night so we could witness constellation events. I stopped being too lazy to get off the couch if someone reported seeing a rainbow.

My "Hell Yeah" methodology applied to work opportunities too. I've said "Hell Yeah" to things I wasn't sure I could do but wanted to be *able* to do.

Over time, I began to identify with "Hell Yeah" so much that some of my Epic Adventure clients assigned me a new trail name—"Shell Yeah."

Sometimes, if I'm feeling flat or a little bored with my life, I'll think of this trail name and am able to tap into a more enlivened version of myself.

The Time "Hell Yeah" Led to Head Banging and a Ride with Elvis

It was in the spring of 2017 when I really cranked up my "Hell Yeah" philosophy. My family took a road trip that included camping and hiking, and, at the end of it, a fancy hotel, dinner out, and a Utah Jazz basketball game.

Midway through our trip, after a long day of hiking in Colorado's Garden of the Gods, we headed back to our hotel to shower and clean up. Our sons hinted that they felt like they had earned some "privs" (privileges, which, for our boys, meant video games and other screen time), and Jerry and I saw an opportunity for a date. (Can I get a "Hell Yeah"?)

While Jerry was in the shower, I googled Electronic Dance Music (EDM) in Colorado Springs and, to my delight, there was a well-known DJ performing at a club called Rawkus. I suggested it to Jerry, and after looking at me long enough to confirm I was serious, he agreed.

Our adventure started when our Uber driver showed up: a kind and outgoing woman in a maroon minivan. On her dashboard was a bobblehead Jesus and, clipped to the visor above the passenger seat, were wallet-sized photos of two young, adorable children, a girl and a boy. The van had the vague fragrance of a lemon grove, which I assumed was emanating from the yellow pine tree air freshener dangling from the volume knob on the van's radio.

"Where would you like to go?" she asked.

"The Rawkus," I said.

"Rawkus, huh? Feeling raucous tonight, are we?"

Jerry and I laughed. "Yes!"

"Wow," she muttered. "I didn't see that coming."

As our driver pulled out of our hotel parking lot, she asked us what kind of music we'd like to listen to.

"You can pick," I offered. She pressed some buttons on her stereo and on came a hip-hop song that was, according to the stereo display panel, by Big Sean. It was so loud we could feel the bass thumping underneath our seats and up against our backs and heads. As our driver maneuvered through Friday night traffic, the van's windows rattled and the Jesus on the dashboard bobbed about wildly.

With our ears ringing, we hopped out, and our driver yelled, "Have fun—dance like you don't know anyone!" I made a mental note to give her a rave review. We found our way to the front entrance. The club wasn't open yet, but the sign on the door indicated it would open in fifteen minutes, so we started a line. As others began to arrive, they sat or stood near the entrance. They were several years younger than us. I felt self-conscious. It seemed like everyone who showed up looked at us with curiosity. Whether it was because we were wearing collared shirts or because we were older, I don't know, but we were obviously a novelty.

When the doors finally opened, we were the first to step onto the dance floor. Jerry got a beer, and I held a bottle of water as we waited for the first of many DJs to arrive and start the beats. A man and woman came over to us and introduced themselves. The conversation was awkward—it reminded me of a networking event, where people randomly come up to you and introduce themselves. After some polite small talk, the man asked, "Is this your first rave?"

Panic flooded through me. *A rave?* I thought frantically. *Are we at a rave?* My mind flashed to a scene of a festival of people who were high out of their minds and possibly some orgies going on. (I don't get out much!) But as I returned to the present, I quickly realized this didn't look anything like that. Jerry responded that we had never been to a rave before. The couple wished us a good time, then walked away.

We danced for hours. All around us, people jumped and bent at the torso and banged their heads up and down. Even though I felt certain we'd pay a physical price for it the next day, we followed suit. The music was electrifying, and we jumped, danced, and head-banged our guts out.

As soon as there was a break in the music, we drank water like it was our job. We were drenched in sweat, and Jerry said he was stoked. "I love the powerful bass," he said, raising his voice so I could hear him. "I can feel it reverberating through my entire body!" I agreed—it was invigorating, to say the least.

That said, we knew we must have looked like we had gotten off the train at the wrong station. During the course of the night, people of various races, genders, and ages came up to us and boisterously offered hugs and high fives. A few of them remarked, "It's so great to see *you guys* here."

One person approached me and politely but skeptically asked, "So, you really like this music?" What a dumb question, I thought. Wasn't it obvious? I responded, "Yes. I love it!"

After dancing to another DJ set, we had head-banged ourselves to exhaustion and finally left the dance floor and requested an Uber. My Fitbit reported sixty-four thousand steps, thirty thousand of which (twelve miles worth) were from dancing. (I know—who wears a Fitbit to a rave? A dork.)

When we got into our Uber, "Jailhouse Rock" was playing quietly from the stereo, and our driver was none other than Elvis. As soon as we were buckled in, Elvis asked us if we liked Elvis. We assured him that we did. Jerry repeated how awesome Elvis's music is, and in response, the driver changed songs to "Love Me Tender" and started singing loudly:

Love me tender

Love me sweet

Never let me go

You have made my life complete

And I love you so . . .

There's a difference between singing out loud and performing. Our driver was performing. And his performance was stupendous. It felt like we were in a dream. After "Love Me Tender" came "I Did It My Way" (which I think is originally a Frank Sinatra song, but this version was covered by Elvis). As we approached our destination, I told Elvis that "I

Did It My Way" was a favorite of mine. "I love it so much," I said, adding, "you are a spectacular singer." And I meant it.

Then, Elvis offered, "If you like, I can drive around a few extra blocks so you can hear it to the end?"

Hell Yeah! "Yes, please," I said.

Elvis crooned, "Yes, there were times, I'm sure you knew / When I bit off more than I could chew / But through it all, when there was doubt / I ate it up and spit it out / I faced it all and I stood tall / And did it my way . . ."

The song ended, and so did our ride and our unforgettable night. We gave our personal Elvis a generous tip and made our way back to the hotel room and our sons. It took a while to come down from the high of our experience, but I knew, even at the time, that it would be an experience we'd never forget.

These "Hell Yeah" experiences make me feel young again and more fully alive, and I can't recommend them enough.

Next time you're standing at a crossroads between being responsible or bold, reasonable or ecstatic, ask yourself: *What would happen if I said hell yeah?* The choice is yours—and so are the thrills, if you choose correctly.

How to Create More Unforgettable Moments

When we reach the end of our lives, we won't remember everything—it's simply not possible.

Nobel Prize–winning psychologist and behavioral economist Daniel Kahneman observed that we have roughly twenty thousand thoughts each day. That's six million thoughts a year. Trying to hold onto all of them is impossible, and I'm not sure we'd want to even if we could. What we *will* remember are the moments that break the rhythm of the ordinary— the ones that elevate us, inspire us, bring us laughter, impart joy, or leave us awestruck. These moments stand out because they are infused with emotion, significance, and meaning.

As Dan and Chip Heath explain in *The Power of Moments*, the most vivid and enduring memories come from "peak moments"—experiences of Elevation, Pride, Insight, or Connection (EPIC). These are the moments that lift us above the mundane and make us feel profoundly alive.

Picture the spontaneous laughter that binds us during an unforgettable evening, the surge of pride in conquering something we thought was impossible, or the insight that alters our perspective forever. These deeply felt experiences imprint on our hearts, crafting the story of who we are at our cores. They remind us about what it means to truly live and about what matters most to us. Such experiences enrich our lives and make us happier and healthier.

Lesson 6
Cherish Your People

Our People Make Us Better

We were standing victoriously, with our arms in the air, on the summit of the fourth and final mountain of our expedition. We were giddy.

We had reached the summit and were done climbing mountains, and the next day we'd return to civilization, where we'd be able to reconnect with our loved ones, enjoy a hot shower, and sleep in a bed. After fourteen days of camping and hiking, nothing sounded better.

At the beginning of our NOLS expedition, we were strangers with little in common. The only thing we had in common was that we had self-selected to embark on an epic adventure. But by the time we reached our final peak, I felt intimately connected to Antonia, Lauren, JJ, Patrick, Marc, Jon, Cutter, Chris, and Amy. They had all found their way into my heart, and now that the expedition was coming to an end I felt like a better person as a result of having spent time with each and every one of them.

There are a lot of bears in Alaska. Just weeks before our NOLS course, there had been a bear attack on a course in another region of Alaska. The injured victims survived, but when our course started, the event was still fresh. From the start, our instructors warned us to go above and beyond when it came to our bear safety protocols. We carried bear spray and were trained how to use it. We secured our food in bear-proof containers and even set up a "bear fence" around our backcountry kitchen at each of our camps.

We were required to travel with a minimum group of four—this meant never going to the bathroom alone, even if we had to go number two. We were able to find the humor in it all, referring to these as "group poops" and "social dumps," but the fact was, it required a lot of vulnerability from all of us. Shared vulnerability does a lot of heavy lifting when it comes to creating a stronger bond among a group and its members.

Nothing transforms a group of people—especially strangers—into a team as well as doing something challenging together. When we do something that feels hard, and maybe even impossible, we emerge from it stronger than we were before. But even more importantly, we're transformed by the people with whom we share the experience.

Who's on Your Short Rope?

In the wilderness, whenever traveling over uncertain and potentially dangerous terrain, mountaineering guides will often use a safety technique called "short roping." All team members are attached to one another using a relatively short length of rope, typically five to fifteen meters long, so that their guide can ensure their safety and reduce their risk of slips and falls.

For example, when crossing a glacier, if someone were to fall into a crevasse—a deep, open crack in the ice—the rope becomes a literal lifeline. When the team is roped up and alert, they can act quickly to hopefully prevent that person from falling to their death.

It's a dramatic image—but it's also an apt metaphor for the impact people and our relationships with them have on our health, our well-being, and our ability to stay upright when life gets uncertain and particularly challenging.

The people in our lives, and the quality of our relationships with them, have a direct and profound impact on us. The people we spend time with influence how we live, if and how we lead, how we show up in our various roles, what we're able to achieve or not achieve, and if and how we weather life's storms.

When it comes to our health and self-care, we often turn to checklists that include things like exercise, diet, and sleep as the main categories to pay attention to. These are all important—and I will discuss them later in further detail—but in my humble opinion and experience, our people and relationships must be just as high of a priority.

The late Jim Rohn used to say, "We're the average of the five people we spend the most time with." I believe this—I have seen and experienced it. We must have people in our corner who will be honest with us, who want the best for us, and who see and believe in our potential. We must have people in our lives who will hold our feet to the fire and who won't let us off the hook when we're pursuing something that's important to us.

Reflect on the people in your life and the quality of your relationships with them. Consider your goals or any changes you're wanting or need to make. Is there someone you're spending a lot of time with who is at odds with these goals? If so, what are some steps you could take to spend less time with them? Conversely, is there someone you'd like to invite into your circle—someone who could help level you up and provide the support you need to soar? If so, what are some steps you could take to discover such a person, and how might you invite them into your life?

We Must Overestimate Our People

We can go further than we think when someone else thinks we can. As leaders, whether in the workplace or at home, we must overestimate our people. We must see their potential so we can help them become the person or leader they aspire to be—the person they *can* be.

In my work, I often guide leaders up tall mountains, figuratively and literally. Their mountain could be a hard change they need to make in their life, asking for a promotion, or requesting a raise. It could be finding their way through a divorce they didn't choose. It could be breaking a habit that's causing them or their family or their leadership to suffer. It could be learning a new skill or speaking up at a meeting when their usual style is to simply observe.

It could be climbing a tall mountain in Wyoming or making their way up Angels Landing (clinging to the chain so they don't fall over the fifteen-hundred-foot cliff). It could be crossing a high, swift river on a backpacking trip. It could be learning to rock climb or doing their first rappel over a steep cliff into a slot canyon. As a coach and guide, my mission is to inspire and help people climb the mountains they're not sure they can climb. My purpose is not to rescue people when times get tough, but to support them and help them believe in their abilities.

One of the reasons I chose to become a coach is that I have always been someone who believes in others' potential, often more than they do. I can see people's greatness, and I like to call it forth and to offer them my support and guidance.

I encourage my clients to dare to do challenging things that are meaningful to them, and I help them through the crux—the most difficult part of a climb. I may offer to carry some of their load, share strategies with them, and do all I can to help them find their way through, but I never do the work for them. We are more capable than we think we are. But sometimes, we're blind to this unless and until someone else sees and points it out.

According to Adam Grant in his book _Hidden Potential_, when we support and believe in the potential of others, we create a ripple effect of growth. By uplifting others, we elevate the entire system. Overestimating our people doesn't just apply to our teams in the workplace. As parents, it's important for us to believe in our child's potential—to believe they can go further than they think they can.

When my boys were toddlers, I had the idea to take each of them on a "mother-son rite of passage" adventure the summer before they entered high school. I designed a four-day backpacking adventure in our backyard, Wyoming's Wind River Range. I looked forward to spending such meaningful one-on-one time with each of my sons during this formative time in their lives, but I also hoped the experience would empower them. The itinerary I designed included a solo mountain climb on one of the days.

We'd wake up at 4 a.m., and then my son would climb Mitchell Peak by himself. Even though it was my idea—one that I put a lot of thought into and felt strongly about—this part of the adventure always made me doubt myself. I worried, *Am I being reckless by encouraging my fourteen-year-old son to climb a mountain on his own?* But I knew deep down that my sons were capable and I trusted the version of myself who thought this was a great idea. I wanted them to be inspired to climb mountains in their lives as they got older, and my hope was that each son would return from the mountain climb with more confidence in himself and his abilities. I also hoped my relationship with each son would grow and the experience would have a lasting impact on our relationship.

I enjoyed my final mother-son expedition for our youngest son, Finis (Fin), in July 2021. All three adventures went beautifully and are among my most cherished memories. Each son climbed the mountain successfully, and on our final night at camp, we shared meaningful conversations and made promises to one another—promises we still revisit today.

As a mother, I'm particularly hard on myself. I worry whether I'm good enough and whether I provide all that my sons need. Having the idea for these expeditions with each of my sons was one of my best ideas ever and is something I'm proud of.

Over the years, I have personally experienced so much growth and fulfillment due to others' belief in me. I would not be who I am without the encouragement and support I received from others when I doubted my abilities.

I will forever be grateful to those who have believed in me and who continue to inspire and support me in my dreams. Being this person for the people in my life and work is one of the greatest honors and most fulfilling aspects of my existence.

Not the Feedback I'm Going For

A handful of times I've received feedback along the lines of, "I was going to quit," or, "I felt like quitting, but I didn't because I didn't want to disappoint you." Each time, I experienced a twinge of sadness, because this is not the feedback I'm going for. I don't ever want my clients to do something for purposes of not disappointing me.

But, in these cases, the person climbed a mountain they weren't certain they could climb. They put in for a promotion they were afraid they weren't qualified for and got it. They had a difficult conversation with someone they led and it went wonderfully, improving their relationship and impact. They made a hard change, and it transformed the whole trajectory of their life for the better. Or they made a personal dream come true for their family.

They did these things. I didn't. But the difference-maker was that someone believed in them and their abilities when they did not.

People Are the Beating Heart

People are the beating heart of our organizations. While systems and strategies provide structure, it is human connection—our shared values, collective effort, and emotional commitment—that brings meaning to our work, life, and cultures.

People are not just resources; they are the storytellers, problem-solvers, and relationship-builders who shape our culture and create a lasting impact. People drive innovation and growth. By valuing and empowering individuals, we can cultivate an environment in which people feel seen, heard, and inspired, enabling them to contribute their best work and amplify the mission at the core of their organization.

As humans, one of our most basic yearnings is to belong. Belonging is a fundamental human need to feel accepted, valued, and connected to others or to a place, group, or purpose. It is the experience of being a part of something larger than yourself while feeling seen, respected, and valued for who you are. Belonging provides us with a sense of emotional safety, connection, and purpose, and experiencing a sense of belonging is crucial for our emotional well-being, mental health, and overall life satisfaction.

As humans, we yearn to be accepted and valued for who we are. We spend so much of our time at work that, while there, we want to feel connected—we want our presence to be valued and our contributions to matter. According to Brené Brown in *Braving the Wilderness*, we often confuse fitting in with belonging, but they are not the same thing. According to Brown, fitting in is being someone else in order to be accepted. Belonging is being accepted for who we are.

Brown argues that true belonging begins with belonging to yourself. She defines this concept as being deeply connected to who you are at your core and standing authentically in your values, even when it feels uncomfortable or isolating to do so. Once a person has cultivated a relationship with themselves, there are steps they can take to overcome their loneliness and increase their sense of belonging.

Unfortunately, these steps will not be easy, considering the person who is suffering from loneliness and lack of belonging may feel more like retreating and hiding than putting themselves out there. These steps require intention and practice but are likely to pay off.

Nurture any existing relationships you have. Check in with a family member via text or ask a friend if they want to go for coffee.

Dare to be vulnerable. Share your feelings of loneliness with others and consider asking for help. You can go to someone in your life or find a therapist online.

Accept invitations to events. Is there a family gathering happening for the upcoming holiday or a friend's birthday party this weekend? Even though it's difficult when you feel lonely, make an effort to show up and stay awhile.

Consider joining a club or other meetup group. This is also a great way to find a new hobby.

Volunteer your time and services. Doing so will connect you with new people. Studies also show that when we do acts of service, we feel better about ourselves.

Finally, practice active listening—show genuine interest in others and what they have to say. This will help you connect in meaningful ways.

"A Meaning Crisis"

In recent years, you may have noticed an increase in workers quitting their jobs before they have another lined up or "quiet quitting"—staying despite feeling overwhelmed and disengaged. This is because the combination of economic instability and remote work, especially post-pandemic, has resulted in a sense of disconnection and disengagement for many employees.

In his 2023 book *The Song of Significance: A New Manifesto for Teams*, Seth Godin addresses what he perceives as a "meaning crisis" in the modern workplace. He argues that traditional work models often leave individuals feeling disconnected and undervalued, leading to a lack of purpose in their professional lives. Godin advocates for a shift toward creating environments where work is meaningful and individuals can find significance in their roles.

Godin and his team surveyed ten thousand people across ninety countries. They asked them to describe the conditions for the best job they've ever had. There were fourteen choices to choose from, and the top four vote-getters were:

1. I surprised myself with what I could accomplish;

2. I could work independently;

3. The team built something important; and

4. People treated me with respect.

In short, Godin encourages leaders to enroll, empower, and trust their people. A culture of belonging and meaning won't spontaneously appear on its own. This culture must be intentionally designed and continually fostered. You're not just a leader—you're a human. And, as a human, you need to work to accept and value others for who they are. Embrace their differences and offer them the support they need.

For Christmas a few years ago, I made a plaque for each of my sons that had musician Thelonius Monk's words, "A genius is the one most like himself," burned into it. The reason I love this statement so much is because it inspires us to dare to be our authentic selves. What would it be like if we could show up to our workplaces, communities, and families being unapologetically ourselves—bringing the gifts that are unique to us? How different would we feel if we were not only accepted but felt valued and embraced for being who we are?

Loneliness

Loneliness is the subjective emotional experience of feeling disconnected and isolated from the world. Although being physically alone is often a catalyst for loneliness, it's not a defining feature. Sometimes, the worst loneliness is not the feeling you get when you're sitting in an empty room, but when you are in a crowd of people and you feel invisible, like you don't belong. At its heart, loneliness is rooted in a lack of meaningful connection.

I work with and know many people who struggle or have struggled with loneliness. Maybe they've taken a new job and don't know anyone at their new organization, or maybe they've moved to a new city where they don't know a single soul. Maybe they feel misunderstood in their family or lonely in their marriage. Maybe they lack confidence and feel generally unworthy of love and attention.

The rate of people experiencing loneliness was increasing even before the COVID-19 pandemic. According to a May 2018 Cigna survey of ten thousand Americans, close to 50 percent reported frequently experiencing loneliness. The rate was significantly lower (20 percent) in the 1980s. I can't imagine what the rate of loneliness in the United States is now, during a time when people are spending most of their free time alone in their homes looking at their screens and when remote work has become so commonplace.

In addition to being a cause of emotional suffering and despair, experiencing loneliness also negatively impacts our physical health, leading to high blood pressure, heart disease, obesity, a weakened immune system, anxiety, depression, cognitive decline, and Alzheimer's disease. According to some studies, it has been estimated that loneliness can shorten a person's life by as many as fifteen years.

Most people will experience loneliness at some point of their life. For some people it can be so challenging that it may feel impossible to overcome. While I feel blessed to have so many wonderful people in my life, I have occasionally experienced loneliness.

Small Acts of Kindness Make a Difference

Mostly, we don't want to harm each other.
We want to be handed our cup of coffee hot,
and to say thank you to the person handing it.
To smile at them and for them to smile back.

—Danusha Laméris, "Small Kindnesses"

We can all do our part to be kind. Maybe it's looking up and meeting the eyes of the barista or smiling and greeting the person at checkout. Acknowledging someone's presence and doing something that demonstrates we see them can make their day better. Perhaps even their life.

It's not a stretch to say that treating someone with kindness and compassion can save a life. It costs us nothing to be mindful of the people we interact with, to acknowledge their presence, and to offer kindness. Next time you run an errand, leave your phone in your pocket and look up and around you. Acknowledge every person whose path you cross.

I don't know about you, but I want to be a person who is not too busy to be thoughtful and kind.

Strong Teams Make Mountains Smaller

When I'm at the foot of a mountain, I find that it appears to be less steep and intimidating if I'm with people I like, love, and respect. Turns out it's not just my imagination that this is the case. There is science (a study about "geographic slant") that supports this. Whether it's an actual mountain in the wilderness or a challenge you're looking ahead to in your life or work, tackling it with people you like and respect will make it seem more manageable and less formidable.

So, regardless of what form your current mountain takes, remember that strong teams, families, relationships, and friendships will make it seem less formidable.

Thirty-Two Years of Marriage: A Hard-Earned Celebration

In August 2024 as Jerry and I approached our thirty-two-year wedding anniversary, I reflected deeply on our relationship.

Choosing to spend my life with him was one of the most important and life-altering decisions I've made. Although our marriage is far from perfect, it's been an amazing journey. This is not an accident—we didn't leave it to chance. Over those three decades, we worked at it by making an effort to be thoughtful and intentional.

I met Jerry at a wedding in Omaha, Nebraska, in August 1992 when I was a bridesmaid and he was a groomsman. At the time, he was living in Dayton, Ohio, working as a physical therapy tech in the Air Force, and I was in Missoula, finishing journalism school at the University of Montana.

We met during the wedding rehearsal and proceeded to flirt and dance all night after the wedding. After the memorable night, we promised to keep in touch. It was a time before cell phones or email, so we wrote letters and had weekly long-distance phone calls. When we could, we traveled back and forth between Montana and Ohio to spend time together. In the process, we fell in love.

Our first Epic Adventure together occurred almost a year after meeting, and to this day, it remains a cherished memory. Little did we know at the time that the experience would provide such accurate foreshadowing for what would happen in our many years together that followed.

Our First Epic Adventure

It was August 1991. At the time, Jerry was a marathon runner, and I had a love for outdoor adventure.

We both had a penchant for doing hard things, so I came up with the idea to embark on a backpacking adventure. We would have just one night for our adventure, and I chose our destination—Sapphire Lake in the Bob Marshall Wilderness. The route I picked was labeled "strenuous."

The night before our adventure, Jerry's flight was delayed, and he didn't arrive until after midnight. We had some catching up to do and didn't get to bed until 2:30 a.m. So, when the alarm buzzed, we opted to hit the snooze button. But we had an Epic backpacking adventure planned and the clock was ticking, so eventually we dragged ourselves out of bed.

We were backpacking rookies, and as such, we were appropriately penalized. Theoretically, since we were only going for one night, it should have been easy to keep our loads light. But our gear was cheap, which meant it was heavy and bulky. We filled our backpacks with bottles of wine and other luxuries, along with things we needed.

Our packs were heavy, unwieldy, and towered over us when we put them on. (They were so heavy that our boots sank into the ground whenever we stood still.) We paid for our late start by sharing the first five miles to the popular destination, Upper Holland Lake, with dozens of other hikers. The temperature was in the 90s, and we huffed in the blazing heat while steadily gaining 2,100 feet in elevation. Despite our discomfort, our stoke was high and the views were breathtaking.

About an hour into the hike, my feet started protesting. I could tell they had swelled from the heat, effort, and altitude. My hiking boots were brand new and turned out to be too small. Soon, my every step became agonizing. I couldn't wait to soak my aching feet in Sapphire Lake—that is, if we ever made it there!

At Upper Holland Lake, we took a brief rest to gulp water and gnaw on some jerky. The route's "strenuous" rating turned out to be accurate. We still had another mile to go that would gain another thousand feet of elevation on steep switchbacks. The afternoon sun was high in the sky and, as the day grew hotter, the mosquitoes became unbearable.

By the time we reached Sapphire Lake, the crowds had thinned, and we had the lake and all the beautiful scenery to ourselves. Newly in love and having not seen each other for four months, we decided our sore feet could wait and found a soft spot in the dirt to roll around in.

After our romantic interlude, we unintentionally fell asleep for two hours, waking up to discover we each had severe sunburns on half of our bodies. Oops. The effort it had taken to get to Sapphire Lake had left us in rough shape. Every muscle in our bodies ached, my blistered feet were barely functional, and Jerry had a headache from the altitude. Now, we could add severe sunburns to the mix.

Since we had only one night, we quickly got to work. Jerry pitched the tent while I crawled around camp on all fours because my feet hurt too much to stand.

I managed to start a fire. Our final stretch had taken us through a marsh, and we had been too tired to remove our boots, so they were soaking wet. We hoped the fire would dry them and also keep the mosquitoes away. For dinner, Jerry cooked fettuccine alfredo with pepperoni, fresh black pepper, and parmesan cheese. We devoured it, licking our plates clean to save the effort of washing dishes.

Exhausted and stuffed, we forced ourselves to get up and finally head to the lake with a bottle of wine. We found a perfect granite slab slanting into the water, sat down, and submerged our sore feet in the icy water. Jerry opened the wine, and we passed the bottle back and forth.

As the sun set, the lake and surrounding wilderness were painted in stunning pinks, oranges, and reds. Later, lying on our backs on the slab, we watched the stars emerge and fill the sky. We named constellations and reveled in the silence, broken only by the occasional *blerp* of fish nipping at the lake's surface. Then, something extraordinary happened: The sky exploded with purple, pink, and neon-green waves. Aurora borealis. The northern lights. We gasped as we watched the most vibrant waves of color pulse and ripple across the sky. We had not expected this, and it felt like a miracle.

Eventually, we could keep our eyes open no longer. Jerry headed back to our camp to add some more logs to the fire—he wanted to ensure our boots would be dry by morning. He returned to lay back down beside me, and we fell fast asleep under the color-filled sky.

The next morning, Jerry woke me with a kiss. Under a now bright-blue sky, the lake was tranquil, its surface dotted with ripples from feeding fish.

After lingering to take in the breathtaking view, we limped back to camp to make coffee and oatmeal. I noticed there was a circle of charcoal and ashes where the fire had once burned.

I started gathering our boots and discovered there were only three—two of Jerry's and one of mine.

Where was my second boot?

My first thought was that a wild animal had stolen it during the night, so I scanned the surrounding area, searching behind trees and beneath bushes frantically. Upon closer inspection though, I spied the charred remains of my right boot in the campfire. I unleashed a torrent of f-bombs. With no backup footwear, I would have to hike the return seven steep and rugged miles in one boot.

The hike was pure agony. My swollen feet throbbed, and my bootless foot, protected only by a thick sock, constantly picked up thorns and stickers. Jerry, ever the supportive partner, lightened my load by taking extra gear and insisted we rest often.

By the time we reached the car, we were utterly exhausted. The return hike had been a suffer fest, but despite the hardships, we couldn't stop talking about the adventure's highlights. The stunning views, the romantic moments, the unexpected northern lights, and even the mishaps made it unforgettable. As we made the drive back to Missoula and I nursed my aching feet, I thought, *If these are the sorts of things that are possible when I'm with Jerry, then I want more.*

Four months later, when Jerry was traveling to Missoula to spend Christmas with me, he rallied the flight crew and passengers on his plane as it prepared to land to help him surprise me and ask me to marry him. I said, "Yes!" and it remains one of the best decisions of my life.

Thirty-Two Years Later

Our marriage has been nothing short of a great adventure. Together, we have raised three wonderful sons, and they are our greatest blessings. Each of them was conceived in the wilderness, and we've raised them largely in the outdoors—which I can tell you doesn't happen without a lot of intention, patience, and resolve.

Like most adventures, our marriage has been full of discovery, learning, inspiration, awe, and fulfillment. But it has also included hardship, uncertain terrain, detours, poor communication, and stretches of monotony. There is no single secret to our long marriage, but if we had to sum it up, we might say: "Hikes, happy hours, hot tubs, and hammocks."

We have always enjoyed hiking with each other, setting out at sunrise and ending at sunset. We commemorate our wedding anniversary each year by going on an epic hike as long in miles as our marriage is in years. We also have a tradition of going out for what we call "golden-hour happy hours."

During the pandemic, we did this three times a week, but now that life is back to normal, we enjoy these weekly. We also love sitting in the hot tub and hanging in the hammock in our backyard while listening to our favorite music, or at a favorite campsite up in Sinks Canyon during summer.

These may seem like little things, but when you make a habit and a long-term tradition out of them, they end up equating to something significant: connection.

When our sons were young, Jerry and I came up with a strategy for how to keep the intimacy fire stoked in our relationship. Our strategy worked so brilliantly that I often share it with people I know and work with, especially people who are parents and at the start of their parenting journey. Without intention and a strategy or plan, keeping the intimacy fire stoked will be challenging at best. At least for us, simply having "date nights" wasn't sufficient.

My Best Half

Whenever I make a post on social media for Jerry's birthday or for our anniversary, I often refer to him as my "best half." And I mean it with all my heart. Sometimes, in response to my calling Jerry my best half, my closest girlfriends give me a hard time.

They adore Jerry and think he's wonderful, but they don't want me to sell myself short. I appreciate their sentiment, but I stand by my comment. The truth is, I'm a tall order, and it takes someone very special to want to—and be able to—be married to me, let alone *stay* married to me. Jerry's a trooper.

For my forty-second birthday, I decided I wanted to climb Wind River Peak in a day. This was no easy feat. It would be a thirty-four-mile roundtrip hike with a five-thousand-foot elevation gain that included climbing a mountain at the halfway point, and to do it in a single day and somehow make it back to town in time for our middle son's championship baseball game scheduled for 7 p.m. As a result, we would have to start at a ridiculously early time. Jerry and I had climbed the mountain years earlier as part of a backpacking trip—he knew how challenging this would be. But I leveraged my birthday to request it of him, and he obliged.

When we were halfway up the mountain, post-holing at altitude through thigh-deep snow, Jerry let out a loud sigh and exclaimed, "Why couldn't you just want expensive jewelry?"

Like I said, he's a trooper. (I don't deserve him!)

Marriage, like any adventure, is unpredictable and requires perseverance. Choose your partner wisely and, once you find the right one, be thoughtful and intentional with how you nurture your relationship.

Friendship: A Balm for Life's Journey

"A friend is one who overlooks your broken fence and admires the flowers in your garden."

—Unknown

I think a lot about friendship these days, how blessed I am to have the friends I do. Friendship is one of the most profound and universal human experiences. It transcends age, culture, and geography, providing a connection that nourishes the mind, body, and soul. More than just a social bond, true friendship serves as a cornerstone of emotional resilience, physical well-being, and personal growth.

In a world that often prioritizes productivity and individual achievement, the role of friendship is a reminder of our shared humanity and the importance of connection. At its core, friendship offers a safe haven for emotional support.

Life is unpredictable, often presenting challenges that feel too heavy to bear alone. In those moments, a friend provides comfort, understanding, and reassurance. Research has shown that individuals with strong social ties recover more quickly from stress and trauma. A simple conversation with a trusted friend can diffuse anxiety and bring clarity to difficult situations, creating space for healing and growth.

David Whyte, in his essay "Friendship" in his book *Consolations*, writes:

> *Friendship is a mirror to presence and a testament to forgiveness. Friendship not only helps us see ourselves through another's eyes but can be sustained over the years only with someone who has repeatedly forgiven us for our trespasses as we must find it in ourselves to forgive them in turn. A friend knows our difficulties and shadows and remains in sight, a companion to our vulnerabilities more than our triumphs, when we are under the strange illusion, we do not need them. An undercurrent of real friendship is a blessing exactly because its elemental form is rediscovered again and again through understanding and mercy.*

As we navigate the complexities of modern life, we need our friends more than ever.

I've had the honor of facilitating several custom Epic programs for groups of friends. Last year, I guided two doctors and longtime friends through Zion to celebrate their 50th birthdays—and their friendship. A few years ago, I facilitated a program for a group of women that included one who had recently lost her only son. Her sister-in-law organized the experience to offer healing support through the wilderness, love, and presence of close friends. I've also led an Epic for two couples who are all best friends, and witnessing their connection deepen in new ways while experiencing an adventure together felt like such a privilege.

Most recently, I returned from leading an Epic program with 13 breathtaking forces of nature—women ages 42 to 69: Susan, Mia, Mona, Stephanie, Jill, Alexia, Jennifer, Ilana, Jocelyn, Rachel, Joanne, Coretha, and Doreen. I'll be forever grateful for how they showed up—daring big, leaning in, laughing hard, and sharing deep conversations and unforgettable joy. What emerged was a powerful circle of connection and deepening friendship. As if that weren't enough, they invited me into their sacred circle. As a result, I got more out of the program than I gave. Friendship isn't just a comfort. It's a necessary balm. A vital, grounding force.

A Tribute to My Dear Friend "SoX"

I've been devastated about the passing of one of my very best and closest friends, Kathy (Browning) Kramer. She died on July 4, 2024, while mountain biking in southern Colorado.

Our friendship first blossomed when Kathy made me and my family a pan of lasagna and some brownies after my youngest son was born. That was eighteen years ago. I loved and adored Kathy, whom I fondly called "SoX." (SoX was the trail name that friends and I gave Kathy during a 2013 backpacking trip in the Wind Rivers because every day, she would surprise us with a different, decorative pair of knee-high socks that she wore proudly with her shorts and hiking boots.)

Among other things, Kathy and I shared a love of nature and the outdoors. For several years during late spring and early summer, it was common for us to wake early and drive to the mountains to catch the sunrise and view wildflowers; their colors popped during first light.

We enjoyed countless adventures in the wilderness, "happy hour" walkabouts, coaster bike rides, and meetups, taking road trips, dancing our guts out to reggae performances, and sharing so many thoughtful conversations. Kathy and I were always either goofing around and laughing our asses off or having deep and meaningful conversations.

Even before her hearing loss was significant, Kathy and I could sit together—enjoying each other's company in the grass at City Park while admiring the long shadows of the giant cottonwoods as the sun set, hiking or skiing down a trail, or in her truck—and there would be periods of comfortable silence. I really appreciated that we didn't need words to find our time together meaningful. Last June, a couple weeks before she died, Kathy and I enjoyed a 2.5-hour "happy hour" Facetime call that was so rich. I loved seeing her face and spending time with her.

Our time together filled my cup, and my stomach muscles were sore from all the laughing. In the years before she passed, Kathy had endured some unimaginable challenges, and on our call, she said she was finally in a wonderful place. She said she felt at peace. SoX was light, happy, and inspired about her life.

I miss her so much! Without her, I feel short of air—breathless—as if a vital part of me has gone missing. And yet I know she is not gone. I feel her presence everywhere. Whenever she was in nature, Kathy wore a constant, soft smile. I can picture her on July 4, riding her bike, smiling, and feeling blessed to be doing something she loved so much, surrounded by natural beauty. And how beautiful, and fitting, that my dear SoX's final rest was in a field of wildflowers.

Rest in peace, dear SoX. I love you forever!

Making Friends

It can be challenging to cultivate new friendships or rekindle past ones, especially as we reach midlife. Many women struggle to nurture their friendships when raising a family or working full time, and often the friendships that were once so meaningful to us unintentionally fade.

Then, once we're empty nesters or at a place in our lives when our schedules aren't as demanding, we yearn for friendship. It can be hard to know where or how to find it.

Women aren't the only ones who struggle with friendship in midlife, however. Recent studies indicate that middle-aged men in the United States are experiencing heightened levels of loneliness. Research published by the American Psychological Association reveals that US adults in midlife report significantly higher rates of loneliness compared to their European counterparts, a trend attributed to factors like weaker family ties and greater income inequality. This growing prevalence of loneliness among middle-aged men underscores the need for targeted interventions to foster social connections and support mental health within this demographic.

Regardless of your gender or age, if you feel a gap in your life that a friendship might be able to fill, consider the following strategies for developing new friendships:

Reconnect with old friends. Reach out to former friends to rekindle your connections. You might find that they thought of you recently or that you have something new in common.

Join groups. Participate in clubs or activities that match your interests, or branch out and explore new interests.

Volunteer. Doing community service is a great way to meet other like-minded people.

Use social media or apps. Use platforms like Meetup to find local events and groups or give Bumble BFF a go.

Attend local events. Engage in community gatherings, workshops, or seminars that interest you, and challenge yourself to strike up a conversation.

Take classes. Join courses to develop your hobbies or skills as a way to connect with others.

Be open. Smile, initiate conversations, and above all, show genuine interest in others.

And finally, be persistent. Building friendships takes time. Keep trying! One day, you'll be surrounded by supportive people, grateful you refused to give up your search.

Talk to Strangers

In October 2016, I boarded a flight to Detroit. As usual, I greeted the passenger beside me, but then quickly put in my earbuds—a signal that I wasn't available for conversation.

This is a habit I've developed when traveling alone, prioritizing solitude over connection. But, as we landed and I took out my earbuds to hear the announcements, I ended up striking up a conversation with the woman seated next to me.

She was warm and kind, and as our conversation unfolded, she shared that she was visiting her nephew who had been paralyzed after a drunk driver ran into him decades earlier. Now, at forty-nine years old, her nephew had pneumonia, and his organs were beginning to shut down. As tears filled her eyes, she said she feared he was likely approaching his end, and she was visiting him to say goodbye.

As I listened and blinked back tears of my own, I touched her arm gently. "I'll keep you, your nephew, and your family in my thoughts and in my heart," I told her.

That brief interaction stayed with me, her story replaying in my mind during the days that followed. Strangers like her remind me of Martin Buber's idea of the "I & Thou" moment, where two people connect deeply, transcending small talk and creating something that feels sacred, even if only fleetingly.

Later that day, I requested an Uber to take me to the General Motors Renaissance Center so I could tour some of Detroit on foot and check out the Detroit Riverwalk. I struck up a conversation, and learned his name was Phil. He shared that he'd retired from General Motors five years earlier so he could care for his wife, Susan, during her second round of cancer.

"She died one and a half years ago," he said, his voice full of emotion. "She was a wonderful woman. I know all husbands say that about their wives but, truly, she was an angel. I miss her so much."

He added that his two grown daughters, who live in Florida, talked him into driving for Uber. "It gets me out of my quiet and empty house and off my couch, and it's an effort to meet and talk to people."

His willingness to share his story reminded me of the beauty in weak connections—the brief but meaningful encounters we share with people we may never meet again.

Once at the Renaissance Center, in an effort to find my way to the Riverwalk, I introduced myself to a stranger in hopes he could point me in the right direction. He introduced himself as Casey, and he was kind enough to guide me to the scenic path and share insider tips about exploring the city. When I later found myself in an unfamiliar, deserted area, feeling vulnerable and a little unsafe, I texted him for advice. He quickly responded, giving me instructions for where to go to be able to find an Uber. (Casey was a "trail angel"—one of those people who appear just when you need them most.)

My final connection of the day was my Uber driver back to the hotel, Richard. In our conversation, he told me he transported vehicles for Chrysler for twelve years. "But I gave it all up so I could pursue my passion for music and be more available to my wife and kids," he said.

When we eventually arrived in front of my hotel in Birmingham, Richard shared one last detail: He was a triplet. Not only that, but their names were, "Tom, Dick, and Harry."

"No way!"

"Yes way, ma'am," he said, "We are Tom, Dick, and Harry!"

As he opened my door for me, he remarked, "Young lady, thank you for being my first-ever Wyoming customer."

His joy was infectious.

As I prepared for bed and reflected on my day, I realized the highlights of my trip weren't the sights I had seen but the strangers I had met. Every connection felt like a gift, adding depth and meaning to my experience.

This and many experiences like it have taught me that each encounter, no matter how fleeting, is a chance to connect, to see and be seen. When they happen, they make life feel a little fuller, a little brighter, and a little more significant. Since that trip, I've made a conscious effort to be more open and willing to engage with people while traveling and in other public settings. I challenge you to give it a try.

Don't Underestimate "Weak Ties"

Sitting in the window seat of a plane headed to San Francisco for a work trip, I ditched my headphones and introduced myself to the middle-aged woman next to me.

Her husband was snoring next to her, and we struck up a lively conversation that resulted in us ordering glasses of wine and sharing about certain aspects of our life, with many giggles. The stories she shared were delightful, and our encounter was so touching and meaningful. I was almost disappointed when our plane began to prepare for landing.

The woman and her husband had a tight connection, so they had to hurry and rush ahead of the other passengers to try to reach their gate on time. We hugged goodbye, and I watched as my new friend and her husband raced off. We had exchanged only our first names, so there would be no future interactions, but it didn't matter. Our brief encounter had been lovely.

Research shows that brief interactions with acquaintances, or what scientists refer to as "weak ties," contribute significantly to our mental and physical well-being. Studies by sociologists highlight the value of weak ties in expanding our social networks and exposing us to new ideas and opportunities. Research suggests that small, positive exchanges with baristas, clerks, and other acquaintances boost happiness, reduce loneliness, and foster a sense of community.

These simple interactions, while seemingly insignificant, can uplift us emotionally and provide a sense of belonging. By engaging in casual conversations and acknowledging others in our daily lives, we not only improve our own well-being but also contribute to a more connected and compassionate society.

My favorite story from *The Moth* is called *A Phone Call* by Auburn Sandstrom, a story of a young woman who makes a call for help. It's free on *The Moth* website. Check it out. It's well worth your ten minutes. The story is hopeful.

People Are the Most Important Thing

I am so inspired by what people have to say when they're approaching the end of their lives. I am profoundly moved by their wisdom. As anyone in my life will tell you, I've devoured all the TED Talks, books, and insights from friends that delve into the thoughts and reflections of individuals with terminal diagnoses or those simply approaching their final days.

For the last fifteen years, I have thought about my mortality every single day. I have tried, in earnest, to live my life intentionally, treating each day as if it could be my last. And I've gotten pretty good at it. But I can't do it as well as someone who has been given a terminal diagnosis or who is ninety years old.

When you ask people who are approaching the end of their life, "Tell me—tell us 'mortals,' what is the most important thing?" All of them say, "The people in your life." I have a feeling that you already know this; we all know this. But if you're like me—human, imperfect, and fallible—you often take for granted the people you love the most.

When I was working with a coach ten years ago, we were on a phone call and she asked me, "Who are your most important people?" I remember thinking that it was a softball of a question because, of course, I knew who my most important people were. But I was invested in the work, so later that night, I gave it some careful thought.

Who are my most important people? I reflected and proceeded to make a list in my journal. My beautiful mother was near the top. My mom has struggled with multiple sclerosis for forty-two years. She's a breast cancer survivor and, in recent years, she has been in the early stages of dementia. Most recently, she's been diagnosed with Parkinson's. I don't know what I'll do when I lose her. She's precious to me. Of course, death is a part of life, and no one is unaffected. I'm sorry for those of you who have lost people you loved.

As I considered my most important people, I resolved that I wanted to spend more time with my mom. We live in the same town, and, over the years, we've shared most holidays together. We have weekly traditions and have traveled together extensively, but my family is usually in tow. I realized I wanted more personal time with just my mom. So, I proposed that we have a tea date every Wednesday afternoon. That was about twelve years ago, and while we haven't had perfect attendance—my parents travel a lot, and so do I—my mother and I have enjoyed hundreds of tea dates. And now, especially given my mom's health and declining memory, I cherish those meetups more than words can say. Having tea with my beautiful mother on Wednesday afternoons is one of the best ideas I've ever had.

Is there someone in your life you would like to spend more time with? If so, how can you make that happen? And what are you waiting for?

Because people are the most important thing.

Lesson 7
Tend to the Pebble in Your Shoe

Tend to the Pebble

"It isn't the mountains ahead that will wear you out; it is the grain of sand in your shoe."

—Unknown

As my clients and I stand at the trailhead with our backpacks on, finally ready to embark on our Epic Adventure, I offer the first—and most important—instruction: "If you get a pebble in your shoe—or if something just doesn't feel right—please speak up so we can tend to it."

Most of us will not speak up or tend to it. We don't want to call attention to ourselves or hold others up. We tell ourselves it's no big deal, it's just a small thing, we'll just focus on something else. We think it will resolve itself and everything will be fine.

When we do this, we do so at our peril, because the pebble in our shoe seldom goes away and rarely, if ever, resolves itself. What usually happens is the pebble turns into a hotspot, then the hotspot turns into a blister, and now every single step we take feels like we're walking on broken glass. The pain we experience prevents us from being able to fully appreciate the journey. It limits our ability to enjoy, engage, and contribute to the expedition. To be an effective and impactful leader of others, we must first be a good self-leader. If we can't take care of ourselves, how can we effectively lead others?

On a wilderness expedition, if it starts raining and a member of our group refuses to put on his rain jacket, he puts himself and our entire expedition at risk. Firstly, his refusal to properly take care of himself negatively impacts him. His clothes, which are in limited supply, will get drenched, and he risks getting hyperthermia. But if he gets hyperthermia, it's not just bad for him—it's bad for our group.

His health becomes a concern, and he can no longer meaningfully contribute to the expedition. We may even have to arrange for his evacuation, which is no small thing, given we're in a remote wilderness and a long way from help. If only he would have tended to the "pebble" earlier and put on his rain jacket when it started raining.

We all have a pebble in our shoe from time to time, possibly more than one. Your pebble could be anything that's making your life or leadership more difficult. Maybe it's a health issue or diagnosis. It could be a relationship you're in that's not serving you, a secret you're keeping, or a difficult conversation you need to have with someone you love that you're putting off. It could be an addiction or a concern about another harmful behavior. It could be anything you're doing or not doing that's negatively impacting your journey and your life.

One of the reasons we avoid tending to the pebble is that we think of it as a personal problem. But I've learned the pebble in our shoe is never just *our* problem. The pain and discomfort caused by our pebble negatively affects the way we show up, the depth and quality of our relationships, our ability to effectively lead others, and our impact on the people around us.

Responding is a huge part of living and leading. While we cannot control our circumstances, thankfully, we *can* control how we respond to them. Tending to the pebble in our shoe—taking care of ourselves—is within our control. It's something we all can do. That's not to say it's easy.

Tending to our pebble may cause or require a disruption in our life. The first step to tending to the pebble is being honest with ourselves. We must acknowledge the pebble and the harm it is doing. Even taking that simple step can make us feel like help is on the way—like we've started the process of tending to the issue. This is no small thing, and trust me, you will feel better about yourself when you do. I have had many pebbles in my shoe over the years. Some have caused me tremendous physical pain and suffering, and others resulted in the decline of my physical and mental health.

One particular pebble, left unchecked for two years, caused me deep personal shame, which limited my participation in some key relationships. Tending to it involved some of the most challenging inner work I've ever done, but confronting the pebble and doing the necessary work led to a deepening of those relationships. When we tend to the pebble in our shoe—when we do the work to take care of ourselves—everything improves. Often, we will even be transformed by the experience.

I encourage you: Tend to the pebble. Because in my experience, it's not the tall mountains ahead or our big audacious goals that will do us in, but the pebble in our shoe.

Self-Care Is Not Selfish

In a world that glorifies productivity, self-care is often dismissed as indulgent. But taking care of yourself isn't selfish.

There's a good reason that when you're on an airplane, the safety instruction is: "In case of emergency, place your own oxygen mask on first before helping others." You can't take care of others if you don't take care of yourself first.

The Pebble in Your Shoe Could Be Shortening Your Life

According to research, 35 to 50 percent of premature deaths are linked to personal behaviors within our control—things like physical health, mental well-being, diet, sleep, and stress management. These are the most common pebbles in our shoes, the small discomforts we ignore until they become too big and problematic to ignore. I hope this section inspires and motivates you to tend to the pebbles in your shoe.

Finding My Way Back to Health

"I'm not training for any event other than my life."

—my dear friend Debra, in an interview I did with her
that inspired me during my health transformation journey

When my husband and I sold our first company in fall 2008, I had space and time to reflect and take stock of my life for the first time in years. What I realized was sobering. There were all kinds of pebbles in my shoe: I was thirty-five pounds overweight, tethered to my gadgets, drinking wine on too many weeknights, and sinking into depression.

Each night, after Jerry and the boys had fallen asleep, I waged a battle of self-loathing. I berated myself for another day gone by without making a change. Night after night, the weight of my own disappointment crushed me. It was relentless. Then, one morning in May 2009, something shifted. I woke up and knew I couldn't endure another night of self-directed punishment. The stakes felt high, and I was desperate, which led me to do something I seldom do: Ask for help.

I started with Jerry. Through tears, I told him how low I had sunk and how desperate I felt. I shared with him my commitment to turning things around and asked for his support. His response was immediate, loving, and unwavering. For the first time in a long time, I didn't feel alone in my fight.

Next, I went to my doctor and admitted the extent to which I was struggling. I was prescribed a short course of antidepressants—a step that felt both humbling and hopeful and helped create just enough space for the next right steps.

Then, I reached out to Steve, a friend who is an exercise physiologist, respected fitness expert, and gym owner. I asked him to train me, believing that if I could rebuild my physical health, my mental and emotional health would follow.

It helped that I had some self-awareness. I knew, for example, that I wasn't good at moderation. I've never been able to eat a single serving of cookies, potato chips, or ice cream. In the early 1990s, I had an unhealthy soda habit. One day, after my drive home to Wyoming for a visit from college in Montana, I was cleaning out the car and was astonished when I saw how many empty pop cans had accumulated during the ten-hour drive. (I couldn't carry all of them into the house in one trip.) The next day, I decided I would quit soda pop cold turkey, and I haven't had a soda since. I would need to have a similar all-or-nothing approach for this.

I also knew I needed accountability. As a writer and long-time blogger, I decided to share publicly about my health journey. I committed to sharing regular updates on my social media platforms and on my blog. I shared not only my weekly progress but intimate details, including my weight, body fat percentage, measurements, and fitness milestones when I met them. By putting myself out there, I knew I'd be more likely to stay the course.

While weight loss was my initial goal, fitness would be my first priority. I wanted to be capable and strong enough to enjoy adventures with my family and friends and fit enough to consider any epic adventure that came my way.

Steve introduced me to high-intensity interval training (HIIT). Initially, I resisted, convinced that long cardio sessions would be the key to improving my fitness. But he explained that HIIT would boost my cardiovascular fitness, burn fat efficiently, and improve my metabolic health, all in a short amount of time. He also said it would improve my endurance and strength.

Steve also wanted to incorporate strength training. He said building muscle could help me lose weight and increase my endurance. This was crucial, because I had my sights set on tackling long hikes in my backyard, Wyoming's Wind River Range. So, once a week, my training session with Steve focused on resistance training and lifting heavy things. I can still hear Steve saying, "The stronger your foundation, the more endurance you'll be able to build on top of it."

At first, I worried about getting too big—I didn't want to be too "bulky." But I trusted Steve, and I started getting stronger even as I was getting smaller. Once I was reaping the benefits of my physical training, I shifted my focus to weight loss. I knew I needed to apply the same rigor I had applied to my fitness to my nutrition. Research and conversations with friends who had successfully lost weight suggested that 80 percent of weight loss comes down to diet and nutrition.

At the time, my daily meals were carb-heavy—peanut butter and jelly toast, cereal, sandwiches, pasta, chips, and pizza. I made the personal decision to eliminate all complex carbs for one year. This was before the paleo diet had a name, but essentially, I created my own version—let's call it "Shelleo."

I had to be strict. According to some research, we spend an average of four hours a day resisting temptations. Every time we must resist giving in to a temptation costs us self-control and willpower, a resource that is in finite supply. In an effort to experience significant results, I decided to break up with carbs.

I cleaned out our cupboards as a result: all cereals, crackers, breads, and pastas—gone. (I even recorded and shared a video of me removing these carbs from my cupboards, with The Greg Kihn Band's "The Breakup Song" for a soundtrack.) I was setting myself up for success. It helped me to remind myself—often several times a day—that this wasn't forever. Just one year.

The impact was immediate and profound. Within weeks, I experienced a surge in energy levels. My blood sugar stabilized, eliminating the constant crashes that had left me feeling sluggish and irritable. Without the insulin spikes from processed carbs, my body started burning fat for fuel instead of relying on glucose. I went off antidepressants.

My mental fog lifted, my sleep improved, and I felt a level of clarity and vitality I hadn't experienced in years. Not only was I losing fat, but I was also regaining control of my body and mind. In eighteen months, I lost thirty-one pounds and 16 percent body fat, but more importantly, I got my energy and vitality back. I was re-inspired about what was possible. During that transformation, I managed to: set the women's pull-up record at the gym at the time (twenty pull-ups in a row), bench-press my body weight (135 pounds) five times, deadlift my body weight twenty-nine times (I stopped when my grip finally failed), do fifteen front squats at my body weight, and do thirty-one dips.

It turned out that when I tended to my health, everything in my life improved. The biggest benefit of my newfound health and fitness was that I felt like a more active participant in all areas of my life.

Go Out into the Woods

"Go out in the woods, go out. If you don't go out in the woods, nothing will ever happen, and your life will never begin."

—Clarissa Pinkola Estés, *Women Who Run with the Wolves*

By early 2010, I had found my way back to health, yet I still struggled with some depression and anxiety.

With summer approaching and my newfound high level of fitness, I hoped hiking would help alleviate some of the depression I was experiencing and inspire me about what might come next professionally. I committed to solo hiking on Fridays and found opportunities throughout the week to hike with family or friends. At first, I went on three-mile hikes, then four, five, and six. Soon, I was up to twelve miles, and I could feel myself getting stronger and more capable with every step.

I challenged myself to see how far I could hike in a single day, and by spring 2010, I had hiked several sixteen-mile routes and even a particularly rugged twenty-four-mile trek. In May of that year, I completed the forty-five-mile Rim-to-Rim-to-Rim of the Grand Canyon in a day and several twenty- to thirty-mile routes in my backyard. In 2011, I hiked a fifty-mile traverse of Zion National Park in a day, climbed some mountains in Wyoming, and embarked on a NOLS course.

Once I started hiking, I never stopped. In the last fifteen years, I've walked approximately 35,000 miles. I've logged many of these miles while hiking with my family in Wyoming's Wind Rivers and in other natural destinations in the West, including Yellowstone, Grand Teton, Arches, Canyonlands, Zion, Bryce Canyon, and Grand Canyon national parks, and in Vancouver, B.C., Washington, Oregon, California, and Hawaii.

A significant amount of miles were hiked/walked during our family's epic adventures in Switzerland, Italy, Iceland, and Spain, and while leading clients on guided Epic Adventures. I've logged many miles while walking during my coaching calls, a practice I've continued since becoming a coach fourteen years ago. Hiking and walking haven't just improved my fitness—they've reshaped my mind, opened my heart, and helped me navigate some of life's hardest transitions.

It was also during my long hikes in the wilderness that I had the inspiration to start Epic Life Inc. in 2011 and to offer guided Epic Adventures to coaching and leadership clients who were looking for something particularly inspiring and transformative. If you ever find yourself in a mental and physical health rut, or if you're simply feeling lost, overwhelmed, or stuck, I have one piece of advice for you: Go out into the woods. Your life will start back up, and you might just find your way back to yourself.

Spend Time in Nature

Time in nature, no matter the duration, provides healing. Research from the University of Exeter found that people who spend at least 120 minutes per week in natural environments report significantly better health and well-being than those who don't. Other studies show that being in green spaces lowers cortisol levels and reduces stress, lowers our blood pressure and heart rate, and supports cardiovascular health.

Spending time in nature enhances immune function by increasing exposure to beneficial microbes found in natural settings, improves our cognitive function and memory, sharpens our focus, and inspires creativity. A little time spent outside has been shown to reduce symptoms of anxiety and depression and to improve our emotional resilience.

Despite all this growing evidence of the physical, emotional, and psychological benefits of spending time in nature, most American adults are barely stepping outside.

Recent surveys show that most Americans spend less than an hour a day outdoors, with over a third logging thirty minutes or less, and nearly one in five spending under fifteen minutes in nature each day. That's barely enough time to drink a cup of coffee, let alone reset your nervous system or feel the sun on your face. When you add it up, many Americans are spending fewer than four to seven hours a week outdoors—less time than we spend scrolling social media in a single day.

This is a tragedy! In a country filled with vast public lands, local parks, and beautiful open spaces, this disconnection from the natural world isn't just a missed opportunity—it's a crisis. I would even call it a state of emergency.

You don't need a wilderness or a national park to reconnect with the outdoors—nature is closer than you think. Even in the busiest urban environments and with jam-packed schedules, small shifts can bring big benefits.

Step outside for your morning coffee. Eat lunch on a park bench instead of at your desk. Walk or bike instead of drive when you can. Open a window and let fresh air hit your face. Sit on your front steps at sunset.

Even just ten to fifteen minutes a day outside—in a courtyard, on a balcony, under a tree—can help clear your mind, lower stress, and make you feel more grounded. The most urgent advice I can offer in this field guide is: Go outside, even for ten minutes. You will be better for it!

Bonus recommendation: Watch the movie *Perfect Days* directed by Wim Wenders. (If you find the movie to be slow, it's because it is.) I found the movie to be so very inspiring. In addition to being an invitation to simplify one's life and to find the wonder in the ordinary, it's a beautiful reminder that no matter how routine our lives are, there is so much beauty to see and experience if we'd only step outside and open our eyes.

Our Sitting Is Killing Us

We get old when we stop moving. It's that simple.

If you don't believe this, think about the last time you sat in a car for three hours. When you got out, did your hip flexors feel stiff? Did your low back feel sore? Maybe your knees felt swollen or tight? That's just a small example of what happens when we become sedentary.

Over time, inactivity doesn't just make us feel stiff. It deteriorates our health and shortens our lifespan. Unfortunately, we are sitting more than ever before. While part of this is due to lifestyle and habit, it's also a byproduct of modern society—one that prioritizes convenience, screen time, and desk work over natural movement. It's killing us, in some cases literally. Research has linked prolonged sitting to an increased risk of obesity, heart disease, diabetes, cognitive decline, poor posture that can lead to skeletal issues, weakness, loss of muscle, and early death. One study published in *The Lancet* found that sitting for more than eight hours per day increases the risk of early death by up to sixty percent.

The rise of streaming services, social media, and gaming has led to a massive shift in how we spend our leisure time. The average American spends more than seven hours per day looking at screens—phones, computers, TVs—which usually involves sitting. The way we work today, especially given the rise in remote work, also plays a factor. Many jobs require sitting for more than eight hours a day.

Screen time has kept us indoors. It has replaced outdoor activity, limiting our natural movement and reducing our exposure to the mental and physical health benefits of being outside and in nature. Our transportation habits aren't helping. Cities and suburban sprawl encourage driving rather than walking or biking for errands. And, for the many people who work at an office, they spend one to three hours per day sitting during their commutes to and from work.

The good news is that small changes can make a huge difference. We can combat the effects of a sedentary lifestyle by taking active breaks, using a standing desk, and getting outside daily. Many leaders I know and work with have walking meetings with their colleagues and teams.

Personally, for more than a decade (and weather permitting), I've turned my coaching calls into "walk and talks." I do this because I'm a better listener and more creative—essentially, I'm a better coach—when I'm sauntering than when I'm sitting indoors looking at a computer screen.

The bottom line is that sitting is a silent killer, and the antidote is simple: Move more. Start small. Take that first step. Your life will improve immediately.

Move More, Live More

I've just turned fifty-seven years old, and I can proudly say I've lived an active life. Apart from those couple of years when I struggled with depression and found myself in a health rut, movement has been a constant in my life. Back in the early years of operating Epic Life, many of my coaching and Epic Adventure clients were obsessed with their Fitbits, determined to hit their ten thousand steps each day.

I was happy for them, but at the time, I didn't see the appeal. I was hiking regularly and lifting weights a few times a week. I was getting all the exercise I needed. I wasn't Fitbit's target market. My perspective shifted when I came across Dan Buettner's "Blue Zones" research, a study of the world's longest-lived populations.

Buettner, a National Geographic explorer and longevity expert, identified five regions where people consistently live to be one hundred years old or more, and who are living not only longer but more vitally. His research revealed that people who live in the Blue Zones don't run marathons or spend hours lifting weights in the gym. Instead, they move naturally and frequently throughout their day—walking, gardening, doing manual labor.

They live in environments that encourage—and often require—consistent, low-intensity physical activity. Their mobility isn't a task to check off; it's a way of life and common practice among all the Blue Zone populations. This intrigued me and caused me to consider my daily habits. Despite my hiking and strength training, I was spending hours each day sitting at my laptop. Eventually, I caved and purchased a Fitbit.

What I discovered was eye-opening: On non-hiking days, I was quite sedentary. I started making small changes: walking instead of driving, taking movement breaks every hour, bouncing on a rebounder for ten minutes at a time at regular intervals. It wasn't long before I averaged more than twenty, thirty—sometimes forty—thousand steps a day.

I started walking during all of my coaching calls and whenever possible while running errands, and my average daily step count climbed to more than twenty thousand, not including my hikes. I had never felt better—mentally, physically, emotionally. My joints were less stiff, my inflammation decreased, and my energy soared. I became intimately aware of my world through movement: I knew exactly how many steps it took to walk to the grocery store, the post office, my sons' schools, the bakery, and my office. Walking became not just exercise but a way of life.

By the time our family took our first European trip—a month-long, eight-country adventure in 2016—movement was second nature to us. We designed an itinerary that was as active as it was immersive. Each time we arrived in a new country, we'd walk one to three miles to our Airbnb or apartment—and that was just the beginning.

We explored cities, climbed towers, wandered through ancient streets, and hiked rugged trails. By the end of our epic European journey, we had averaged 24,500 steps per day per person—totaling over three million collective steps. All told, we each walked 370 miles during our month in Europe. The experiences were made possible because of our active lifestyle.

In London, we walked the River Thames, stood before Big Ben, explored the Tower of London, and immersed ourselves in Shakespeare's *The Taming of the Shrew*. In Munich, Germany, we wandered the Englischer Garten, climbed hills to see the Glockenspiel, and sipped beer at the historic Biergarten before venturing into the Bavarian Alps. In Switzerland, we hiked twenty-four miles in Lauterbrunnen, where waterfalls were everywhere and the cows' bells echoed in the crisp mountain air. In Zermatt, we climbed to breathtaking alpine lakes and stood in awe of the Matterhorn.

In Italy, we trekked the cliffs of Cinque Terre, climbed the steps of Florence's Giotto's Bell Tower, and stood beneath Michelangelo's *David*. We walked in the footsteps of great historical figures—across the Ponte Sant'Angelo, inside the Colosseum and the Vatican, through ancient catacombs and the Sistine Chapel, and all the piazzas that make up Rome. In Portugal, we strolled Lisbon's colorful, steep, and hilly streets, explored São Jorge Castle, and kayaked through sea caves along the stunning Algarve coast.

That first European adventure whetted our family's appetite for even greater explorations. Since then, we have completed a 160-mile backpacking pilgrimage along the Camino de Santiago and embarked on a three-week Epic Adventure in Iceland.

These journeys have deepened my belief that movement is not just about health—it's about fully experiencing the world. The more we move, the more we're able to see and experience.

The simple act of walking helps us fully engage in our lives. When we walk, we are more awake, and the result is we notice more. So, whether you walk to the store, hike a mountain, or simply get up every hour to move— never stop.

You don't stop moving because you get old; you get old because you stop moving.

Walking: Not Just for Our Physical Health

The benefits of walking extend far beyond the physical. The act of putting one foot in front of the other is deeply ingrained in human evolution, and science confirms that it has profound effects on the brain and body. One of the most fascinating aspects of walking is how it engages the rhythmic movement of both sides of the body, known as "bilateral stimulation."

When we walk, we activate both hemispheres of the brain and enhance their communication. This process mirrors a key mechanism used in Eye Movement Desensitization and Reprocessing (EMDR) therapy, which is widely used to help people process trauma and anxiety.

Bilateral stimulation allows us to process emotions, reframe thoughts, and reduce stress. Research also shows that walking in a natural setting can lower cortisol levels, decrease symptoms of depression, and even boost cognitive function. Not only this, but researchers at New Mexico Highlands University found that the impact of walking increases blood flow to the brain, improving oxygen delivery and strengthening memory recall. A Stanford University study revealed that walking boosts working memory, the type of memory responsible for short-term decision-making and problem-solving.

I don't mean to boast, but my memory is one of my greatest assets. I receive feedback all the time from friends and clients about how excellent it is. I remember conversations and things people have shared with me years later, even if we've lost touch or are no longer working together. I can't help but think this gift is due to the endless hours I've spent wandering in the woods and mountains.

Regular walking has been linked to a reduced risk of cognitive decline and dementia. A study from the University of Pittsburgh found that older adults who walked six to nine miles per week had greater gray matter volume in their brains compared to those who were sedentary. More gray matter means better memory, problem-solving, and overall cognitive function. Another study from Harvard Medical School found that walking stimulates the growth of new brain cells through a process called neurogenesis, particularly in the hippocampus: the region of the brain responsible for learning and memory.

Walking also enhances synaptic plasticity, meaning it helps brain cells communicate more efficiently, leading to sharper thinking and improved recall. All my best ideas, inspirations, and aha moments have occurred while I was walking or hiking. When German philosopher Friedrich Nietzsche said, "All truly great thoughts are conceived while walking," he wasn't just speaking from personal experience, although he had plenty.

A 2014 study from Stanford University found that walking increases creative output by an astonishing sixty percent compared to sitting. Movement enhances divergent thinking, allowing the brain to form new connections and generate original ideas. This is why many of history's greatest thinkers—Aristotle, Nietzsche, Virginia Woolf, and even Steve Jobs—were known for their daily walks. It's not just about moving the body; it's about unlocking the brain.

Mood follows action. Walking facilitates a sort of emotional reset. When we walk, our body releases endorphins and serotonin, natural chemicals that boost our mood and reduce stress. Walking outside in natural light has the added benefit of helping to regulate our circadian rhythms, which improve our sleep quality and energy levels.

For centuries, walking has been used as a form of meditation and self-reflection. Many spiritual traditions emphasize the power of walking—whether it's a pilgrimage on the Camino de Santiago, a Buddhist walking meditation, or simply the practice of taking contemplative walks in nature. Walking provides a rhythm, a cadence that helps us slow down, breathe, and reconnect with ourselves. Its repetitive motion and steady pace allow thoughts to flow more freely, offering clarity and insight that are often elusive in the noise of daily life.

The beauty of walking is its simplicity. Most everyone can do it, and it doesn't require expensive equipment, a gym membership, or a complicated plan. We just need to step outside and start moving. So, lace up your shoes, step outside, and start walking. Your body, brain, and soul will thank you, and everything in your life will improve.

How To Get Your Kids to Hike

If you'd like to be an active family, you'll need to commit to it. Raising an active family requires intention and a lot of extra effort. It can take twice as long to get out the door as well as multiple trips to the car when loading (and later unloading) all the necessary gear required to care for a baby or keep a toddler well and happy while outdoors and beyond the creature comforts of home. There might be bribing and nagging involved. There will almost certainly, at times, be complaining.

We raised our sons largely outdoors. I can still remember when I was pregnant with our first son, Wolf, and the many conversations Jerry and I had before his birth about how we wanted to raise our family. Jerry and I have always loved adventuring, and we felt strongly that time outdoors needed to be a significant part of our family life. Our strong intention and commitment were necessary. Without that kind of reflection, I'm not sure we would have been successful.

Those days when we were raising our sons, when they were babies and until they were in their teen years, were years when Jerry and I had a fair amount of work stress and the usual demands that make it not easy to raise a family.

As I write this, our sons are now ages eighteen, twenty-three, and twenty-five. We did the heavy lifting, so you don't have to. Well, you'll have to do some heavy lifting, because it's par for the course, but hopefully our tips and tricks will help.

In short, here's my best advice on this matter: Be the captain. Be serious about instilling an active lifestyle in your family. When your kids are young, don't ask them, "Do you want to go hiking?" Instead, smile and enthusiastically announce, "Today, we're going hiking!" Although subtle, this important difference really matters if you truly want to make spending time outdoors one of your family's values.

Even though our sons loved being outside and were usually happy campers once on the trail, I doubt they would have said *yes* most of the time if we had asked if they wanted to go hiking. Kids are human—we're designed to pick the path of least resistance, and the reality is that even children who love the outdoors will often choose the easiest option when given a choice.

To help in our quest to raise our boys in the outdoors—and to raise hikers—we created a bit of magic we called the "Trail Fairy." Jerry and I would sneak ahead and tuck little bags along the trail, each with a tiny treat and a handwritten note cheering the boys on, always signed, "Love, the Trail Fairy."

Just when they were nearing their wit's end, our sons would stumble upon these little treasures. It felt as if the forest itself had been watching, celebrating their effort—and it always gave them much-needed pep in their step.

As our boys got older, if Jerry and I had asked our sons what kind of international trip they'd like to take during their 2018 summer vacation, I doubt they would have picked a backpacking pilgrimage on Spain's

Camino de Santiago. (Although I did take this into account and added time at the beginning and end for leisure and fun in Paris, Madrid, and Barcelona.) Feel free to judge me, but I wasn't above bribing.

For our boys, food has always been their love language, which seems like a small and reasonable price for Jerry and me to pay. As long as we kept them fed and included some of their favorite, non-healthy indulgences, they could go for quite a long time! We have landmarks along some of our most-traveled local hiking routes with names like "Root Beer Rock," "Butterfinger Point," and "Skittles Cave." These were landmarks we'd encourage our boys to hike to before we'd stop—yet again—when they needed a break or a snack.

At the time, with their little legs, these points seemed so far apart from one another. We still hike these trails, and it takes about three minutes to travel between these beloved landmarks. But back when our boys were especially young and little, it may have taken fifteen to thirty minutes to get from one to the next.

To any parents out there, it's about the journey, so embrace it—I promise you, it's worth it!

Boost Your Longevity

Keeping healthy for the sake of adding years to our lives is not enough—we need to add life to our years. Health span is the number of years we remain strong, mobile, and independent. The key to achieving this? Resistance training and cardiovascular fitness.

Dr. Peter Attia, a leading voice in longevity science, and Dr. Stacy Sims, an expert in midlife women's physiology, both emphasize that building strength and cardiovascular fitness are the most effective ways to improve health span. They argue that without deliberate effort, we lose muscle mass, cardiovascular capacity, and metabolic flexibility—all major predictors of longevity and well-being. *Outlive: The Science and Art of Longevity*, by Dr. Peter Attia, with Bill Gifford, is an excellent resource and a book I highly recommend.

One of the most significant predictors of longevity is muscle mass and strength. Grip strength, leg strength, and overall muscle mass are directly correlated with lower, all-cause mortality rates. We should actively strength train to avoid losing three to eight percent of our muscle mass per decade after age thirty, increase our bone density to reduce our risk of osteoporosis and fractures, and improve our metabolic health to improve our insulin sensitivity, regulate our blood sugar, and lower our risk of falls in old age.

If you're feeling confident about your longevity status, I suggest you give the following tests a try. First, try the sit-to-stand shoe test: Can you put on your socks and don and tie your shoes while standing on one leg, without assistance or leaning on anything? This test, promoted by movement expert Kelly Starrett, is a simple yet powerful indicator of mobility, balance, and lower-body strength, all of which are key factors for long-term independence. Another test is the grip strength hang test. To do it, try hanging from a pull-up bar for at least thirty seconds. How did you do? Are you as prepared for old age as you think you are?

One of the strongest predictors of longevity is VO2 max: a measure of the body's ability to use oxygen efficiently. Those with higher VO2 max levels live longer and have a lower risk of cardiovascular disease, dementia, and metabolic disorders. Attia emphasizes a three-tiered approach to cardiovascular training: zone 2 training (low-intensity, long-duration), high-intensity interval training (HIIT), and strength/resistance training.

Zone 2 training provides the longevity base and involves sustained, low-intensity activity where you can (barely) carry on a conversation while feeling slightly out of breath. Such training improves mitochondrial function, metabolic efficiency, and endurance, all key markers for aging well. Brisk walking, cycling, rowing, or hiking are all great examples of zone 2 training. Attia recommends spending three to four hours per week training in zone 2.

The benefits of zone 2 training are many, including: enhancing fat metabolism and insulin sensitivity, improving mitochondrial health, reducing risk for neurodegenerative diseases, and supporting long-term cardiovascular efficiency.

HIIT training involves short bursts of high-intensity effort followed by recovery periods. Examples of HIIT training include sprinting, rowing in intervals, and doing cycling sprints. Attia recommends performing one to two HIIT workouts per week. Personally, my favorite way to incorporate them is by turning to my Peloton, but an elliptical trainer or treadmill will do the trick if you're limited to the indoors.

I start my HIIT sessions with a five- to ten-minute warmup, then I perform ten thirty-second, all-out sprints, each followed by thirty seconds of easy, recovery pedaling. I end each workout with a five- to ten-minute cooldown.

Another go-to HIIT workout is to replace the aforementioned with ten one-minute stand-up sprints followed by ninety seconds of easy pedaling and recovery. (If you're new to HIIT training, start small and work your way up. And remember—anything is better than nothing.)

In addition to incorporating zone 2 and HIIT training into your weekly exercise, you need to lift heavy things. There's no other way to put it— we must double down when it comes to building and maintaining our strength, and the effort you put into your strength today will determine your capacity to explore, adventure, and fully engage with life in your sixties, seventies, eighties, and hopefully beyond.

Dr. Peter Attia recommends resistance training two to three times a week. Focus on compound movements (training several muscles at once) and heavier resistance (lifting heavy for fewer reps). Start now, seek support, and train with purpose to give your future self the gift of strength, resilience, and freedom.

If You're Suffering Any of These Symptoms, You Might Be a Woman in Her Midlife

Five or six years ago, I regularly walked into rooms in my house and forgot why I was there. I misplaced keys, and words vanished mid-sentence. It was scary—I worried about early-onset Alzheimer's or dementia.

Then I started waking at 2 a.m., often drenched in sweat. My body felt unfamiliar, my mind foggy, and my patience evaporated. The smallest irritation sent me into a mini rage.

If you're a woman in your late thirties to early sixties experiencing any of these symptoms (or the other twenty-eight possible ones) and wondering, "What the hell is happening to me?" you're not alone or crazy. For years, women's midlife symptoms were often dismissed by doctors as inevitable inconveniences of aging. Thankfully, science is catching up to what we've known deep down: This isn't just aging—it's perimenopause and menopause. And these hormonal shifts affect every system in our bodies.

Most of us learned menopause means hot flashes and periods ending. But perimenopause, the hormonal transition leading to menopause, lasts for years and includes symptoms like brain fog, mood swings, anxiety, depression, weight gain, insomnia, night sweats, reduced sex drive, joint pain, thinning hair, heart palpitations, vaginal dryness, gut issues, frequent UTIs, burning mouth syndrome, and more wrinkles— just to name a few. Welcome to perimenopause and menopause, where declining estrogen profoundly impacts our brain, bones, metabolism, and cardiovascular health.

Historically, women's health was an afterthought in medical research. The flawed 2002 Women's Health Initiative study generated fear around hormone replacement therapy (HRT), leading millions of women to miss out on treatments that could have improved their quality of life and health.

Fortunately—and finally—the tide is turning.

Documentaries like *The M Factor* (free on PBS) and the book *Estrogen Matters* by Drs. Avrum Bluming and Carol Tavris highlight extensive research supporting estrogen therapy. We now understand that estrogen plays a crucial role in brain health, possibly linking menopause to women's higher Alzheimer's risk. Starting HRT within five to ten years post-menopause had reportedly been linked to reduced cognitive decline.

Personally and professionally, I've known many women who've suffered needlessly due to misinformation or inadequate treatment. My own struggles with anxiety and depression after turning forty were likely symptoms of perimenopause. I blamed stress, stagnation, or lack of effort, not realizing my brain was reacting to declining estrogen.

Had I known then what I do now, I would have considered HRT sooner. (While hormone replacement therapy can offer significant relief and health benefits, it isn't suitable for everyone, so always consult closely with your healthcare provider.)

The strength training, interval work, and recovery practices that my friend and trainer, Steve, introduced me to in 2010 when I was in my early forties became foundational practices that I've kept up for fifteen years. It turns out these methods align perfectly with Dr. Stacy Sims' current recommendations for midlife women. (Thank you, Steve!)

Dr. Sims suggests women adjust training during midlife, focusing on heavier loads and fewer reps to counter muscle loss and hormonal shifts. Jump training, like box jumps, helps maintain power and bone density. She recommends consuming 0.7–1.0 grams of protein per pound of body weight daily.

I highly recommend Sims' book *Next Level: Your Guide to Kicking Ass, Feeling Great, and Crushing Goals Through Menopause and Beyond*. I strength train two to three times weekly, focusing on squats, swings, pulls, and presses, alongside functional movements like lunges, carries, step-ups, and grip-strengthening exercises. These activities support longevity and independence. Contrary to popular belief, endless cardio and calorie restriction are ineffective and potentially harmful during menopause. Instead, advocate for yourself.

If a doctor dismisses your concerns as "just aging," find another. Seek menopause-informed providers who take your experience seriously. By embracing strategies tailored to midlife physiology, you won't just maintain vitality and strength—you'll thrive through the transition. You don't have to suffer!

Eat Well to Live Your Epic Life

Food is one of the most powerful tools we have. What we put into our bodies directly impacts how we feel, how we move, and how we think. It's never too late to start taking your nutrition seriously and making meaningful changes. This is not to say it's easy, especially since the modern American diet is full of hidden threats—most notably sugar and processed foods.

The average American consumes sixty-eight grams of added sugar per day. That may not sound like much until you realize it amounts to fifty-five pounds of sugar per year. Fifty-five pounds! Imagine lugging around a fifty-five-pound sack of sugar and spooning it into your mouth every single day, because that's essentially what most of us are doing (often without even realizing it). To put this in perspective, the American Heart Association recommends no more than twenty-five grams of added sugar per day for women and thirty-six grams for men. Most of us are consuming nearly three times that amount.

It starts subtly. You reach for a sweet snack in the afternoon—perhaps a quick fix to combat fatigue. The sugar rush feels good, giving you a burst of energy until it fades, leaving you even more drained. Over time, these constant blood sugar spikes and crashes begin to take their toll, leading to insulin resistance, a primary driver of type 2 diabetes and metabolic syndrome.

Your body struggles to process the constant influx of sugar, forcing your pancreas to work harder and harder until it can no longer keep up. Meanwhile, silent but deadly inflammation spreads throughout your body. Chronic sugar consumption fuels systemic inflammation, which has been linked to an increased risk of heart disease, autoimmune disorders, and even neurodegenerative conditions like Alzheimer's.

The very foods meant to provide energy begin sabotaging your long-term health. After such excessive and accumulative sugar consumption, your liver, which is tasked with processing the excess sugar—especially fructose—starts to accumulate fat, leading to non-alcoholic fatty liver disease (NAFLD).

This condition, once rare, is now rampant, impairing detoxification and metabolism. What was once an occasional indulgence has turned into a metabolic burden that slows your body's ability to function efficiently. Alcohol contains a significant amount of sugar, especially in sweetened drinks like cocktails and wine, which can contribute to metabolic issues, insulin resistance, and inflammation over time. As people age, increased alcohol consumption is linked to heightened risks of cognitive decline, liver disease, cardiovascular problems, and impaired immune function— even at moderate levels.

Excess sugar intake has been directly linked to memory impairment and cognitive decline. Studies show that excessive sugar consumption increases your risk of dementia by disrupting neural pathways and fueling neuroinflammation. Have you ever experienced "brain fog"—difficulty concentrating, poor memory recall, and mood swings? These are all consequences of a diet high in sugar.

Your immune system also suffers. High sugar intake suppresses immune cell activity, making your body more vulnerable to infections and slowing down recovery. It's no coincidence that people who consume large amounts of sugar often experience sluggishness and frequent illnesses.

Sugar accelerates aging. Glycation, a process in which sugar molecules attach to proteins and fats, damages collagen, leads to premature skin aging, wrinkles, and loss of elasticity. This internal breakdown makes a person look and feel older than their actual age. At the same time, weight gain becomes nearly inevitable. Sugar consumption leads to constant cravings and excessive hunger, driving fat accumulation, particularly around the abdomen. This visceral fat is the most dangerous kind, increasing the risk of cardiovascular disease, metabolic disorders, and even some cancers.

Finally, the gut, which plays a vital role in overall health, takes a hit. Excess sugar feeds harmful gut bacteria, reducing beneficial microbes that are essential for digestion and immune function. Over time, this imbalance contributes to bloating, poor digestion, and increased gut permeability, also known as leaky gut syndrome, which has been linked to inflammation and chronic illness. But it's not just our sugar consumption that's making us unwell. The average American now consumes over 60 percent of their calories from ultra-processed foods.

These foods are engineered for convenience and taste but are stripped of essential nutrients, packed with preservatives, and full of additives that negatively impact our metabolism and energy levels. When we eat more whole, unprocessed foods, everything changes—our energy levels, ability to focus, resilience, and even our emotions. A well-nourished body doesn't just survive; it thrives.

What I've come to understand—both with my own health and that of the people I work with—is that health isn't about deprivation or discipline for its own sake. It's about feeling strong enough to do the things you love, resilient enough to handle anything life throws your way, and energized enough to be fully present for it all. It's about being able to hike that mountain, chase after your grandkids, or simply wake up feeling good in your body. So, start where you are.

Reduce your sugar intake. Eat real food. Drink more water. Your body will thank you—not just today but years from now, when you realize that feeling great in midlife is a critical part of this journey that is your epic life.

Eat for Your Mental Health

What we eat also profoundly affects brain function, mood, and resilience. Dr. Chris Palmer, a psychiatrist and researcher who is leading the charge in the emerging field of metabolic psychiatry and author of *Brain Energy: A Revolutionary Breakthrough in Understanding Mental Health—and Improving Treatment for Anxiety, Depression, OCD, PTSD, and More*, has pioneered research showing that mental health disorders are not just psychological—they are metabolic conditions.

The same dysfunction that contributes to obesity, diabetes, and heart disease also plays a role in depression, anxiety, and bipolar disorder. One of the biggest dietary culprits? Once again, sugar.

Excess sugar consumption fuels chronic inflammation, insulin resistance, and mitochondrial dysfunction, all of which impair brain health. Blood sugar spikes and crashes lead to mood swings, fatigue, and poor concentration. Chronic inflammation is directly linked to depression, anxiety, and cognitive decline. Mitochondrial dysfunction reduces the brain's ability to produce energy, causing brain fog and fatigue. Gut-brain disruption weakens mood regulation by feeding harmful bacteria and starving beneficial microbes.

Palmer's work and research has shown that nutritional interventions can significantly improve—and in some cases even reverse—mental health conditions.

A ketogenic diet (a diet high in fat and low in carbohydrates) can have the effect of stabilizing our mood and improving symptoms of bipolar disorder and schizophrenia. Increasing our healthy fat intake through omega-3s (from salmon, walnuts, and flaxseeds) supports our brain function and reduces depression. Fermented foods (such as kimchi and kefir) and fiber-rich vegetables enhance our mental clarity. Dr. Palmer's work is redefining mental health treatment, proving that food is medicine—not just for the body but for the mind.

To Be More Present in Your Life, Practice Mindfulness

We are more distracted than ever. Pinging notifications, endless to-do lists, and mindless scrolling consume our attention, fueling stress, anxiety, and burnout. Nothing has helped me mitigate distractions, respond thoughtfully, and reclaim my focus as much as practicing mindfulness.

Intrigued by research on how mindfulness could reduce anxiety, increase creativity, and make us more present, I attempted to incorporate it into my daily routine. I found it frustrating. I believed mindfulness meant silencing my thoughts, but my overactive mind had other plans. I would sit for ten minutes, agonizing over my inability to calm my racing thoughts, and conclude I wasn't "good" at it. So, I quit.

Then, in 2013, I attended the Wisdom 2.0 conference in San Francisco, and it changed my mind—or shall I say, my mindfulness? Jack Kornfield, a Buddhist teacher and psychologist, compared our attention to a puppy—distracted and darting in every direction.

Just as we gently guide a puppy back to the path, mindfulness is about kindly redirecting our attention over and over again. It's not about clearing our thoughts completely but training ourselves to notice them without judgment. This simple shift helped me reframe my practice.

I learned to see my mind as the sky and thoughts as passing clouds—transient and ever-changing. When we observe our thoughts rather than letting ourselves get swept up by them, we clear space in our minds. Being mindful enables us to create a pause between stimulus and response during which we can thoughtfully choose our response rather than react mindlessly.

After that conference, I committed to ten minutes of mindfulness five days a week. I started with the Headspace app and gradually expanded my practice. Today, mindfulness is woven into my life in many ways, helping me feel more present, alive, and connected. Yet, despite overwhelming evidence of its benefits, many still don't practice mindfulness.

Let's keep it simple. Harvard psychologist Ellen Langer, the "mother of mindfulness," gives us a simple instruction of how to practice mindfulness: "Actively notice things." She argues that the opposite of mindfulness isn't distraction—it's mindlessness.

One of my favorite ways to practice mindfulness while working to "tame" my overactive and at times inhospitable mind is to work to memorize my favorite poems. Focusing on the words of my favorite poems helps keep my mind engaged and keeps it from wandering to unhealthier places. (And I have memorized poems to show for it.)

Start small. Take notice of your surroundings. On my Epic Adventures, I encourage clients to pick something in nature—a leaf, a tree, the sound of a river—and focus on it for two minutes. Over time, this practice strengthens our ability to pay attention, making us more engaged in our lives. Mindfulness isn't about perfection—it's about presence. We only have one life. To be mindful is to be present and awake for it.

To Live Well, Sleep Well

I've been a "health nut" for most of my life. I've prioritized exercising and moving throughout my day, healthy eating, and taking care of my mental health. It wasn't until recently that I added getting good and regular sleep to my priorities.

Naively, I used to think the purpose of sleep was simply to give our brains a break—a chance to rest and recover. I couldn't have been more wrong. It turns out that when we sleep, our brain doesn't shut down—it goes to work. There's an incredible amount of work to be done by our brains and bodies, and much of it can only be done when we are asleep.

Matthew Walker, PhD, a renowned neuroscientist and sleep expert, explains that our brain engages in a remarkable array of processes during sleep that are essential for our physical, emotional, and cognitive health. These processes require us to sleep long enough—and deeply enough—to reach specific stages of sleep. It's recommended that adults get seven to nine hours of sleep per night, yet research shows many of us fall far short of this goal.

The effects of inadequate sleep ripple across every aspect of our health. Most people don't realize the full extent to which the quality and quantity of our sleep shape our well-being. Sleep deprivation has been linked to an increased risk of heart disease, diabetes, depression, and obesity. Chronic poor sleep is also associated with impairments in memory, learning, decision-making, and emotional regulation—all of which are precursors to broader neurological conditions. No amount of exercise or healthy diet can make up for the negative effects of poor sleep.

Studies show that poor sleep quality and disorders like sleep apnea and insomnia are associated with a thirty-three percent higher risk of dementia and a greater likelihood of developing Alzheimer's or Parkinson's disease.

Fragmented or insufficient sleep contributes to inflammation, oxidative stress, and vascular damage, which erode cognitive function over time.

Sleep plays a critical role in regulating our hunger hormones: ghrelin, which stimulates appetite, and leptin, which signals fullness. When we're sleep-deprived, our ghrelin levels increase, our leptin levels drop, and we're more likely to overeat due to an increased craving for high-calorie, carbohydrate-rich foods. Chronic sleep loss also disrupts our metabolism, impairs our insulin sensitivity, and increases our risk of weight gain. Research shows that sleeping less than six hours per night is associated with a fifty-five percent higher risk of obesity.

Sleep deprivation doesn't just make us tired—it makes us less intelligent, literally. Without sufficient sleep, the prefrontal cortex, responsible for decision-making and problem-solving, becomes impaired. At the same time, the amygdala, the brain's emotional control center, becomes hyperactive, making us more emotionally reactive and less able to manage impulses. Sleep is also essential for memory consolidation and learning; without it, we struggle to absorb and retain new information, feel foggy, and find it harder to think creatively or make sound judgments. The bottom line is quality sleep is not optional. It's a necessity for living your epic life.

I've struggled with insomnia for as long as I can remember. Poor and restless sleep is how my stress tends to manifest. Unfortunately, this can make a stressful time even more challenging. This combined with everything I learned about sleep motivated me to make it a priority in my life.

Three years prior to writing this book, I bought an Oura Ring to track my sleep and Heart Rate Variability (HRV)—a marker of central nervous system health that is closely tied to rest. During my first full year of tracking in 2022, I averaged six and a half hours of sleep per night.

In 2023, I boosted that to seven hours per night, and by the end of 2024, I averaged seven hours and twenty minutes per night. Within the first thirty days of 2025, I increased my average to seven hours and forty minutes per night. If you're considering tracking your sleep, consider purchasing an Oura Ring, WHOOP Strap, Fitbit, or Apple Watch.

In addition to tracking all kinds of health measures and markers, these devices provide insights into your sleep patterns, helping you identify areas to improve, such as increasing REM or deep sleep percentages. I've found it helpful to create a consistent schedule, improve my sleep environment, watch what I eat and drink, and move my body during the day.

I'm also mindful about my use of sleep aids, which I occasionally use to help get to sleep, including Advil PM, Tylenol PM, and Benadryl. While these are probably okay to use occasionally, it's best not to rely on them too heavily or consistently. For some years, lack of exercise, poor nutrition, mental health struggles, and inadequate sleep were pebbles in my shoe—nagging discomforts that I ignored.

Tending to these pebbles helped me reclaim my energy, clarity, and strength. When we care for ourselves, we don't just survive—we thrive. And most of all, we're able to live our most authentic and epic lives.

Lesson 8
Be All In

Be All In

Have you ever rappelled down the face of a mountain or leaped from an airplane? To do either of these things requires being all in, with both feet. You can't do them part way. Staying committed to your authentic life is similar.

You must be all in. You must commit to it—and choose to live it—again and again. Committing is one of the hardest things any of us can do. People who hire me to be their coach are often already aware of the goals they'd like to achieve or the changes they want to make. What they need help with is staying committed. After all, that's where most of us fail.

How often do we decide, with conviction, that we're going to eat more vegetables, spend less time on our devices and screens, do more yoga, or spend more time with family? We might remain committed for three days, three weeks, three months, or even three years, but eventually, we fall off the wagon. We let ourselves off the hook, out of our commitment.

I had signed up for the Brooks Range expedition because it was in Alaska and I figured, what better way for me to see and experience such a vast wilderness than by taking a NOLS course there? But one of the practical reasons I chose it was to become more skilled, confident, and comfortable in and around rivers.

Someone I knew had drowned while attempting to cross a swift river in the high country. Since then, despite the fact that there are many rivers flowing through my favorite hiking routes in Wyoming, I found myself gripped by fear whenever the rivers were running high. I hoped that by immersing myself in rivers, I could not only confront my fear but emerge more capable for the sake of my personal and professional adventures.

Early on in our expedition, I volunteered to be the "leader of the day." All that meant was that, for that day, I'd be responsible for getting our group from point A to point B.

Because a good leader doesn't do everything, I delegated Antonia to be our point person. The trek to our next camp was about seven or eight miles away, and she would choose our route and lead us there. Right away, within the first mile, she led us across the river and back a half a dozen times.

I was—how shall I say this?—not happy. My discomfort mounted as we stood together, our feet submerged in the river, splashing our calves. I decided to make an executive decision. I called everyone together and announced, "Guys. We are soaking wet. We have six miles left and ten days left in the expedition. We're going out of the river."

I could tell not everyone agreed with me, but they obliged and followed me out of the water. Once on solid ground, we found ourselves trekking through alders, which are thickets of shrubs and small trees. Their dense and mangled growth created a thick and tangled underbrush, making it challenging to pass through. We were poked and prodded, stabbed and jabbed by their branches, which would snap and threaten to hit the person behind us. The thickness and density also made it difficult to see if any bears or moose were bedded down in the trees. We hiked miserably for some time.

Once through the alders, we emerged to find ourselves on a steep sidehill far above the river. Much of the Brooks Range is alpine tundra—even on level ground, the hiking was laborious as our feet sank into the tundra with each step. Add steep sidehill to the mix, and it was hard going. The river had been an excellent choice because, unlike this route, it followed a level course. As we made our way up the steep hill, I noticed we were all spread out. Everyone was disengaged, each in their own personal hell. As we struggled up the uneven terrain, I recalled one of my goals for the course was to spend time in rivers, to learn and improve my skills, yet here I was, avoiding the river.

I chided myself and proceeded to put myself through a wrath of self-criticism that was, thankfully, short-lived. I yelled to gather everyone up, and announced, "I'm sorry. My bad. This was a terrible idea. We're going back down to the river."

As we found our way back to the river, there was a huge ice formation in the water. Streaks of turquoise-blue light reflected in the ice, bright and sparkling. It was a stunning sight and the only thing like it we'd see during our entire expedition. We would have missed it if we'd stuck to my plan to avoid the river.

How often do we do this? We decide, with conviction, that we're going to make a change and live an authentic life, but when the conditions aren't perfect, we let ourselves off the hook.

The danger when we do this is we often tell ourselves: *It's not that I won't do it—I'm just not going to do it right now.* The risk is if we're not mindful, days can pass, weeks, months, years—perhaps a lifetime–and the thing we wanted so badly to do? We never did it. And sometimes, it's too late; we no longer can.

I wonder what's harder: having the courage and doing the hard work that living your epic life requires, or not doing it and someday wishing you had?

Living Your Epic Life Requires Knowing Who You Are and How You Want to Be

If living an authentic life were easy, everyone would be doing it. It's difficult work, in large part due to the level of commitment required. But before we can even commit to living an epic life, we need clarity: What exactly are we committing to?

Over the years, I've done the work, tested and taught the strategies, and dug into the research so you don't have to. And here's the biggest insight I've learned from the research and from my own experiences: Commitment starts with identity.

I find that my clients often find it difficult to articulate exactly *who* they want to be. But when I ask, "*How* do you want to be?" most have a much clearer idea. I created an exercise called "Five Ways to Be." Take some time to reflect on how you want to be as a person. Don't rush this—take the time you need to reflect deeply on your life and the person you aspire to be.

Come up with five words to describe the five ways. Then, for each word, write one to two sentences about *why* that quality is important to you. (This second step is important because it will act as a powerful motivator when your resolve is tested. And you can be sure, it will be tested.)

For each way/word, brainstorm a list of five to ten things you can do to practice being that way. Some of the actions should be so easy that you have no excuse to not do them, but there should also be a few that require you to stretch and play bigger than normal. Out of all the exercises I like to implement in my coaching work, this is the one that often leads to the greatest and most profound changes in a person's life, so don't underestimate its value. Doing this work will help you be the person you wish to be and will be the key to living intentionally.

In 2010, when I found myself thirty-five pounds overweight, drinking wine on too many weeknights, addicted to my gadgets and devices, and depressed, I was devastated. I knew I needed to transform my mental and physical health. But when I had this realization, I was even more bothered by the fact that I could be caught so unawares in the first place—that I could end up on a path that was not the one I expected to be on. (This is what happens when you're not paying close attention, when you're not awake and living intentionally.)

I spent a lot of time walking alone in the mountains and the woods pondering many big life questions, but the one that kept coming back to me was, *What kind of person do I want to be?* (Or asked another way: *How do I want to be?*)

This central question helped me think about the various roles I filled in my life and to take them into consideration, especially since some of them involved my most important relationships. I also considered my goals and ambitions and thought about the various qualities that could help me achieve them. I brainstormed a list of people I admired, those who inspired me, and what traits of theirs stood out and why.

After a lot of reflection, by early 2010, I had my five ways/words: disciplined, courageous, fun, inspired, and humble. (These words described the type of person I wanted to be.) Let me share about one of the words here—*disciplined*.

I knew transforming my health would require self-discipline. But I also wanted to be the kind of person who followed through and did what she said she would do.

At the time, I was working while raising three young sons. I didn't have much free time, so if I wanted to work out, I had to find a time to do it when nobody needed me. I chose 4:30 a.m. and I committed to working out four days a week.

In the beginning, every time the alarm shattered my slumber, I was tempted to push the snooze button, but as I reached to do so, I would envision a disciplined version of myself and remember that *she* set this alarm. I trusted her and reminded myself that no one ever regrets working out, but most regret not working out. It worked.

Over the course of eighteen months, I completely transformed my mental and physical health, but when I reflect on my successful transformation, these accomplishments aren't what I'm most proud of.

What I'm most proud of is that, for fifteen years, I've sustained the changes I made and the many good habits I formed.

Eighteen months of discipline and commitment were all it took for those habits to become a part of me. They're no longer to-dos. I don't view any of my health habits as chores—they are part of who I am.

In 2018, years after my personal transformation, I came across James Clear's *Atomic Habits*, a book that has sold more than fifteen million copies worldwide, making it one of the best-selling self-improvement books of all time. Clear gave words to what I had intuitively done: I had tied my goals to my identity. Clear argues that the most lasting change comes from identity change. But what does that mean? He explains it this way: The goal isn't just to get fit; it's to become a fit person. The goal isn't just to write a book; it's to become a writer. The goal isn't just to parent better; it's to become the kind of parent you admire.

To tie my 2010 words (*disciplined, courageous, fun, inspired,* and *humble*) to my identity, I aimed to be a disciplined, courageous, fun, inspired, and humble person.

Setting my sights on these qualities as part of who I aspired to be is what I was really going for, even more than the outcomes I hoped they would lead to. When you align your goals with the type of person you want to be, your actions become a natural extension of your identity.

Clear refers to this process as "casting votes" for your future self. Each small action is a vote that affirms and provides evidence that you are—and can be—that type of person.

Identity → Process → Outcomes

When trying to make changes in their lives, people often start with the outcome, such as, "I want to lose twenty pounds." But if the goal is *only* tied to the outcome, the result is often temporary. Instead, start with identity, determining the type of person you want to be, then determine the processes you'll put in place to practice being that type of person. Your desired outcomes will follow.

In 2010, I decided I wanted to be a disciplined person. From there, I came up with several steps to take that would help me become that. And lo and behold, I became a disciplined person. It's now part of my nature to be disciplined, and it's no longer one of my five ways/words. When you transform your identity, the changes are profound. They reshape how you see yourself and how you show up in the world.

Change Is Hard

Transformation isn't pretty, and changing your life is hard work. You will face many challenges, and the list of barriers to change is long. First, know yourself. A lack of self-awareness will make it impossible to create lasting change. Without self-awareness, it will be nearly impossible to come up with a winning strategy for how to successfully change your life.

I would not have succeeded at transforming my health if not for the self-awareness that I'm terrible at moderation. It was also helpful to know that I'm impatient and that I didn't want my transformation to be slow and steady, but dramatic and more immediate. A lack of self-awareness is a common reason people struggle to make lasting change.

Laziness is a barrier for most of us when it comes to making change that lasts because it's human nature to choose the path of least resistance. Another barrier is ambiguity, which can sabotage even our best intentions.

Without specificity—such as defining *what* change we want, *why* it matters, and *how* we'll achieve it—we'll likely fail in our commitment. "Be healthier" or "get stronger" are not achievable goals. They're vague aspirations, and we need them instead to be specific and measurable.

Forgetfulness is a barrier to making lasting change. According to research, we forget about fifty percent of what we learn within twenty minutes of learning it, and we forget about seventy percent of what we've learned within a twenty-four-hour period. We often experience what's called the intention-action gap, which describes the disconnect between what we plan to do and what we actually do. Without cues, reminders, or systems in place, we easily forget to act on our goals, allowing old habits to persist.

This work is important because it takes only a second to forget our intention and fall off the wagon. For just a few seconds, we might forget we're giving up chocolate and accept a piece of chocolate we're offered. One way to be less forgetful is to practice being the opposite—mindful. When we practice mindfulness, we learn how to become an observer of our thoughts, which provides us with a brief pause during which we can thoughtfully choose to resist a temptation and stay the course. Our brains are wired to seek ease and avoid discomfort, which makes breaking old habits and forming new ones difficult.

For this reason, comfort is a frequent barrier to our ability to create lasting change. Twenty-five percent of adults in America consider themselves procrastinators. We like to put things off, especially things we don't love doing, that are hard to do, or that we're scared to do. But one of the greatest dangers of procrastination is that if we're not careful, such procrastination can continue for days, weeks, years, and even a lifetime.

We have only one life. Why would we want to wait any longer to become the person we aspire to be? One barrier to change that I personally encounter often is self-criticism. I set the bar for myself impossibly high and then I'm hard on myself if I don't measure up. I tell myself that being self-critical will motivate me to work harder and accomplish more.

But as it turns out, this isn't how it works. There are numerous studies that show we achieve more when we are kind and compassionate toward ourselves, and it makes for a much more pleasing experience.

We Have Limited Willpower and Self-Control

Having limited willpower and self-control is one of the most common barriers to making lasting change. In 1996, psychologist Roy Baumeister and his team conducted a groundbreaking study that revealed a fundamental truth about human self-control: It is a finite resource.

The experiment was deceptively simple. College students entered a room with two bowls on a table, one filled with warm, freshly baked chocolate chip cookies, the other with plain radishes. The students were divided into two groups: One was free to indulge in the cookies but couldn't touch the radishes, while the other was strictly instructed to eat only radishes—no cookies allowed. Afterward, all participants were given an unsolvable puzzle and told to work on it for as long as they could. The results were astonishing: Those who had resisted the cookies gave up significantly sooner than those who had been free to enjoy them. Why? Because their self-control—the same mental energy required for discipline, decision-making, and perseverance—had already been depleted. They had spent so much effort resisting the temptation of the cookies that, when another challenge arose, they had nothing left to give.

This finding was revolutionary. It showed that self-control is not an endless well but a limited resource, drained by every decision, every act of resistance, every moment of restraint. We don't just use self-control for avoiding temptations; we use it for managing our emotions, staying focused, making decisions, and following through on commitments. Once it runs low, we become vulnerable to shortcuts, indulgences, and impulses in all areas of life. But that's not all.

Did you know that willpower is directly tied to glucose levels? Every time we make a decision or resist a temptation, our brain burns glucose—the primary fuel it runs on. That means after a stressful day filled with decisions and challenges, our mental reserves have been depleted. This is why, for so many people, the wheels come off around 5 p.m. By that time, their self-control and willpower have been exhausted. There's no resolve or fortitude remaining, and they give up on the good fight and cave to their temptations and bad habits.

I have a weakness for Dairy Queen Blizzards—I call it my "DQ dilemma." There isn't a DQ in my small town, so I don't get to indulge often. However, when I drive the nine hours to Zion National Park to lead my Epic Zion programs, I drive by seven Dairy Queens along I-15 in Utah.

I set out on my trips to Zion determined to wait for my return trip to treat myself to a Blizzard. My diet and nutrition are always dialed in at a high level in the days leading up to my Epic programs, so it makes sense to save my Blizzard for the way back as a celebration of an Epic-program-gone-well.

But here's the problem: Each of the seven DQ signs I pass while traveling south in Utah tempts me to have a Blizzard and forces me to remake my decision. Should I give in? Should I resist? I can say no the first time. And the second. And even a few more, but typically by the time I reach Beaver, Utah—six temptations later—my self-control is spent, and almost every time, I cave. If those Dairy Queens didn't exist with their signs taunting me at every exit and if I didn't have to make that decision over and over again, it wouldn't be an issue.

But because I'm constantly exerting willpower, I eventually run out of it. This is what happens in our daily lives: The more temptations we face, the more self-control we burn until finally, we relent. Understanding that willpower is a limited resource is crucial to making lasting personal change. The key isn't to rely on discipline alone but to strategically conserve it.

"The Rider and the Elephant"

We tend to favor immediate gratification over long-term benefits. This is called "present-time bias," and it makes it particularly difficult for us to stick to new habits, let alone make lasting change. Imagine you set a goal to wake up early and go for a morning run. The night before, you feel motivated and committed. You lay out your running shoes, set your alarm, and tell yourself, "Tomorrow, I'll start fresh."

But when the alarm rings, your brain betrays you. The logical part of you—the one that wants to be fitter and healthier—knows you should get up. But another, deeper part of you only cares about right now. The warm bed feels too good. The future benefits of exercise feel distant and abstract, while the immediate comfort of hitting snooze is tangible and tempting. This is an example of present-time bias, our tendency to prioritize immediate pleasure over long-term rewards even when we know better.

It's why we struggle to save money when we could spend it now, why we plan to eat healthy but reach for junk food, and why we promise ourselves we'll start a habit tomorrow, but when tomorrow comes, we procrastinate yet another day.

One thing that makes it hard to stay the course on the hard changes we're trying to make is the fact that we have two minds that are both always on: our rational mind and our emotional mind. Jonathan Haidt, a social psychologist, professor, and bestselling author, uses the metaphor of "the rider and the elephant" to illustrate the conflict between our rational and emotional selves. The rider represents our rational mind—the part that sets goals, makes plans, and understands what's best for us in the long run. The elephant, on the other hand, is our emotional, instinctual mind—the part that craves comfort, pleasure, and immediate gratification.

The problem? The rider may hold the reins, but if the elephant decides to charge toward what feels good in the moment—sleeping in, eating the cookie, skipping the workout—it's no contest. The elephant is too big and powerful. This is why self-discipline alone often fails. We assume we can "think" our way into better habits, but logic isn't enough when the elephant is in control. To truly overcome present-time bias, we need to work *with* our psychology, not against it. We need to get the rider and the elephant to work together.

In my favorite 201 1 *Radiolab* podcast episode called "You v. You" that I revisit often and share with coaching clients who are struggling to make a hard change, neuroscientist David Eagleman discusses the challenge of resisting immediate temptations in favor of long-term goals. Such temptations can be tough to overcome because our brains are wired to prioritize immediate rewards over future benefits.

To overcome this struggle, Eagleman suggests creating immediate emotional salience for the future outcome. By associating the long-term goal with a strong, immediate emotion, we can make the future consequence feel more relevant in the present moment, thereby enhancing our motivation to resist temptation and stick to our desired behavior.

For example, let's say I've committed to a fitness goal of going to the gym after work Monday through Thursday. But by the time Wednesday rolls around, I'm feeling exhausted and overwhelmed at work, and the couch is calling my name. I've already gone Monday and Tuesday, and I tell myself I'll "just skip today and make it up tomorrow."

But I know this is the moment when my resolve tends to unravel, and where I risk falling back into old patterns. To stay on track, I could tap into emotional salience by visualizing something deeper: how proud I'll feel a month from now when I've honored my word to myself, how much stronger and more confident I'll feel in my body, or how I want to model consistency and self-respect for the people I love.

That deeper emotional connection to *why* I set the goal in the first place is what helps me override the temptation in the moment and keep my commitment.

Commitment Tools and Strategies

So, you have a goal, and you want to follow through with it. How do you put everything you've learned into practice? The following are some tools and strategies I've learned during my journey that I often teach in my coaching, leadership programs, and workshops. I invite you to test-drive all of these to find the strategies that are most effective for you. Pick three or four of them to start. Please include #1 no matter what, though.

1. First and foremost, reflect and gain clarity about who/ how you want to be.

You can start with the Five Ways/Words Exercise. For example, if you want to be a fit and healthy person, you will need specific goals that are consistent with how a "fit and healthy person" behaves. Knowing, and being clear about, who/how you want to be is the first step to making lasting personal change.

2. Be honest with yourself.

The humanistic psychologist Carl Rogers said, "The curious paradox is that when I accept myself just as I am, then I can change." Rogers believed that to grow and change, we must cultivate an environment of acceptance, authenticity, and understanding.

3. Determine and understand your "tendency."

Understanding how you respond to expectations can be a game-changer when it comes to making lasting change. In The Four Tendencies, Gretchen Rubin identifies four "tendency types" based on how we meet internal and external expectations: upholders, questioners, obligers, and rebels.

The most common type, obligers, readily meet others' expectations but struggle with their own, meaning they're far more likely to stick with a habit (like exercising) if they're being held accountable by an external source, such as a workout partner or group class.

Knowing your tendency will help you leverage strategies that work with your nature, not against it. I highly recommend taking the Four Tendencies quiz (gretchenrubin.com/quiz/the-four-tendencies-quiz), because knowing your tendency is a simple yet powerful tool for creating lasting change and living your epic life.

4. Preload your decisions.

Preloading decisions is the practice of making choices in advance to reduce friction, conserve willpower, and to increase the likelihood of following through on your goals. This concept, popularized by Chip and Dan Heath, recognizes that decisions are hardest when made under stress, fatigue, or temptation—so by deciding ahead of time, you remove uncertainty and emotional resistance.

One of the most important things we can do if we are to live an epic life and be the people we aspire to be is to schedule and account for the things we commit to. Scheduling my long solo hikes on Fridays means that when Friday morning arrives, I don't have to deliberate whether I'll go hiking or not. It's been decided. Packaging food in single-serving containers or signing up for something that requires you to stay accountable, such as a gym or group class, are two excellent examples of preloading decisions.

Do you want to save more money? Setting up automatic contributions to a 401(k) is one way we do this, and it works. Can you imagine if every month you were asked if and how much you'd like to contribute to your 401k? It wouldn't work very well. But because it's preloaded in advance, it's a non-issue. Preloading sets you up for success by removing the temptation to change your mind and opt out during a moment of weakness.

5. Create emotional salience for the outcome you're working toward.

If I'm working to cut out sugar and junk food and I'm faced with the temptation to grab a candy bar or donut, I could say, "Nothing tastes as good as healthy and strong feels." I could picture how I'd look and feel if I stayed the course versus if I gave into what would be only a few minutes of short-term pleasure. I could also remind myself, "Short-term pain for long-term gain.

6. Remember the "fresh start effect."

This is the psychological phenomenon where certain time markers—like a new year, birthday, a Monday, or the start of a new month—create a mental reset, making us more motivated to pursue goals and make lasting changes. These moments feel like a clean slate, helping us reframe our identity. Leveraging the fresh start effect can improve our chances of success.

A study by Dai, Milkman, and Riis (2014) found that people are more likely to initiate aspirational behaviors—such as dieting or exercising—following landmarks like the start of a new week, month, or year. Research indicates that individuals are sixty-three percent more likely to stay committed to a goal when they begin at the start of the week.

7. Shrink the change.

Breaking big, intimidating tasks into smaller, manageable steps makes the goal or change feel more achievable.

Instead of committing to an overwhelming hour-long workout, start with ten minutes a day and build from there. Rather than overhauling your entire diet at once, begin with one improvement, such as making and packing a healthy lunch to bring to work.

Instead of tackling cleaning your entire house at one time, commit to organizing just one drawer or shelf or scheduling in a daily ten-minute session to build momentum.

8. Make it fun.

When something is enjoyable, it stops feeling like "work"—and that makes it far easier to stick to a new healthy habit or change you're trying to make. If you're new to exercising, you might make it fun by turning it into a game. Instead of forcing yourself to run on a treadmill (which might feel like a chore), you could join a dance class, hike a scenic trail, or use a fitness app that rewards you for hitting milestones.

9. Pair a should-do task with a want-to-do task.

Temptation bundling is a powerful strategy that pairs something you want to do (a temptation) with something you should do (a beneficial habit). Research shows that when we link enjoyable activities to difficult tasks, we not only make them more fun, but we increase the likelihood of long-term consistency. I have put this one to the test with several habits, including one where I get to watch a favorite Netflix show only when I'm doing my twenty minutes of elbow planks and yoga stretches three times a week.

10. Create multipliers.

Stanford Professor Jennifer Aaker defines a "multiplier" as a single activity that fulfills multiple goals simultaneously. Multipliers are powerful because they allow you to achieve multiple goals with a single action, making habits more efficient, enjoyable, and sustainable.

For example, once a week, my husband and I ride our bikes to a park for golden hour, bringing a bottle of wine and a cribbage game. This one simple action helps me achieve four meaningful goals at once: spending quality time with my husband, inserting more fun into our relationship, getting some light exercise, and enjoying time outdoors.

11. Try habit stacking.

To habit stack, attach a new habit you're trying to form to a habit you already do. When I committed to drinking more water, I made a rule: Every time I walked into the kitchen, I had to drink a full glass of water. It became automatic because it was linked to an action I already did throughout the day.

Another example is when I first started practicing mindfulness in 2013—I used the time it took for my tea kettle to heat up and whistle to simply sit, do nothing, and observe my thoughts. This made mindfulness an effortless part of my daily routine without feeling like I had to "find time" for it.

12. Make a "Ulysses Pact."

A Ulysses Pact is a commitment strategy where you preemptively bind yourself to a future course of action, eliminating the option to back out when temptation strikes. Named after the Greek hero Ulysses, who tied himself to his ship's mast to resist the sirens' song, this strategy helps you stay disciplined by removing decision-making power in moments of weakness. By making a strong commitment in advance, you protect your future self from making impulsive choices and ensure follow-through on your goals.

If you struggle with social media distractions, you could use an app blocker to lock yourself out of certain apps during work hours. When I was transforming my health in 2010, I knew I needed consistency but also knew I hated running on pavement. So, I pre-committed to hiking three days a week—and if I skipped, my only option was to make up for it with a run on the paved streets around my neighborhood. The thought of that was so unappealing that I never skipped a hike.

13. Rally support and public accountability.

One of the most effective ways to stay committed to a goal is to make it public—whether it's sharing it with friends, family, or a community. When others know what you're striving for, you create a sense of external accountability, making it harder to back out. For example, if you commit to running a marathon and announce it on social media, your public declaration increases your likelihood of following through.

When I needed to transform my health in 2010, I decided to blog and openly share my journey, including stats like my weight, body fat percentage, and measurements as well as milestones reached. Telling the public and my social networks about my journey held me accountable and made it more likely that I would stay the course.

14. Avoid the "just this once" trap.

Clayton Christensen was a Harvard Business School professor, author, and one of the most influential business thinkers of our time. In his book How Will You Measure Your Life?, Christensen wrote that it's easier to stay committed 100 percent of the time than only some of the time. Why? Because the moment you allow yourself an exception—telling yourself, "just this once"—you open the door for future compromises. Allowing yourself such exceptions creates a slippery slope and prevents you ever from being fully committed.

I May Not Wake Up Tomorrow

"We are breathless, but we love the days. They are promises. They are the only way to walk from one night to the other."

—Nina Riggs, *The Bright Hour: A Memoir of Living and Dying*

I don't want to die. I love my family and friends and my life so much that, even if I live to be eighty-five, it won't be long enough. Still, I think about death and my mortality often, and on purpose. But it hasn't always been this way.

Lori was a wife, mother, grandmother, sister, aunt, and friend to many—including me. Sometime around the second week of October 2011, she stopped by my house unexpectedly while I was struggling over things related to someone's death. I invited her in, and we had a meaningful conversation, which included her sharing about an epic biking adventure she had recently embarked upon in California.

After a time, she got up to leave. I walked her out and we stood for a moment next to her car in my driveway. Before getting in her car, Lori squared herself in front of me, using her hands to hold my shoulders to ensure I was paying attention. She looked directly at me with her lively, sparkly eyes, and said, "For whatever reason, that day was the day that man was meant to die. I believe we each have a time that we're meant to die."

Just days later, on October 19, Lori died suddenly from an aneurysm. She was only fifty-two. Lori's passing struck me hard, not only because she was a family friend and we loved and adored her but also because of the impassioned words she had shared with me just days earlier in my driveway.

Her belief that we all have our time to die, even if we don't know it, took on new meaning. At her funeral, as I reflected on Lori's life, I wondered whether she somehow knew her life would be short. Of course, I'm not suggesting that she really did know what was going to happen, but I wonder whether she had a sense of it, because she lived every day so fully. She was exceptional that way.

Other friends and acquaintances have died too early, and their lives were lived similarly. As I left each of their funerals, I was sad about their passing, but I was also inspired by their examples. I experienced a new sense of urgency about my life, and I resolved to live more purposefully.

Over the years, I've shared with a handful of people who are close to me that I have felt as if my life will be short. I have really believed it, even though as far as I know, I have no terminal cancer diagnosis or serious illnesses. I'm going on fifty-seven years old at the time I'm writing these words, and by all indications (other than the occasional aches and pains in my neck and lower back), I am quite healthy. So, why do I believe my life will be short? Could it be because I've practiced believing it, every day, for more than a decade?

In late 2011, I wrote a personal manifesto for how to live my epic life. *I may not wake up tomorrow* is the last statement. Since writing the original manifesto, I've been reading it every morning. The manifesto, which I've updated several times since writing its original version many years ago, continues to guide me in how I live my life.

Life is short and *live each day as if it will be your last* are not original ideas. We hear these often. But in my experience, it's one thing to endorse a slogan or belief and another to work to believe and embody it. While I hope every day that it won't be my last, I decided in late 2011 following Lori's premature death that I wasn't going to take any chances. I was going to act and live each day as if it were. The following is the current version of my manifesto. It includes most of my original statements, plus numerous additions and updates I've made over the years.

My Personal Manifesto (2025)

Pay attention.

In everything I do, I think first of my family.

I have meaningful relationships with each of my sons. I make efforts to have a rich connection with each of them, and they know, and can feel, my love. I will be the best mother I can be. I will show my sons my love and support. I will love them unconditionally, and they will feel this from me.

As a mother and parent, I will work to grasp less.

I show Jerry my love, and we make efforts to have a rich and meaningful connection and partnership. We make time just for the two of us. We support each other's growth and find opportunities to grow as a couple.

I will acknowledge and apologize when I have screwed up, especially in my relationships.

Spend time with our dog (Chewy). Play and cuddle with him and take him hiking.

I make time to spend with my parents.

I keep in touch with my sisters and brother.

I value my friends and friendships.

I make an effort to nurture them.

I am a great listener.

I know myself, but I'm always changing.

I promise to keep learning about myself.

I reflect, and am grateful, every day.

I am kind. To everyone.

I will be of service to others.

I love my whole life, the wondrous and ordinary parts and the challenging and sad parts. Obstacles teach me.

I create fun. I can turn drudgery into adventure.

Every day, I make time to lighten up and play, at least a little, snd to experience joy.

I'm at choice. I'm not a victim. I get to choose my existence.

I will respond, not react.

I am curious, and I follow my curiosities.

I will work to be more patient.

I love solitude and spend a lot of time alone.

I am courageous; I dare to fail.

I will be afraid of failing, but I will still dare to fail.

Sometimes I will fail. When I do, it won't be for nothing.

I'll learn and grow from the experience.

I am humble.

Frequently, I will go without. I'll continue to fast regularly.

I'll also allow for some indulgences.

Read. Every day.

I will wake early often and watch the sun rise.

I will also see some sunsets.

I want to be the person who gets up off the couch to see a rainbow or who sets her alarm to see a meteor or other stellar, constellation-related events.

Once in a while, I'll sleep in.

I will choose often to travel the scenic and more interesting route instead of the shortest, most direct one.

Write. I am a writer. Act like one.

Live more. I want to be the person who takes a plunge in a frigid mountain lake in the wilderness, not the person who watches, safely and so reasonably, from the shore. (Keep adding more "Hell Yeah" experiences to my life.)

I practice. Everything.

I don't want to be so hard on myself.

I will practice self-compassion.

Most of the time, good enough is good enough. Seriously!

I will do what's right.

I inspire others to climb mountains they're not certain they can climb (real mountains and the mountains in their life, and/or their leadership).

Talk less but say more.

I am as healthy and as fit as I can be so I can consider any epic adventure that comes my way.

I am serious, and I'm a goofball.

I take life very seriously.

And I also don't take life very seriously.

I am generous.

I champion others.

I am on time, or early.

Every moment counts. (Remember Seneca's words, "Life is long enough if you know how to use it.")

Don't view anything as a waste of time, and it won't be.

I may not wake up tomorrow.

Notice that all the statements that make up my manifesto are things over which I have control. This is important, since my manifesto serves as a sort of to-do list. My manifesto is more specific than necessary, but I wanted to name items like sunrises and books and particular relationships because, in doing so, I'm reminded of the kind of essence I want to embody.

Since making it, I have seen more sunrises and sunsets. I've seen more rainbows and constellation events. I've slept in more! I've played hard and been more of a participant in my family. I've viewed drudgery differently and have become more generous. I've kept my fitness at a high level and practiced everything that's important to me.

I've read more books than ever before, and I've made strides toward being less self-critical. I've been more loving with Jerry and my sons, and we've had more meaningful connections as a couple and as a family. I have tried to be a better friend. I've dared to fail often, and I *have* failed, which means I've learned. I've written more often. This book is evidence of that. I've done a mostly good job of living each day as if it could be my last.

As a life coach and guide, my mission is not to inspire people to be like me or to have a life like mine. I want to inspire people about their own lives—to help them imagine who and how they want to be and the kind of life they'd like to live.

Writing a personal manifesto is a meaningful process that requires one to take stock of one's life. It's an invitation to be in the driver's seat of your life, to be the hero in your story, and to decide how you'd like to live your life. We can see our priorities by looking at how we spend our time. I like to encourage people I know and work with: "Let's say you have only one week left to live. Now look at your calendar. Would you change anything? If yes, make the changes."

I'm a voracious reader, and I have a particular fascination with books and stories written by people who are approaching the end of their lives. As hard as I try to view each day as a gift and live each day as if it could be my last, I can't do it as well as someone who knows they are dying or who is, say, ninety years old. As a result, I'm deeply inspired by the wisdom and generosity offered by people who know their end is near.

One of my favorite genres of books is what my friend Jamie refers to as "dying books," books written by people who are approaching the end of their lives, either as a result of a terminal diagnosis or they're up there in age and later in their life. (See some of my very favorites in the list of books/sources near the back of the book.) In addition, I'm a fan of the ancient philosophy of Stoicism.

In the last decade, I've read many books about Stoicism and by Stoics like Marcus Aurelius, Seneca, and others. The Stoics used the phrase "memento mori," which means "remember you must die," to create urgency and meaning in their lives. Marcus Aurelius, emperor of Rome from 161–180 and a Stoic philosopher, considered it imperative to keep death at the forefront of his thoughts. In his *Meditations*, Aurelius wrote to himself: "You could leave life right now. Let that determine what you do and say and think."

My interest in Stoicism has inspired me to add two significant practices to my life. The first is the concept of negative visualization. Negative visualization is essentially the practice of imagining you've lost someone you love, or your job, or your home, or all of them. It is the act of imagining that your worst fears have come true. By thinking about losing someone or something we love, we're likely to cherish them more and stop taking the people and things we love and value for granted. We're more likely to make it a point to appreciate who and what we have in our life.

Another practice of mine inspired by Stoicism has been incorporating a meditation practice at the end of the day. Many of us do this already. We lie in bed at night and play back the day like a movie in our minds. Most of us tend to judge ourselves and what occurred. I prefer to evaluate rather than judge to make the process constructive rather than damning, which is not only not helpful but, in many cases, harmful.

Every night, I reflect on my day, holding it up against the calls to action in my manifesto, and I ask myself things like, "Could I have handled that conversation with more patience?" and, "Darn. When Fin was asking me about Friday night, was I looking at him or my phone?" and, "I need to check in with Mom and Dad," and, "It's been a while since I connected with my siblings," and so on.

We have only one life, and our time is our life. I challenge and invite you to reflect deeply on your life. Determine the ways you wish to be and the things you need to do—and have present—to live your most authentic life. Write these in a personal manifesto, which will serve as the instructions for how to live your epic life.

Do this, and it will change your life.

Establish Your "Rumble Strips"

Living an epic life is as much about keeping the things that don't serve us out as it is about ensuring all the right things stay in. Sometimes, as we reflect on changes we'd like to make, it can be worthwhile and helpful to consider what we don't wish to have in our lives—the behaviors and elements that could sabotage it. I call the exercise of identifying these "rumble strips."

Rumble strips are grooved patterns cut into the pavement along highways in Wyoming and other states to alert drivers. When a vehicle's tires hit these strips, they produce a loud noise and vibration, acting as a warning system that wakes the driver up if they're nodding off or otherwise distracted. When I'm working with someone and trying to help them change their life, I will often ask them to list behaviors or actions that would cause them to veer away from their authentic, epic life.

Examples of items that commonly show up on people's rumble strips lists are excessive alcohol or drug use, not spending adequate time with family and the people they love most, saying yes to too many people, and not taking care of their own health.

Being clear about our rumble strips can be an effective tool in helping us stay committed to being the person we aspire to be and to staying on our authentic path.

A "Forever Project"

In the pristine waters of Yellowstone Lake—at the heart of the world's first national park—an invisible battle has been raging for nearly three decades. Once, the native Yellowstone cutthroat trout thrived here in astonishing numbers, their vast migrations feeding grizzly bears, otters, ospreys, eagles, and countless other species. But in 1994, biologists made a chilling discovery: Non-native lake trout had invaded the lake. Illegally introduced, these deep-dwelling predators multiplied rapidly, preying on cutthroat trout. Their negative impacts on the surrounding ecosystem had a rippling effect.

Unlike cutthroat, which spawn in shallow tributaries where wildlife can easily access them, lake trout reproduce deep in the lake—out of reach of bears and birds. As the non-native lake trout numbers exploded, cutthroat populations plummeted by over ninety percent, leaving vast sections of Yellowstone's backcountry eerily silent. The once-reliable food source for countless animals was vanishing at a horrifying rate.

In response, an all-out restoration effort began. Since the 1990s, and with major intensification after 2009, a massive gill-netting operation has targeted lake trout, removing more than 4.3 million fish. Biologists have also developed techniques to destroy lake trout eggs before they hatch, attacking the invaders at every stage of their life cycle. The effort has cost tens of millions of dollars, but slowly, the cutthroat are returning.

The lake trout will never be completely eradicated, and the work to protect cutthroat will never be finished. When I was operating our Yellowstone business and reporting on the story, one fisheries biologist referred to the effort as a "forever project." The same could be said about living your epic life. To live authentically is not just about cultivating what we need to have in an epic life, it's also about keeping out what doesn't serve us. Just as Yellowstone's biologists must be relentless in protecting the cutthroat, we must remain vigilant in protecting what matters most in our lives.

The effort to live our most true and fulfilling life is never finished. Living your epic life is a forever project.

The Chinese Bamboo Tree

To plant a Chinese bamboo tree is to commit to a process of dedication, patience, and unwavering belief. It begins simply: You plant a seed. Then, for five long years, you must return to the same patch of soil every single day, tending to it with water, care, and faith—despite seeing nothing. No sprout. No sign of life. Just bare earth. Five years of effort with no visible reward.

But beneath the surface and out of sight, something powerful is happening. The bamboo is building an intricate, deep-rooted foundation—one strong enough to sustain the towering growth to come.

Then, almost suddenly, after years of what looks like stagnation, the first green shoot breaks through the soil. And in just six weeks, it may surge to an astonishing ninety feet high. Our most extraordinary growth isn't the result of a single breakthrough moment—it's built through hundreds of small, seemingly inconsequential actions repeated day after day.

It's not about grand gestures but about showing up, tending to the work, and believing in what's growing—even when we can't see it. Your epic life is no different. To create and live it, you must keep showing up. Keep tending to it. Keep believing in it. And if you remain committed and trust the process long enough, one day, you'll feel it—you will have found your way.

Conclusion
A Call to Adventure

If you wish to live your authentic life, you cannot leave it to chance. It will not just happen. You must imagine it, create it, and step boldly into it. This requires a willingness to venture into the wilderness inside yourself. I urge you to embark on this epic journey.

The most valuable thing I've learned—in all my years of working with others, and in all my fifty-seven years of life—is this: We risk our life when we don't live it.

Set aside time—an hour, a day, a weekend—and step away from the noise, the expectations, the distractions. Seek solitude. Use this field guide as your compass. Reflect deeply. Follow the pull of what feels most true and allow it to lead you home to yourself.

If you do this, I promise . . . the experience will be breathtaking.

Afterword

"I can die now!" The words blurted out of me as I held the printed manuscript of this book in my hands for the first time.

Let me explain. For years, this book existed as stacks of unfinished drafts—original versions, revised versions, newer versions. Every New Year, I resolved: *This will be the year I finish the book.* And yet, year after year, life pulled me in other directions, and I just couldn't get it across the finish line.

In early 2021, long inspired by Gretel Ehrlich's *The Solace of Open Spaces* and Laura Bell's *Claiming Ground*, I bought a historic Wyoming sheepherder's wagon to serve as my writing studio—a room of my own, the perfect setting from which to write. I told my husband and three sons, who were out of breath after pulling the sheepwagon into place near the Popo Agie River, *"Now I'll be able to finish my book!"*

And still, it would take four more years.

Each year I didn't finish, the weight grew heavier. A quiet regret was forming. Not because this book is everything, or because I expect it to be widely read, but because I've needed to get it *out* of me. To lay down all I've learned—all the insights, stories, and wisdom I've gathered.

This book was first written in my mind—over years of wandering in the wilderness, walking alone for hours and miles, immersed in reflection and deep thought. It was written through the work I've done with people who trusted me to be their coach and guide. It was born from a lifetime of experience, an insatiable curiosity, voracious reading, and a love of storytelling that has lived in me since childhood.

It turns out I had to become the person I aspired to be before I could write this book. And, well, that took a while. Almost fifteen years.

Finally, I have given birth to the overdue baby! Since you're holding this book in your hands, it means you've journeyed through it—at least in part. That means so much to me. Thank you. I hope this book has inspired you to reflect deeply on yourself and your life. I hope something in these pages sparked a realization, a sense of recognition, or a longing to live more fully.

I hope it inspires you to live your epic life.

Acknowledgements

This book was not written alone. It may have been conceived while hiking in the wilderness and typed in solitude from my sheepherder's wagon— but it has not been a solo effort. I could not have done this without the love and support of so many extraordinary people.

To my husband, Jerry—the love of my life and my partner in all things. Thank you for sharing this breathtaking life with me. For hiking beside me, even when we didn't know exactly where we were going. Your love, partnership, steadiness, and fierce belief in me have meant everything. Thank you for being such a phenomenal father to our sons, for doing the heavy lifting and the dirty jobs, for being the navigator on all our travels (and somehow never getting us lost), and for holding down the fort while I lead Epic Adventures or travel for work. I love you for always and forever!

To my beloved sons—Wolf, Hayden, and Finis—thank you for being my greatest adventure. Each of you is your own wild masterpiece, and raising you has been the most epic journey of all. Thank you for all the adventures, and for getting up so early on so many mornings to beat the crowds and have nature's wonder all to ourselves. Thank you for the memories, which I hold among the most precious of my life. I'm so proud of the kind, thoughtful, adventurous humans you are. You are the best Wolf, Hayden, and Finis in the world. I love you more than life itself.

To my mom and dad—thank you for everything. For giving me life, and for the gift of our wonderful family. For your steadfast love and support. For being our "epic crew" on countless adventures and family trips. For being such an incredible "Mommom" and "Poppop" to your grandchildren. I love you both so much! Mom—thank you for your zest for life, your selflessness, deep compassion, and fierce resilience. Your joy, even in the face of pain, is a light that guides me, and you taught me what it means to love. Dad— thank you for moving us to Wyoming and planting the seeds of my love for this wild place. For inspiring my journalistic spirit. For hiring me to be an intern to cover the 1988 Yellowstone fires, and for our partnership in *Yellowstone Journal* and *YellowstonePark.com*. You've taught me so much, and your support has been invaluable.

To my sibs—Alicia, Amber, and Michael—I feel so blessed to have you as my siblings and in my life. I love you guys!

To Jamie L.—thank you for finding me again after 30 years, for seeing the writer in me and calling her forth. For your wisdom, belief, and for being so loving and gentle with me when I've asked for hard truths and advice. For the meetups, the endlessly deep and meaningful conversations, moon ceremonies, birdwatching adventures, and so many giggles. I'm so grateful.

To Kathy S. ("Fremont")—thank you for hiking great distances with me, and for climbing mountains you didn't want to climb, just to spend time with me. Thank you for sharing a reverence for wild beauty, and for so many meaningful conversations. Thank you, also, for the misadventures, which continue to bring both depth and laughter.

To Kathy B. ("SoX")—I miss you every day. You understood me in a way few others ever have, and that meant more than words can express. I feel you near so often—when I hear the song of a hermit thrush, when wildflowers bloom, whenever I listen to Xavier Rudd or the Dirty Heads, and in countless other moments. I'll never forget the way you would exhale in the stillness of a beautiful place, or our deep, meandering happy hour conversations beneath the cottonwoods in City Park. Thank you—for the road trips, the reverent silence we often enjoyed with one another, the fires you built (especially on that frozen fat-biking day), and for always bringing the chocolate Pop-Tarts.

To Leann S.—thank you for your friendship, your wise example as a mother, and your companionship on so many long, hard, beautiful hikes. I'm grateful from the depths of my heart.

To Joel K.—thank you for your creative brilliance and partnership, including helping to design our Webby Award-winning *YellowstonePark.com* back in the day. For the thought-provoking conversations, your friendship, and trust. Thank you for introducing me to Gina, and your family—and to Alan.

To Alan W.—thank you for saying yes to the Wind River trip in 2014, and for enduring the mosquitoes, climbs, and unknowns. Thank you for your belief in me, and for introducing me to so many wonderful people, including Marie and your family.

To Jon D.— thank you for inviting me to hike the Grand Canyon Rim-to-Rim-to-Rim in 2010, and for your presence and support during that transformative experience. For the 50-mile Zion Traverse day hike and our Wind River Epic, thank you. I'm also deeply grateful you introduced me to Heather and your family. Your friendship is cherished—and I'm honored by your generosity in writing this book's Foreword.

To Betina K.—I consider meeting and working with you a "life event." Your skillful coaching changed my life, and you inspired my path into coaching. Thank you for your impact on my life—and your friendship.

To Julia F.—thank you for being a grounding force, for seeing me, and for the richness of our conversations and cherished happy hours.

To Susan G.—thank you for our many conversations about books and writing. Your friendship, support, example, and encouragement have meant the world to me.

To Sharon T. ("SFA," aka Sharon From America)—thank you for being such a dear and present friend during a time of transformation and reinvention. Our *Folklore* visits were sacred!

To Steve B.—thank you for being the trainer and mentor I needed when I was in a health rut post-business sale. You helped me become the fittest and healthiest I've ever been. I still practice everything you taught me, and it continues to serve me well.

To Susan, Mia, Stephanie, Ilana, Doreen, Mona, Rachel, Alexia, Jill, Jennifer, Coretha, Jocelyn, and Joanne— thank you for inviting me into your sacred circle during what has been a particularly tender time. Your presence was a balm, and your sisterhood a gift.

To my Epic clients—thank you for your trust, your courage, and your vulnerability. Thank you for teaching me what it means to lead, to grow, and to be fully human. You inspire me every day.

To all of you who have referred people to me—thank you. Your belief in me means more than I can say.

To my Epic Adventure partners—thank you for helping me deliver unforgettable, transformative experiences. I'm especially grateful to:

— National Outdoor Leadership School (NOLS)
—Jackson Hole Mountain Guides (especially Jason Dittmer and Cat Coe)
—The National Park Service and Zion National Park Commercial Services
— Zion Guru (especially Jonathan Zambella and Audrey Abbott)
— Sierra Mountaineering International (Kurt Wedberg)

Your expertise, support, and partnership are greatly appreciated.

To my NOLS Brooks Range comrades—Jon, Chris, Cutter, J.J., Antonia, Marc, Pat–and our incredible instructors, Amy and Lauren: Thank you for being such an important part of what was an inspiring, informative, and unforgettable experience for me. You all made it particularly meaningful and the experience continues to inform me.

To the wilderness itself—thank you for being breathtaking, and for providing an ongoing platform from which I can examine my life while experiencing astonishing wonder. To my beloved Wind Rivers: thank you for being my cathedral, my refuge, my mirror, my compass.

To Alee Anderson and Deborah Rose—thank you for helping me shape this wild, unruly, deeply personal work into a book. Alee, your early enthusiasm came at just the right time. To you both: thank you for your loving support and guidance, the thoughtful edits, for pushing back on word count (this would've been 400,000 words without you!), and for helping carry this book to the finish line. I'll always be grateful!

To Ryan Aliapoulios, Lily Weiner, Justin Sullivan, and Katie Cosgrove—thank you for your magic on the publishing end. You're all a joy to work with—kind and brilliant at what you do.

To Kristen Ingebretson— thank you for designing the perfect cover, and for your patience and care through every iteration, especially those requested in the eleventh hour.

To Misty Bourne—thank you for your thoughtful copyediting.

To Gail Hudson—thank you for helping me unlock some blocked stories that were preventing me from accessing my authentic voice.

To the early readers—thank you for your encouragement and kind words.

And finally, to you, dear reader—thank you for choosing to read this book. I'm more grateful than I can say.

With all my heart,

Shelli

Leave No Trace

Leave No Trace is a simple but powerful ethic that helps ensure the wild places we love remain unspoiled for future generations.

The *Leave No Trace* principles are promoted by the Leave No Trace Center for Outdoor Ethics (lnt.org), a nonprofit dedicated to protecting the outdoors through education and research.

Please follow these principles when enjoying time outdoors.

7 Principles of *Leave No Trace*:

1. Plan ahead and prepare
2. Travel and camp on durable surfaces
3. Dispose of waste properly
4. Leave what you find
5. Minimize campfire impact
6. Respect wildlife
7. Be considerate of others

To learn more specifics about the above principles, visit lnt.org.

Books, Authors, Poems & Other Sources Referenced in This Book

(listed in the order in which they appear)

Women Who Run with the Wolves: Myths and Stories of the Wild Woman Archetype, by Clarissa Pinkola Estés

The Hero with a Thousand Faces, by Joseph Campbell

Aion: Researches into the Phenomenology of the Self, by Carl Jung

Upstream: Selected Essays, by Mary Oliver

Deep Survival: Who Lives, Who Dies, and Why, by Laurence Gonzales

Waking Up podcast, Sam Harris

Huberman Lab podcast, Andrew Huberman

Gift from the Sea, by Anne Morrow Lindbergh

A Journal of a Solitude, by May Sarton

The Art of Stillness: Adventures in Going Nowhere, by Pico Iyer

No Bad Parts: Healing Trauma and Restoring Wholeness with the Internal Family Systems Model, by Dr. Richard Schwartz

The On Being Project podcast, by Krista Tippett

A Field Guide to Getting Lost, by Rebecca Solnit

On the Shortness of Life: Life is Long If You Know How to Use It, by Seneca, translated by C. D. N. Costa

Man's Search for Meaning, by Viktor Frankl

Get Excited: Reappraising Pre-Performance Anxiety As Excitement (June 2014 article in *Journal of Experimental Psychology*), by Alison Wood Brooks

Mindset: The New Psychology of Success, by Carol Dweck

Cultures of Growth: How the New Science of Mindset Can Transform Individuals, Teams, and Organizations, by Mary Murphy

"Kindness" (poem), by Naomi Shihab Nye

"Have You Ever Tried to Enter the Long Black Branches?" (poem), from *West Wind: Poems and Prose Poems*, by Mary Oliver

Emotional Agility: Get Unstuck, Embrace Change, and Thrive in Work and Life, by Susan David

The Sweet Spot: The Pleasures of Suffering and the Search for Meaning, by Paul Bloom

Transcend: The New Science of Self-Actualization, by Scott Barry Kaufman, PhD

"Shadow and Light Source Both" (poem), from *The Soul of Rumi: A New Collection of Ecstatic Poems* by Rumi, translated by Coleman Barks

Collected Works of C.G. Jung (various volumes), and writings on shadow and individuation

"Joy" (essay), from *Feel Free*, by Zadie Smith

The War of Art: Break Through the Blocks and Win Your Inner Creative Battles, by Steven Pressfield

Hidden Potential: The Science of Achieving Greater Things, by Adam Grant

Self-Compassion: The Proven Power of Being Kind to Yourself, by Kristin Neff

"The Power of Vulnerability" (Ted Talk), by Brené Brown

The Power of Regret: How Looking Backward Moves Us Forward, by Daniel Pink

The Tim Ferriss Show podcast

Debbie Millman, *Design Matters* podcast

"The Way of Love" (poem), by 13th-century Persian poet and mystic Jalal al-Din Rumi, translated by Coleman Barks, in *The Book of Love: Poems of Ecstasy and Longing*

Astro Teller, CEO of X (formerly Google X), Alphabet's "moonshot factory"

Reshma Saujani, founder of Girls Who Code and author of
Brave, Not Perfect

*The Fearless Organization: Creating Psychological Safety in the
Workplace for Learning, Innovation, and Growth,* by Amy C. Edmondson

Right Kind of Wrong: The Science of Failing Well,
by Amy C. Edmondson

Bittersweet: How Sorrow and Longing Make Us Whole,
by Susan Cain

"Failing and Flying" (poem), by Jack Gilbert

Screenwriting (MasterClass) by Aaron Sorkin, masterclass.com

"CV of Failures" (essay), by Melanie Stefan, neuroscientist and lecturer
at the University of Edinburgh; published in *Nature* in 2010

"Invitation" (poem), from *Red Bird,* by Mary Oliver

*Positivity: Top-Notch Research Reveals the 3-to-1 Ratio That Will Change
Your Life,* by Barbara Fredrickson

*The Progress Principle: Using Small Wins to Ignite Joy, Engagement, and
Creativity at Work,* by Teresa Amabile and Steven Kramer

"The Proper Function of Man" by Jack London (also known as his credo)

*Awe: The New Science of Everyday Wonder and How it Can Transform
Your Life,* by Dacher Keltner

An American Childhood, by Annie Dillard

The Power of Moments: Why Certain Experiences Have Extraordinary Impact, by Chip Heath and Dan Heath

Braving the Wilderness: The Quest for True Belonging and the Courage to Stand Alone, by Brené Brown

The Song of Significance: A New Manifesto for Teams, by Seth Godin

"Small Kindnesses" (poem), from *Bonfire Opera*, by Danusha Laméris

"Social Support and the Perception of Geographical Slant" (study), by Schnall, S., Harber, K. D., Stefanucci, J. K., & Proffitt, D. R. (2008), published in *Journal of Experimental Social Psychology*, 44(4), 1246–1255.

"Friendship" (essay), from *Consolations: The Solace, Nourishment and Underlying Meaning of Everyday Words*, by David Whyte

The Diary of Anaïs Nin, Volume 1: 1931–1934 by Anaïs Nin

I and Thou, by Martin Buber

"A Phone Call," a story told by Auburn Sandstrom at The Moth Mainstage, 2015

Perfect Days, a film directed by Wim Wenders, 2023

Outlive, the Science and Art of Longevity, by Dr. Peter Attia

Next Level: Your Guide to Kicking Ass, Feeling Great, and Crushing Goals Through Menopause and Beyond, by Stacy Sims, PhD, and Selene Yeager

The M Factor: Shredding the Silence on Menopause (documentary film), PBS, 2024

Estrogen Matters: Why Taking Hormones in Menopause Can Improve Women's Well-Being and Lengthen Their Lives–Without Raising the Risk of Breast Cancer, by Avrum Blooming and Carol Tavris

Brain Energy: A Revolutionary Breakthrough in Understanding Mental Health–and Improving Treatment for Anxiety, Depression, OCD, PTSD, and More, by Dr. Chris Palmer

Why We Sleep: Unlocking the Power of Sleep and Dreams, by Matthew Walker

Atomic Habits: An Easy & Proven Way to Build Good Habits & Break Bad Ones, by James Clear

The Happiness Hypothesis: Finding Modern Truth in Ancient Wisdom, by Jonathan Haidt

"You vs. You" (podcast episode), *Radiolab*, WNYC Studios, 2011

How Will You Measure Your Life?, by Clayton M. Christensen, James Allworth, and Karen Dillon

The Four Tendencies: The Indispensable Personality Profiles That Reveal How to Make Your Life Better (and Other People's Lives Better, Too), by Gretchen Rubin

The Bright Hour: A Memoir of Living and Dying, by Nina Riggs

The Last Lecture, by Randy Pausch and Jeffrey Zaslow (2008)

When Breath Becomes Air, by Paul Kalanithi (2016)

Tuesdays with Morrie: An Old Man, A Young Man, and Life's Greatest Lesson, by Mitch Albom (1997)

Chasing Daylight: How My Forthcoming Death Transformed My Life, by Eugene O'Kelly

Being Mortal: Medicine and What Matters in the End, by Atul Gawande

To Heaven and Back: A Doctor's Extraordinary Account of Her Death, by Mary C. Neal

The Year of Magical Thinking, by Joan Didion

Proof of Heaven: A Neurosurgeon's Journey into the Afterlife, by Eben Alexander

On Self-Respect (essay), by Joan Didion, published in *Vogue* (1961)

Meditations, by Marcus Aurelius

The Solace of Open Spaces, by Gretel Ehrlich

A Guide to the Good Life: The Ancient Art of Stoic Joy, by William B. Irvine

About the Author

 Shelli Johnson is an entrepreneur, coach, keynote presenter, leadership facilitator travel consultant, writer, and adventure guide. She is also the founder of Epic Life Inc., a company dedicated to helping people live their authentic, epic life.

Before launching Epic Life Inc., Shelli spent 15 years building and running a Yellowstone-based tourism publishing company (and Webby Award–winning website) that promoted travel to the world's first national park. She often went "into the field" to report on and write stories, and to inspire and help people plan a vacation of a lifetime.

Today, she still goes into the field—but with leaders, teams, and individuals navigating the wild terrain of their own lives. Her mission is to help them live the life of their lifetime, and to create more meaning in their life and their work.

Over the past 15 years, Shelli has walked thousands of miles—alone, with loved ones, alongside clients, and during coaching calls. The wilderness has been her teacher, mirror, and compass. Walking is how she finds her way home to herself.

She lives in Wyoming with her husband. Their three grown sons are forging their own paths. Her office is a 100-year-old sheepherder's wagon parked alongside the Popo Agie River.

For more of her writing and to learn about Shelli's work, visit her Substack: *Epic Field Notes*, or check out her websites: YourEpicLife.com, theShelliJohnson.com, and HaveMediaWillTravel.com.

Get the Epic Field Study Guide

This book isn't just something to read. It's something to walk with, wrestle with, and grow with.

Go deeper into the lessons shared in this book by downloading your free copy of my *Epic Field Study Guide*—a companion PDF full of exercises, questions, and trail-tested prompts to help you explore your own breathtaking life.

Download it for free at:

www.YourEpicLife.com/EpicFieldStudyGuide

Or scan this QR code with your phone:

You'll also get access to occasional Epic Field Notes and updates from Shelli!

www.ingramcontent.com/pod-product-compliance
Lightning Source LLC
Chambersburg PA
CBHW021714120626
46545CB00004B/1561